# Migrating to the Solaris™ Operating System

## The Discipline of UNIX-to-UNIX® Migrations

*Ken Pepple*

*Brian Down*

*David Levy*

**Sun Microsystems Press**
**A Prentice Hall Title**

**Prentice Hall PTR offers excellent discounts on this book when ordered in quantity for bulk purchases or special sales. For more information, please contact: U.S. Corporate and Government Sales, 1-800-382-3419, corpsales@pearsontechgroup.com. For sales outside of the U.S., please contact: International Sales, 1-317-581-3793, international@pearsontechgroup.com.**

Executive Editor: *Gregory G. Doench*
Cover Design Director: *Jerry Votta*
Cover Designer: *Kavish & Kavish Digital Publishing and Design*
Manufacturing Manager: *Alexis R. Heydt-Long*
Marketing Manager: *Christopher Guzikowski*

Sun Microsystems Press:
Publisher: *Myrna Rivera*

First Printing
Text printed on recycled paper

**ISBN** 0-13-150263-8

*Sun Microsystems Press*
A Prentice Hall Title

# Acknowledgments

It's difficult to acknowledge everyone who was part of this book. But our thanks certainly go to the following:

Julie Snow for her tireless efforts at keeping us on time and on track, and for her exceptional technical writing expertise. Gary Rush and others in the Sun BluePrints™ program for allowing us to write and publish this book. Enis Konuk and Amanda Blake for understanding the importance of enterprise migration and approving the funding for this effort. Edward Wustenhoff and Mike Moore for developing Chapter 8 "Managing a Migrated Environment." Many thanks to those who offered their time and expertise to review and comment on drafts of the book, including Martyn Cope, James Fan, John S. Howard, Patrick Hudelot, Luiz Juk, Amjad Khan, Tim Mac, and Rob Mowat.

**Acknowledgments from Ken Pepple:** I would like to thank my Sun Professional Services' Asia Pacific practice colleagues, especially Niall Crawford, Laurence Sibley, KC Fung, Ivan Yue, Ken Buchanan, Jeff McIver, and Woon-Taek Park for their informal input during a few weeks of grueling training. I would also like to thank Gary Kelly and Andrew LeStrange for their insights during my frequent trips to Australia. All of these people have wittingly and unwittingly influenced the formation of the ideas and thoughts that have gone into this book.

I would like to thank my brother, Brian Pepple, for the benefit of his Linux expertise. Last, but certainly not least, I would like to thank Shelley and Zeke for supporting me through thick and thin, both home and away.

**Acknowledgments from Brian Down:** I'd like to thank Mike Habeck and Tom Pallmann for allowing me to work on the book this past several months. I'd also like to thank Dean Kemp who hired me and had the vision to start the migration center in Toronto some 10 years ago, as well as Brad Keates for his continued support. I'd particularly like to thank Jef Futch for his vision, energy, and guidance, and for giving me a chance. Additionally, I'd like to thank those on the migration team in Toronto who helped me develop the material for this book: Rob Mowat, James Foronda, Luiz Juk, Roy Kressin, and Julia Vladimirsky.

My biggest thanks go to my sweetie, Veronica Callinan, who put up with the demanding schedule and long hours and to my cat Ralph, who desperately wanted to contribute to this book, judging from the amount of time he spent walking on my laptop keyboard and sitting on the attached mouse.

**Acknowledgments from Dave Levy:** I'd like to thank Sue, Dan, and Ben for putting up with the all the long hours and extra work I brought home while working on this book. I'd also like to thank Steve Beckley and Richard Croucher for their support of my efforts, and Dave Parr for his support while undertaking the field work on which Chapter 11 is based.

**Acknowledgments from Julie Snow:** As a pilot for the Sun BluePrints residency program, this book was written and published more quickly than any book in the history of this endeavour. This accomplishment was a direct result of the tireless efforts of the following people: Our dedicated and talented authors—Ken Pepple, Brian Down, and Dave Levy, all of whom exceeded my expectations; our committed and responsive reviewers, who provided invaluable feedback within days, instead of weeks; our extremely talented illustrator, Dany Galgani; our dedicated editors, Billie Markim and Sue Blumenberg; our supportive management team, Vicky Hardman and Barb Jugo; and our support at Prentice Hall, Greg Doench, Jane Bonnell, and MaryLou Nohr.

In addition, I'd like to thank my husband, Justin Snow. His ongoing support, patience, and humor have made the long days possible and the demanding workload bearable.

# Contents

# Preface

This book is designed to help customers and Sun staff strategically transition the people, processes, and technologies in IT environments to the Solaris™ Operating System (Solaris OS). By explaining how you can use Sun's migration methodology to realize the benefits that can result from a migration effort, we hope to minimize or eliminate the reluctance many people have to undertaking UNIX® migration projects. While we focus on UNIX server migrations, much of the methodology and many of the best practices presented in this book apply to any migration to the Solaris environment.

Using the methodology presented in this book, you should be able to tackle projects ranging from the smallest data conversion to the largest legacy migration project with a repeatable and systematic approach that ensures predictability and success. Along the way, we provide guidance to help you avoid some of the pitfalls that are common to migration projects. The methodology and best practices include:

- Assessing the current environment to migrate
- Planning for a migration project
- Architecting a new target environment
- Implementing a migration by using available tools and processes
- Managing the newly migrated environment

To illustrate the benefits, costs, and requirements of a migration project, we provide the following detailed case studies:

- A small software development company, migrating from Linux to the Solaris environment

- A simple, custom-written application that uses a Sybase database, migrating to the Solaris environment and an Oracle database

- A ledger solution from the financial services industry, migrating from the HP/UX platform to the Solaris environment

# How This Guide is Organized

This guide is organized in the following chapters:

- Chapter 1 presents a brief overview of the historical events that created an environment in which migration was necessary. This chapter describes some of the most common goals, motivators, benefits, and problems of any migration project.

- Chapter 2 explains how UNIX has evolved over the years and describes the major differences between versions of UNIX, while placing other operating systems in context. This chapter also explains why migration is important, what its benefits are, and what the scope of a migration project is.

- Chapter 3 defines the most important terms used in migration efforts and differentiates these terms. In addition, this chapter presents migration strategies, explains the benefits and risks of each strategy, and describes the appropriateness of each strategy for various situations.

- Chapter 4 presents a detailed implementation of the migration methodology and explains how to plan for important project activities and milestones. This chapter also describes the tasks involved in establishing a business justification for a migration effort.

- Chapter 5 introduces Sun's high-level migration methodologies and reviews the roles of the architecture, implementation, and management stages involved in the methodology.

- Chapter 6 explores the tasks involved in architecting a migration solution.

- Chapter 7 describes the steps involved in migrating the current environment to the target environment.

- Chapter 8 explains how management tasks relate to the Enterprise stack (E-stack). This chapter also presents considerations and tools used for managing migrations to a Solaris environment.

- Chapter 9 presents an example of the process involved in migrating from the Linux environment to the Solaris environment.

- Chapter 10 presents a case study that illustrates the methods, tools, and best practices used to migrate a Tru64 environment to the Solaris environment.

- Chapter 11 presents a case study that illustrates the methodology, tools, and best practices used to migrate customers from HP/UX platforms.

- Appendix A presents a sample JScore report and analysis as referenced in Chapter 7.

# Related Documentation

| Topic | Title | Part Number |
|---|---|---|
| Data center consolidation | *Consolidation in the Data Center: Simplifying IT Environments to Reduce Total Cost of Ownership* | 817-3375-10 |

# Web Sites

**Note –** Sun is not responsible for the availability of third-party Web sites mentioned in this document. Sun does not endorse and is not responsible or liable for any content, advertising, products, or other materials that are available on or through such sites or resources. Sun will not be responsible or liable for any actual or alleged damage or loss caused by or in connection with the use of or reliance on any such content, goods, or services that are available on or through such sites or resources.

- BMC Software: tools for systems management
  `http://www.bmc.com`
- Control Objectives for Information Related Technology (COBIT): information about architecture maturity models
  `http://www.isaca.org)`
- Distributed Management Task Force (DMTF): information about Web-Based Enterprise Management (WBEM) standards
  `http://www.dmtf.org`
- Expect tool: tool for automating FTP and NFS
  `http://expect.nist.gov/`
- GNU C/C++/Fortran/Objective C-to-C converter (GCC2CC)
  `http://www.sun.com/migration/linux/gcc2c_tool.html.`
- Halcyon Monitoring Solutions: information and tools for monitoring and managing software
  `http://www.halcyoninc.com`
- IT Infrastructure Library (ITIL): architecture maturity model
  `http://www.itsmf.com`
- The Open Group and UNIX standards:
  `http://www.opengroup.org/`

- PatchPro: tool for patch management
  `http://www.sun.com/PatchPro`
- Sun Migration group: issues database, compatibility libraries, migration kits, and assessment tools for migrating to the Solaris OS
  `http://www.sun.com/migration/`
- Solaris OE Analyzer for C/C++ and Cobol Source Code (formerly, JScore):
  `http://www.sun.com/migration/ntmigration/tools/jscoretool.html`
- SunTone™ Architecture Methodology:
  `http://www.sun.com/service/sunps/jdc/suntoneam_wp_5.2.4.pdf`
- Software Engineering Institute: architecture maturity model
  `http://www.sei.cmu.edu)`

# Typographic Conventions

The following table describes the typographic conventions used in this book.

| Typeface or Symbol | Meaning | Example |
|---|---|---|
| AaBbCc123 | The names of commands, files, and directories; on-screen computer output | Edit your `.login` file.<br>Use `ls -a` to list all files.<br>`machine_name% You have mail.` |
| **AaBbCc123** | What you type, contrasted with on-screen computer output | `machine_name%` **su**<br>`Password:` |
| *AaBbCc123* | Command-line placeholder: replace with a real name or value | To delete a file, type `rm` *filename*. |
| *AaBbCc123* | Book titles, new words or terms, or words to be emphasized | Read Chapter 6 in *User's Guide*. These are called *class* options.<br>You *must* be root to do this. |

# Shell Prompts

| Shell | Prompt |
|---|---|
| C shell | *machine-name%* |
| C shell superuser | *machine-name%* |
| Bourne shell and Korn shell | $ |
| Bourne shell and Korn shell superuser | # |

# Using UNIX Commands

This document does not contain information on basic UNIX commands and procedures such as shutting down the system, booting the system, and configuring devices.

See one or more of the following for this information:

- Solaris Operating System documentation at `http://docs.sun.com`
- Other software documentation that you received with your system

# Accessing Sun Documentation

You can view, print, or purchase a broad selection of Sun documentation, including localized versions, at:

`http://www.sun.com/documentation`

To learn more about Sun BluePrints books, visit the Sun BluePrints Web site at:

`http://www.sun.com/solutions/blueprints/pubs.html`

# CHAPTER 1

# Introduction to Migrations

The 1940s saw the birth of modern computing. With the advent of programming concepts and advances in vacuum tube technology, computers moved from mainly mechanical to electronic devices. However, even at this early stage of development, the seeds of major operational problems were becoming apparent.

In 1946, the first generally recognized computer, ENIAC, was developed. ENIAC could perform 5000 addition, 357 multiplication, or 38 division calculations a second. It covered 1800 square feet, and weighed 30 tons. ENIAC was considered a technological marvel for its use of vacuum tubes and its ground breaking performance. However, changing the programming took weeks, and maintenance was costly.

Two years later, several modifications were made to the ENIAC to simplify programming, increase performance, and ease maintenance. These modifications included converter code for serial operations and switches to control code selection. Of course, to use the new modifications, software, hardware, and maintenance procedures also had to be modified.

In 1949, the Eckert-Mauchly Computer Corporation introduced the BINAC computer, which revolutionized the infant computing field with the introduction of magnetic tape media for data storage. BINAC represented a quantum leap for the fledgling computer industry, setting a pace for progress that continues to this day. However, in that space of three years, we had already discovered the first and most enduring headaches for IT professionals: upgrades and migrations.

This chapter describes some of the most common goals, motivators (drivers), benefits, and problems of any migration project. It contains the following sections:

# Migration Goals

A *migration* is defined as the transition of an environment's people, processes, or technologies from one implementation to another. In the preceding historical examples, migration occurred when researchers wanted to use the new BINAC computer but needed their programs and data from the older systems.

The term *adoption* is used to refer to instances for which you add or change an implementation without changing the interface. On the other hand, an *upgrade* implies changes in the underlying technologies or interfaces, which require substantial application changes. These terms are most commonly used to address hardware and software issues. For example, moving from one version of the Solaris Operating System (Solaris OS) to another, such as from the version 7 of the Solaris OS to version 9, is a common use of the term adoption. In this case, developers add features to a component of the environment without changing the core technology or process employed. The phrase "without changing the core technology or process" differentiates an upgrade from a migration. Additional examples of adoptions are provided in Chapter 3, "Migration Strategies."

Whether you are attempting a migration, adoption, or upgrade, the goal of your project is to replace or enhance the functionality and service levels of your current solution while moving to a new environment.

# Migration Motivators

Now that we've explained what migrations and upgrades are, we need to investigate what prompts them to occur. Unfortunately, the reasons for migrating or upgrading are diverse and plentiful. However, they can be broadly categorized as either originating internally within the organization or being thrust upon an organization by external forces.

Internal business and technical motivators for migrations and upgrades include the following:

- **Business process changes.** Because most IT environments exist to support a specific business and its processes, it is natural that any changes to those processes might require changes to the supporting environment. Most likely, this will trigger an upgrade when an application can add a feature to support the change or a migration when a new solution might be necessary to support the change.

- **Business reorganizations.** Most companies are in near-constant states of organizational flux as they try to maximize profits and minimize overhead in competitive and turbulent economic environments. When a reorganization occurs, the affected business unit's computational support needs often change, prompting retirements of some applications, migrations of others, and the introduction of still others.

- **Changes to corporate standards or strategies.** Today's business dependence on information technology has escalated the rate of vendor change and partnering within many organizations. As one vendor's application or platform is replaced by strategic partnering with another vendor, migration projects will be generated. For example, an organization might standardize its software infrastructure on a Sun™ ONE software stack.

- **Retirement.** All technology has a finite useful life. Whether this life is based on maintenance issues or the availability of more cost-effective competing solutions, all technology is eventually retired. This retirement usually prompts a migration. Examples abound in the IT industry. For example, mainframe technology is rapidly being replaced by less expensive open-systems technology like that provided by the Sun Fire™ 15K platform.

- **Opportunities to improve solution quality.** Many IT solutions fail to deliver their desired benefit to the business. Over time, the business becomes dissatisfied with the solution and embarks on migrating to a new one. This usually occurs only when an implemented solution consistently fails to meet the service levels or functionality required by a business.

- **Introduction or retirement of new business products.** Like business process change, this driver is the introduction or elimination of a product or service that requires IT support. An example would be adding new modules to an enterprise resource planning application.

- **Desire to take advantage of new functionality.** Technology is constantly improving. Much of the focus of this improvement is centered on adding functionality to products. Some new functionality can enable new business opportunities or better support existing business processes. For example, when backup-software companies added "warm backup" technology to their products, users could decrease maintenance downtime and increase business availability, prompting many organizations to migrate to this new technology.

- **Opportunities to reduce risk.** Organizations constantly monitor risks to their profits and survival. With the enormous role that IT solutions play in this survival, it is not surprising that companies migrate away from risky IT solutions. Whether this means they deploy platforms that are more highly available, implement new failover technology, or move away from unsupported products, businesses can migrate to avoid risk. This was never more true than during the pre-Y2K migration frenzy of the late 1990s. While many organizations were relatively sure that their applications would not be affected by the changeover, a large number took the opportunity to migrate off the mainframe platform to reduce their risk.

External pressures also prompt migrations and upgrades. External pressure usually comes from a partner or vendor. The most common external causes of migrations or upgrades include the following:

- **Reaching a technology's "end of life."** Many technology vendors, especially in the software market, build their businesses around upgrade revenues. As part of this business strategy, older versions of their products are deemed to be at the end of their useful lives as newer versions are introduced. This "end of life" (EOL) categorization often signals an impending lack of vendor support (through lack of vendor patches or spare parts) or an increased maintenance cost, which pushes customers to migrate to newer versions or different products.

- **Availability of complementary products.** Few IT solutions are entirely encompassed by one product. More likely, they are a mesh of compatible products that are combined to meet a business need. For example, consider the case in which a company needing enterprise financial support has implemented an accounting package, developed in house on its Digital VAX under OpenVMS. As the company moves to an intranet deployment and wants to add web front ends to the package, it might face the possibility of having to migrate applications, hardware, and operating environments because few web server packages could interface with its proprietary application, hardware, network, and operating system.

- **Opportunities to reduce cost.** It might simply be too expensive for a company to continue to maintain a solution they currently use. By "too expensive," we mean that competing solutions offer a significant savings over the implemented solution. Costs might be incurred through a myriad of different areas including maintenance contracts, staffing, product acquisitions, or environmental factors. Whatever the specific reason, in this case a migration is undertaken in the hopes that after the migration project investment, the new solution will deliver lower costs over its useful life.

- **Improvements to product quality.** Just as vendors constantly add new functionality, they also improve the basic systemic qualities of their products. Most new products provide better performance, fail less often, and are more flexible to deploy.

- **Managing competitive pressures.** Like the internal driver for increasing functionality or lowering costs, competitive pressures can force organizations to change their technology solutions to compete in the marketplace. This was evident in the banking industry when many banks upgraded their systems to interoperate with web banking solutions, which allowed bank account holders to view their balances over the Internet.

- **Managing regulatory pressures.** New government of industry regulations might ban certain processes, alter business practices, or prescribe new rules regarding a current solution. The only avenue to compliance with the new regulations might be to migrate or upgrade technology, people, or processes. Examples of such regulatory changes would be the United States HIPPA laws or European Union privacy rules.

As you can see from the preceding discussion, many of the drivers for a migration project complement each other. In fact, most migration projects have several drivers. Whether your migration drivers are internal or external, it is important to identify these drivers so that addressing them can be one of your project's objectives.

# Migration Benefits

Certainly, with the large number of business drivers pushing migrations and adoptions, there must be real benefits for organizations to perform migrations. The following list shows that most of these benefits fall into the categories of business support, service level improvement, or risk avoidance:

- **Cost savings.** Technological progress might allow you to replace a costly custom solution with common off-the-shelf (COTS) products. New solutions can save money through increased efficiency, and new products might also have warranties that eliminate the need for costly support contracts. Whatever your reasons for undertaking a migration project, cost saving is usually one of the central benefits.

- **Increased efficiency.** New technologies or processes can automate business processes that might have previously been manual processes. They might also simply increase the speed or rate at which existing automated processes run. This is often the case in migrations that replace batch processes with online processes.

- **Improved solution qualities.** The quality of a solution often improves after a migration to new technologies or processes. Whether this improvement is in the area of capacity (reengineering processes, faster hardware, or streamlined code, which can all improve the performance of IT solutions) or availability (new technologies can make products less faulty), there are important benefits for migrations in this area.

- **Improved support.** Migrating to more current technologies usually results in better vendor support because vendors usually concentrate their infrastructure and processes around maintaining currently sold products. While this might not always the be the case, especially when implementing "bleeding edge" technologies, it is generally accepted that the support for and quality of solutions that have been implemented at multiple customer sites will be better than they are for solutions that are implemented at only a few customer sites.

- **Increased competitive advantage.** As an example of the type of competitive advantage that can result from a migration project, consider how approving loans in real time instead of in overnight batches could be a differentiator for a business in the financial industry. To enable this new functionality, it might be necessary to migrate to a new operating environment, application, or platform.

These are just a few of the common benefits of migrations projects. While most of the benefits for your migration projects will fall under one of these headings, you should also be aware of additional benefits that are specific to your organization.

# Migration Problems

Now that we've explained why migrations occur and the benefits an organization can achieve by undertaking them, it's probably unclear why they are so dreaded within the IT industry. The simple reason is something quality advocates like to call "resistance to change." It is a natural reaction to resist change when substantial time and effort to make an environment stable and productive is required. Add to this the element of the unknown—which is often the case when IT personnel are forced to migrate off a legacy system—along with the cost and complexity of the move, and it is no wonder that IT professionals loathe migration projects.

The following list summarizes some of the common problems you are likely to face during a migration project:

- **High cost.** Migrations can be expensive. You will need to pay for additional hardware, software, services, and staff to make your migration successful. Sometimes these costs can be easily estimated before a project begins. What is problematic for most companies is that the costs are often not planned for ahead of time and come as unexpected expenses during or after the project has completed.

- **Complexity.** Migration projects are an order of magnitude more difficult than ordinary new application implementation projects. Applications and processes already in place have a tendency to grow informally without planning or documentation. As a result, it can be difficult to ascertain the true requirements of a migrated solution or even the true state of the current implementation. Compound these problems by dealing with an unfamiliar technology product, and you can see how the complexity of even small migration projects can be daunting.

- **Substantial time and effort requirements.** Closely related to the cost problem, substantial time and effort will need to be expended to successfully migrate even average-sized environments. Often, this time and effort cannot be spared within an overtaxed IT department. This creates a vicious circle whereby the time and effort needed to migrate keeps increasing, along with the urgency of the business driver for migration. Take a mainframe Y2K migration, for example. Most organizations used this as an opportunity to migrate completely off mainframes instead of simply patching and upgrading their non-Y2K-compliant applications. Those who didn't take advantage of that opportunity saw their future migration become more difficult and lengthy.

- **Resistance to change.** People, even highly skilled IT professionals, fundamentally dislike change. This is natural because most change entails increased risk, at least during the migration itself. In addition, it is human nature to become accustomed to the status quo, regardless of how good or bad it is. Resistance to change manifests itself in denial that problems exist, lack of will or direction to make changes, and even sabotage of the change process itself. This is especially true among IT professionals who are highly skilled in a particular technology.

- **Lack of executive support.** As we have seen, migration projects entail cost, time, and effort. Like any large IT project, it is unlikely that a migration will succeed without executive support. Because any migration must be a joint effort between business units and IT, executive ownership is crucial in providing resources, solving disputes, and forging agreements. Involving an experienced and highly skilled project manager, together with a business-driven project-management methodology, can help ensure that you receive the support you will need.

- **Lack of accurate current information.** Sadly, orphaned legacy environments always remain in any organization where, due to neglect or stability, solutions are no longer actively managed. This is usually because the original implementers of the system are no longer with the organization, leaving no one knowledgeable about its operation, design, or maintenance requirements. When the time does come to migrate off this implementation, you are left with nagging questions that cannot be ignored, such as "Where is the source code for this application?" "What users does it serve?" and "What are its availability requirements?" Without accurate information for answering all of these questions and more, successfully migrating to a new solution will be problematic. Many companies experienced this the hard way during their Y2K upgrade. Applications that had been in place for 20 years could not be ported to new platforms or upgraded to alleviate the problem because the original programmer had left the company without securing the source code. These companies were left with the unhappy choice between reverse engineering applications or starting over from scratch.

- **Poor change control.** It is impossible to migrate from a constantly changing or poorly controlled environment. If you cannot take an accurate snapshot of the current state of the environment, your migration will suffer from many of the same ills as it would from your having inaccurate information. Worse yet, the incremental changes will cause expensive rework in development and testing.

- **Inappropriate scope.** As in any large or complex project, it is imperative to control scope. Too narrow a scope might not satisfy the migration drivers, while too broad a scope will surely cause the project to overrun its budget and not complete on time.

- **Limited skills and resources.** Migration projects require the involvement of highly skilled people who are familiar with both the current and the new technology. In addition, large or complex migrations might need a lot of these people. If you do not have people with the right sets of skills or do not have enough of these skilled personnel, your project will likely fail.

- **Unreasonable expectations.** IT departments are usually not very good at setting expectations for end users about the level of service or functionality they will receive. In situations in which end users do not fully understand the current implementation or the new implementation, it is easy to understand how expectations might not be properly set. This misunderstanding can cause a technically perfectly executed migration to appear lacking in the eyes of the end-user community.

- **Poor communication.** IT departments often also communicate poorly to organizations about their intentions and actions. Examples of important communications include downtime for migration activities, new or replaced functionality in the solution, and participation from the end-user community. Poor communication, or the lack of communication, can cause problems before, during, and after a project.

- **Unknown or unproven technologies.** IT personnel tend to resist unknown or unproven technologies. This is quite justifiable because IT personnel are employed to anticipate and prevent failures in their solutions. However, this resistance can also be an unjustified reaction to a loss of technical superiority in the older technology. Either problem must be overcome for a migration project to be successful.

- **Poor quality of the new solution.** Like new applications, some migration projects simply fail. They might not work correctly, might not support the business properly, or might not meet minimum service levels. Of course, these failures result in lost productivity, missed business opportunities, increased cost, and increased resistance to change.

As you can see, the problems that occur during upgrades and migrations are similar to the problems found in new environment implementations. However, because we are not starting with the proverbial "green field," the problems tend to be more complicated and their effects more severe.

# CHAPTER 2

# UNIX Migration Overview

This chapter starts to address the problems we described in Chapter 1. It explains how UNIX has evolved over the years and describes the major differences between versions of UNIX, while placing other operating systems into context. In addition, this chapter explains what the scope of a migration project should be.

This chapter contains the following sections:

- "Brief History of UNIX" on page 9
- "Comparison of Commercial and Derivative Versions of UNIX" on page 13

# Brief History of UNIX

The story of UNIX reads like an ancient Greek epic poem, full of conflict, interesting personalities, and incestuous relationships. It is no wonder, then, that so many histories of this important operating system have been written. While the history of UNIX might seem irrelevant to migration issues, it actually explains many of the problems that arise from today's migration efforts and their potential solutions.

## The Early Years at AT&T

UNIX began in 1969 when Ken Thompson and David Retch developed a new operating system for the PDP-7 computer that had replaced their Honeywell 635 running GECOS (General Electric Company Operating System). They sought to emulate many of the key features of the MULTICS operating system that they had previously worked on while creating with this more powerful computer. The resulting operating systems was dubbed "UNICS" (Uniplexed Information and Computing System), an acronym designed to poke fun at the MULTICS project. Eventually, the name was changed from UNICS to the modern name, UNIX.

Two years later, in 1971, UNIX was ported to the PDP-11/20 to support more users and the roff text formatting system. It was called the First Edition and was the predecessor for all versions of UNIX to come. UNIX would become different from typical operating systems of the day because it was written mainly in high-level languages with only a relatively small amount of assembly code (called the kernel). This made the operating system portable, allowing programmers to rewrite the small kernel for a new platform and simply recompile the high-level code on the new system.

In the following years, Thompson and Ritchie formalized their creation at the ACM Symposium with a paper called "The UNIX Time Sharing System." This paper, and its subsequent publication in the ACM's journal, propelled UNIX to the front of many researchers' minds. However, because of antitrust issues with the U.S. Government, AT&T was barred from manufacturing or selling any equipment that was not related to the telephone business. UNIX and its source code were made freely available to many universities for educational purposes. Two of the universities that received this source code were the University of California at Berkeley (UCB) and the University of New South Wales (UNSW) in Sydney, Australia.

# Berkeley Software Distributions

In 1974, Ken Thompson returned to his alma mater, UCB, to begin a one-year visiting professorship. Berkeley was already running the UNIX operating system on several machines. A group of graduate students, led by Bill Joy and Chuck Haley, began to improve the operating system through additions such as a visual editor (vi), the Pascal compiler, and the C shell. They also began to take an active interest in the UNIX source code, providing fixes and enhancements to the operating system.

In 1977, Joy put together Berkeley Software Distribution (BSD), which bundled these changes with the Pascal system, and distributed it freely to other sites. This led to a Second Berkeley Software Distribution (shortened to 2BSD) in mid-1978, which incorporated even more modifications and additions. The third distribution (3BSD) was ported to the new 32-bit VAX and included a virtual memory implementation. After this third distribution, the United States Defense Advanced Research Projects Agency (DARPA) began funding the distribution as an early part of the Internet.

In October 1980, 4BSD debuted with an improved Pascal compiler and enhanced mail-handling capabilities. As more improvements were made to this distribution (mainly in the areas of performance), AT&T balked at letting Berkeley call their next distribution 5BSD. AT&T's commercial UNIX distribution, System V, had just been released, and they were worried that this might cause confusion in the marketplace. Berkeley agreed to change its numbering scheme for future releases by simply incrementing the minor number. Hence, this release was called 4.1BSD.

1983 saw the release of 4.2BSD, the fruit of a second round of funding from DARPA. 4.2BSD was immensely popular, shipping more copies than all the previous BSD releases combined. The success of the 4.2BSD release was directly attributed to its inclusion of TCP/IP networking and the Berkeley Fast File system, and to DARPA's sponsorship.

Future years saw the release of 4.3BSD in 1986 and 4.4BSD in 1994. However, in the years between these two releases, a bitter lawsuit was contested between Berkeley; Unix System Laboratories (USL) was a spin-off of AT&T that sold and developed UNIX) and a smaller company called Berkeley Software Design, Incorporated (BSDI). AT&T took offense at BSDI selling a version of the BSD and marketing it as UNIX. BSDI claimed that Berkeley's distribution had reimplemented all but six source code files and BSDI had done the rest. After much legal wrangling in U.S. state and district courts, in 1994, USL, Berkeley, and BSDI came to an agreement that amounted to a number of minor changes and the addition of copyrights to files.

Following the end of legal hostilities, BSD was split into 4.4BSD-Lite and 4.4BSD-Encumbered. 4.4BSD-Lite was free of USL intellectual property and became the basis for most of the modern BSD releases today. These include NetBSD, FreeBSD, and BSD/OS (as WindRiver's BSDI-derived release).

# Mach

A third family of the UNIX releases was born in the mid-1980s when researchers at Carnegie-Mellon University developed a microkernel for UNIX. Following UNIX's founding philosophy of small and simple, the developers of the Mach microkernel (as they called it), implemented a minimal set of essential services while providing a framework for the majority of user services.

This approach was popular with vendors because it was unencumbered with the problem besetting BSD, namely, AT&T/USL licenses. Many popular later commercial UNIXes such as NextStep, OSF/1, and MacOS X were based on Mach.

# Commercial UNIX Releases

One of the earliest commercial releases of UNIX came from the Santa Cruz Organization (SCO), which produced XENIX in 1983. XENIX was a variant of the System V Release 3 (SVR3) that ran on Intel 8086-based personal computers. It would later be renamed SCO UNIX.

In early 1982, Bill Joy announced that he was leaving Berkeley for a small workstation company across the San Francisco Bay called Sun Microsystems. He took over the Sun Operating System (SunOS™), Sun's commercial version of UNIX based on 4.2BSD. SunOS 1.0 shipped in 1983.

In 1992, Sun migrated from their BSD-based SunOS to Solaris, which was based on UNIX System V Release 4 (SVR4). Sun had collaborated with AT&T on the development of SVR4, contributing technologies such as Network File System (NFS), virtual file interface (vfs/vnodes), and a new virtual memory system. To help their customers adopt the Solaris OS faster, they created the Sun Migration and Engineering Center in Toronto.

Hewlett-Packard joined the UNIX market in 1986 with their release of HP-UX. HP-UX was originally based on AT&T source code.

IBM entered the UNIX market with their own AIX/RT in 1986. AIX/RT was eventually renamed simply AIX and was originally based on SVR3.

Digital marketed UNIX for their VAX servers under the Ultrix brand name.

In response to Sun's co-development of SVR4, IBM, Digital, HP, and others formed the Open Software Foundation to develop a competing UNIX unencumbered by AT&T intellectual property. This produced OSF/1, one of the first operating systems based around the Mach kernel. OSF/1 debuted in 1990. However, few of the other member groups adopted this UNIX, due to a downturn in the industry. Most notably, HP and IBM chose to continue with their HP-UX and AIX products, incorporating parts of the OSF/1 specification into their products. Digital eventually refined OSF/1 and renamed it Digital UNIX in 1995. After Digital's merger with Compaq in 1999, the product was renamed again to Tru64.

Through industry consolidation, many of the commercial versions of UNIX have disappeared. For example, IBM's acquisition of Sequent resulted in the demise of Dynix PT-X. Compaq's acquisition of DEC, followed by HP's acquisition of Compaq caused development to cease for Ultrix and Tru64. Those versions of UNIX that remain are System V (SYSV) based. There are few significant differences between the leading commercial versions of UNIX that would impede migration projects.

# Linux

The most recent addition to the UNIX family tree is the development of Linux. A simple newsgroup posting by its founder, Linus Torvald, announced its birth in 1991:

> ".... I'm doing a (free) operating system (just a hobby, won't be big and professional like gnu) for 386(486) AT clones...."

Linux was created to be a free operating system by combining Linus's Intel x86 kernel with the GNU project's extensive UNIX commands and utilities. It contains a monolithic kernel with many of the BSD enhancements. Much like the many BSD versions, there are dozens of Linux distributions such as Red Hat Linux, Debian Linux, SuSe, Mandrake, and Caldera. Each represents a slightly different collection of kernel versions and utilities, along with a different target market and philosoph

Linux is not an SVR4-compliant product. While programs compiled on an SVR4 Intel platform are guaranteed to run on another SVR4 Intel implementation, this is not true for Linux. Despite Linux's heritage, source code migration from Linux to the Solaris OS can be quite simple.

# Comparison of Commercial and Derivative Versions of UNIX

As described in the preceding section, because of the common heritage of many of today's operating environments, there are inherently more similarities than differences between versions of UNIX. However, that is not to say that they provide similar functionality or even similar internals. In this section, we investigate some of the specific technical differences you will encounter when migrating between some of the families of UNIX implementations.

## UNIX Standards

UNIX implementations diverge in many fundamental and not-so-fundamental ways. This divergence has led to compatibility issues that many people refer to as the "splintering" of UNIX. Variations in the different file systems, networking frameworks, and virtual memory architectures are often cited as a difficulty for companies deploying multiple UNIX variants. This was especially difficult for companies looking to deploy complex applications. As a response to this issue, a movement was created to standardize a set of interfaces to abstract these complexities from application developers. The most common UNIX standards groups are:

- System V interface definition (SVID)
- Portable operating systems based on UNIX (POSIX) specifications
- X/Open (The Open Group)

Standard interfaces allow an application to interact with the operating system without detailed knowledge of how the functionality is actually implemented. The standard consists of a set of functions and their detailed semantics.

## System V Interface Definition

The System V Interface Definition (SVID) is a standard published by AT&T (which became USL) in 1995 to specify system calls, commands, and utilities. Versions of UNIX that conform to the SVID are permitted to call their operating system "System

V compliant." The current version of SVID, SVID3, corresponds to SVR4. With changes in ownership of the UNIX brand and source code, SVID has been merged into The Open Group's Single Unix Specification.

## POSIX

POSIX is an Institute of Electrical and Electronic Engineers (IEEE) group of standards for operating systems. Unlike SVID, the POSIX standard blends parts of SVR3 and 4.3BSD, not favoring one over the other. This has led to the widespread acceptance of the POSIX standard, especially POSIX1003.1 (POSIX.1), which defines many of the system calls. The following are some of the POSIX standards:

- 1003.1 Mostly seventh-edition system calls without signals and terminal interfaces
- 1003.2 Shell and utilities
- 1003.3 Test methods and conformance
- 1003.4 Real-time topics such as binary semaphores, process memory locking, memory-mapped files, shared memory, priority scheduling, real-time signals, clocks and timers, IPC message passing, synchronized I/O, asynchronous I/O, real-time files
- 1003.5 Ada language bindings
- 1003.6 Security
- 1003.7 System administration topics, including printing
- 1003.8 Transparent file access
- 1003.9 FORTRAN language bindings
- 1003.10 Supercomputing
- 1003.12 Protocol-independent interfaces
- 1003.13 Real-time profiles
- 1003.15 Supercomputing batch interfaces
- 1003.16 C-language binding
- 1003.17 Directory services
- 1003.18 POSIX standardized profile
- 1003.19 FORTRAN 90 language bindings

Solaris, HP-UX, and Tru64 are all POSIX-compliant operating systems. Most of these environments provide both POSIX-compliant calls and their own proprietary calls for important functions.

## X/Open

X/Open was organized in 1984 by a consortium of international computer vendors. Their aim was to develop an open common application environment comprising already existing standards. They published a seven-volume *X/Open Portability Guide (XPG)* that extended the POSIX.1 standard in areas of internationalization, window interfaces, and data management. This led to a host of standards including UNIX95 (Single Unix Standard version 1) and UNIX98 (Single Unix Standard version 2).

In 1993, all the major commercial UNIX vendors declared backing for X/Open, to create a common standard for UNIX. Because these standards had acquired the UNIX trademarks, this became the definitive UNIX definition.

Finally, in 2002, X/Open (now called The Open Group) completed the Single Unix Standard version 3. This unifying standard, which incorporates the X/Open standards and the IEEE POSIX work, now defines the UNIX operating system. The final specification includes over 1700 programming interfaces, organized into five documents covering the following topics:

- Base definitions (XBD)
- System interfaces (XSH)
- Shell and utilities (XCU)
- Rationale (XRAT)
- X/Open curses (XCURSES)

While no vendor has received Single Unix Standard version 3 certification, UNIX98 is still a common standard for many UNIX developers and users. Tru64 (version 5.1), AIX (versions 4 and 5L), and Solaris (versions 7, 8, and 9) are all UNIX98 certified. HP-UX 11i is not UNIX98 compliant, but is UNIX95 compliant.

More information on The Open Group and these standards is available on their Web site at `http://www.opengroup.org/`.

# The Kernel

The UNIX (and Linux) kernel provides a set of common facilities through abstracted frameworks. This provides a flexible operating system that retains its simplicity for developers. Some of the common facilities available on most modern versions of UNIX include:

- Processes scheduling
- Virtual memory
- Executables
- Virtual storage
- Networking
- Device communications

Within each of these abstracted frameworks, interfaces are implemented to support specific technologies. For example, the virtual storage framework allows interfaces for remote storage, such as NFS, as well as local storage, such as a UFS+ file system. The virtual storage facility is very flexible: it allows access to remote or local storage but hides complexity from the developer with its single method of accessing files. The virtual memory facilities hide the complexities of swap space and physical memory by making all available memory appear to applications as one memory space.

While the implementations of the major commercial UNIX kernels differ greatly, the differences are largely hidden from the user and programmer through these abstractions and the standards discussed in the preceding section. However, the areas that the standards do not cover are the major concerns for most porting efforts. These differences are noted throughout this book, when applicable.

# User Environments

All versions of UNIX provide their users with a host of environments in which to work. These environments are divided into two types: graphical and shell. The shell environment is the classic command-line interface (CLI) with the choice of command interpreters. The graphical user interface (GUI) environments provide visual representations through the use of the windows managers such as X11.

## Shells

Four major shells are available today. These include the venerable Bourne shell (sh) and C shells (csh), the Korn shell (ksh), and GNU's Bourne-Again Shell (popularly known as bash). Each of these shells is available on the major UNIX and Linux platforms. However, only a few platforms ship and support all of them.

Although these shells are available on different vendors' platforms, not all of them are implemented exactly the same. This shows up most commonly in shell scripts used to automate repetitive tasks. Usual culprits are differences in quoting rules, command return codes, and environmental variables.

## Graphical User Interfaces

There are three popular GUIs in today's UNIX environments: the common desktop environment (CDE), GNOME, and KDE. Each of these GUIs has its strengths and weaknesses. While CDE is the incumbent, GNOME and KDE are quickly becoming the desktops of choice for many UNIX users.

### CDE Interface

CDE is a reference implementation of a common UNIX desktop user environment. The CDE user interface presented a common desktop across the Solaris, HP-UX, Tru64, and AIX environments when it was introduced. CDE provides the following benefits:

- Clean, easy-to-use interface
- Consistency between UNIX platforms for both users and developers

- Similar metaphors and experiences for experienced Microsoft Windows users
- Several built-in applications

Unfortunately, CDE never lived up to its potential as a common GUI to compete with Microsoft Windows. Because it was developed jointly, its features did not keep pace with other popular desktops. In addition, few productivity application vendors chose to support it. The following figure shows the GUI from the Solaris 9 OS.

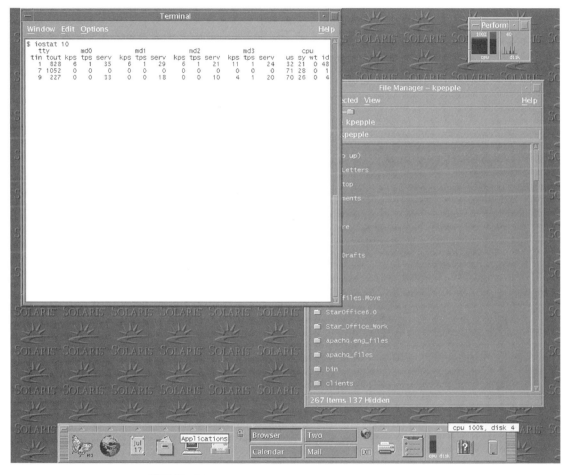

**FIGURE 2-1**   CDE Desktop

## GNOME Interface

The GNOME environment sprang from the open source world as a enabler for Linux's desktop ambitions.

The project comprises the following:

- **GNOME desktop.** A free graphical windows environment designed to run on UNIX and UNIX-like systems (such as Linux).
- **GNOME development platform.** Libraries and tools for developing applications.
- **GNOME Office.** Office productivity applications to rival Microsoft Office.

Some key features of GNOME include the following:

- Attractive and intuitive user interface
- Comprehensive personalization capabilities
- Convenient front panel for rapid access to favorite programs
- Full suite of powerful applications
- Ability to run existing CDE-based and Java-based applications

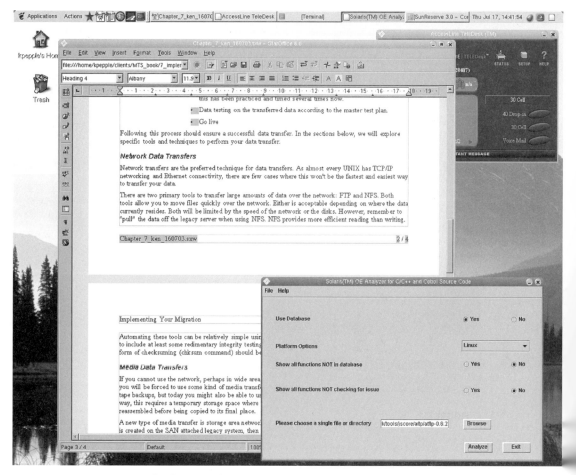

**FIGURE 2-2**   GNOME Desktop

Sun has chosen GNOME as its future desktop, and it is available for version 9 of the Solaris OS and later versions as an optional installation. The following figure shows the GNOME desktop from version 9 of the Solaris OS.

## KDE Interface

The KDE desktop also emerged from the open source world as GNOME's chief competition. Its design goals were slightly different, emphasizing stability and ease of migration for Microsoft Windows users. HP has chosen KDE as their common desktop, and it is available for the Solaris environment. The following figure shows the KDE desktop.

**FIGURE 2-3**   KDE Desktop

# CHAPTER 3

# Migration Strategies

This chapter defines the most important terms in migration and differentiates these terms. In addition, it presents migration strategies, the benefits and risks of each strategy, and the appropriateness of each strategy for various situations.

This chapter contains the following sections:

- "Understanding the Concepts" on page 21
- "Evaluating the Environment" on page 27
- "Examining Strategies" on page 30
- "Choosing a Strategy and Developing Tactics" on page 37

# Understanding the Concepts

Within the context of this book, the term migration is defined as the transition of an environment's people, processes, or technologies from one implementation to another. While somewhat open ended, this definition allows us to discuss migration in a number of different contexts:

- The migration of common off-the-shelf (COTS) software from one platform to a larger or smaller similar platform
- The migration of data from one database to another, possibly similar data storage technology
- The migration of a custom-written application from one platform to a different platform and operating environment

These examples have different inputs, different execution strategies, and dissimilar functional outcomes, but they are all migrations in that the IT functionality has been moved from one platform to a different platform. It is this varied scope that affords the term "migration" its varied interpretations.

# Consolidation

Migration is often confused with the act of *consolidation*. *Webster's College Dictionary* defines consolidation as, "the act of bringing together separate parts into a single or unified whole." As defined in the Sun BluePrints book *Consolidation in the Data Center*, by David Hornby and Ken Pepple, consolidation should be thought of as a way to reduce or minimize complexity. If you can reduce the number of devices you have to manage and the number of ways you manage them, your data center infrastructure will be simpler. This simplicity should contribute to efficiency, and consistency should contribute to lower management costs in the form of a reduced total cost of ownership (TCO).

While consolidations involve migrations as applications and business functionality are moved to a single machine, migrations do not necessarily involve consolidation. The value proposition realized by migration relates to improved quality of service (QoS) and reduced TCO realized as a characteristic of the new platform, environment, and overall IT infrastructure.

# Adoption

Frequently, the release of a new edition of an operating environment might require that the platform's operating system (OS) be replaced with a more up-to-date version, a practice referred to as *adoption*. Depending on the changes introduced in the new version, upgrading to a new version of the current OS might be as difficult as migrating the application to a completely different OS, even though the hardware platform remains the same.

Usually, applications that must be moved to a newer version of the same environment have to be tested to determine whether they provide the same functionality in the new environment. This can be a time-consuming, as well as expensive, process. If test suites designed to verify critical application functionality are not available, they will need to be developed, at considerable time and expense.

Application programming interfaces (APIs) are the touch points between applications and the operating environment. In addition to defining APIs, the Solaris environment also supports the concept of the application binary interface (ABI), the description of these APIs used by the application executable at a binary level. This definition enables you to compare the API usage of an application executable created in one version of the OS to the binary description of interfaces supported by a different release of the OS. Consequently, compatibility between different versions of the OS can be guaranteed without any examination of the source code used to create the application.

In most cases, binaries created under an earlier version of the OS require no change. However, should any incompatibilities exist, specific APIs that don't conform to the ABI definition of the new OS can be identified. Tools exist to support the static analysis of the application binary. Sun's `appcert` tool identifies differences so that they can be remediated prior to moving the application. This technology enables migration engineers to ascertain whether an application can be moved without problem to a newer version of the OS.

Moving applications from an older version of the Solaris OS to a newer version is referred to as *adoption* rather than migration. This distinction is made because the use of stable API standards, backward compatibility, and an ABI and tools enables you to verify and compare application interface usage, thereby guaranteeing that an application will run without problem in the new OS. In most cases, adoptions do not require recompilation, although using a later version of the compiler might provide performance benefits.

## The E-Stack

Before we introduce migration and porting, consider the following figure, which illustrates what we call the Enterprise stack or E-stack.

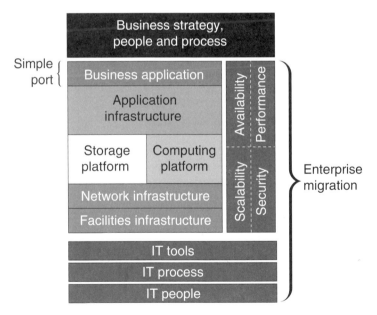

**FIGURE 3-1**   E-Stack Model for Enterprise Infrastructure

This construct is used as a model of the infrastructure of the enterprise. At the top of the stack, the business strategy, people, and process are defined. The high-level functions that occur here are usually controlled by an executive team. These functions provide logistical support to enable business functions, in addition to the unique value-added functions that differentiate one enterprise from another. The outputs of this level of the stack must be implemented by the lower levels. Typically, applications are used to implement and execute business processes.

The next section of the E-stack represents the execution architecture, which is composed of the following items:

- **Applications that support business functionality.** Changes in business processes most likely require changes in the application layer. Consequently, a rapidly evolving business must be able to implement application change in a timely manner. Business segments that are not subject to frequent change are less likely to require an agile development or runtime environment to effect application change.

- **Application infrastructure that supports the applications.** Modern implementations of this layer include web servers, application servers, middleware, and database technology that support a typical n-tiered architecture. For older, legacy applications, the application infrastructure layer is composed almost entirely of the OS. Applications in this layer are written to interact with the APIs provided by the OS vendor and software provided by independent software vendors (ISVs).

- **Computing and storage platforms.** These hardware components enable the application infrastructure. This layer of the stack is usually composed of a heterogeneous mix of hardware provided by a number of different vendors. As we will see, industry consolidation within the hardware manufacturing segment might require changes at this level of the stack. Unless the vendor has gone to great lengths to support backward compatibility, changes to the computing and storage platforms will require changes to the layers above them in the stack.

- **Network infrastructure.** In today's environment, the ability to communicate over a network is critical. This infrastructure can be based on any type of networking technology, from low-speed dial-up to fiber-optic, high-speed backbones. Many legacy applications and their interfaces were designed and developed before the advent of networking technology. They depend on antiquated, proprietary interconnect technology, which might include a series of screens for data entry or possibly thick-client technology. These applications are not web enabled.

- **Facilities infrastructure.** Frequently overlooked, this layer provides critical support to the stack elements above.

The upper portion of the E-stack that defines the execution architecture supports a number of systemic properties that are key to any enterprise. Availability, scalability, measurability, and security are all desirable but can be implemented only to the extent that they are driven and supported by the execution architecture and its components.

The lower portion of the E-stack represents the management architecture. These tools, people, and processes implement the management infrastructure for the enterprise and combine to control, measure, and manage the execution architecture. Tools can be used to monitor capacity, utilization, and throughput, and to help ensure that service levels can be met. Processes are in place to support change, service, deployment, and maintenance. These tools and processes are selected, developed, and administered by the IT staff. As change is effected within the E-stack, IT staff must be made aware of all changes. Training must take place to ensure that people understand the management process, as well as the execution architecture.

As you can see, all the elements of the stack support each other. If the facilities do not provide adequate power or air conditioning, the results will manifest themselves in the computing and storage platforms. If the computing and storage platforms do not support the application infrastructure, the application will not be able to function correctly and service level agreements will not be met. This would mean that the business function and requirements mandated and defined from the top layer of the stack could not be implemented.

The following table outlines the relationship between consolidation, migration, and adoption.

**TABLE 3-1**    Consolidation, Migration, and Adoption

| Term | Definition |
|---|---|
| Consolidation | The act of reducing the complexity in a data center |
| Migration | The act of moving technology from one platform or OS to another |
| Adoption | The act of moving from an earlier version of the Solaris OS to a later version |

# Porting

As illustrated in the E-stack shown in FIGURE 3-1 on page 23, the term *porting* applies to applications rather than infrastructures. In particular, it is usually used in discussions about custom-written applications and refers to modifying or normalizing the code of an application so it can be recompiled and deployed on a new hardware platform that supports a different OS. Wherever possible, coding standards (ANSI, POSIX, and the like) should be adopted to minimize potential future changes that might have to be made.

Porting is inherently associated with modifying the code base of an application so that the functionality provided by the APIs of the existing OS and supporting software products is replicated in the new target environment. This is typically done by developing compatibility libraries that map the older APIs to the new environment. Vendors might provide these libraries to ease the burden of migrating applications to their environments, but in many cases, you will have to develop compatibility libraries yourself.

Porting the application requires minimal understanding of the logic or functionality of the application. It is a somewhat mechanical effort for making the application compatible with the new environment.

A porting strategy requires you to integrate the application with a new development environment, as well as with a new operating system. While source code, scripts, and data are moved, compilers, source code repositories, and software tools are replaced by new versions that are compatible with the target platform.

When porting an application, you must also migrate any supporting third-party software. If the software is no longer available, you will have to find similar software and integrate it into the application. Should the amount of integration become excessive, the migration might begin to look less like a port and more like a rearchitecture effort, as described later in the chapter. Ensure that you determine the availability of third-party software used by the application before choosing a migration strategy.

# Migration

The term *enterprise migration* refers to the process of migrating all layers of the E-stack, not only the application that supports business functionality. This is a very involved exercise that will have a greater impact on the entire IT staff than other strategies do. For example, migrations include the following changes:

- Management policies present in the old environment must be migrated to the new environment.

- Tools used to monitor and manage the execution environment must be replicated.

- Supporting software, in the form of third-party products provided by an ISV, or locally written scripts to manage applications and data, must be integrated into the new environment.

- People must be trained to administer the new hardware platform and operating environment.

- Adding a large symmetric multiprocessor compute platform might justify the use of a multithreaded architecture for the application.

- Implementing a Storage Area Network (SAN) rather than attached storage might enable other applications to fully utilize storage resources that were previously unavailable.

- Adding networking capabilities might eliminate the need to transport and mount tapes.

- Web-enabling an application might reduce the need for proprietary terminal interfaces or thick-client technology.

- Changing hardware might require changes to the facilities to support more, or possibly less, power and cooling.

- Creating new tiers in the architecture might allow for the use of cheaper, more cost-effective hardware to support that portion of the application, which might, in turn, support greater availability and supportability.

- Using a modern programming language might enable the application to leverage more new third-party software, reducing the need for costly in-house development.

# Evaluating the Environment

The migration solution you choose should be based on how an application fits into the overall IT environment. Consequently, you must evaluate the existing environment to determine both how the application meets business needs and how effective it is.

Adequacy of meeting business needs relates to the application's ability to support the business functionality of the enterprise. Adequacy of meeting business needs can be defined as follows:

- The time required to introduce new features
- The ease of use of the application
- The ability to support the functional requirements of the enterprise
- The ability to support the future growth of the enterprise

Whereas the adequacy of meeting business needs relates to the application's ability to meet the current and projected functional needs of the enterprise, IT effectiveness measures the application's use of technology. IT effectiveness can be defined as:

- Total cost of ownership (TCO)
- Technological stability
- Functional separation
- Service level issues
- Implementation technologies

The comparison of an application's IT effectiveness with the adequacy of meeting business needs is represented in the following figure.

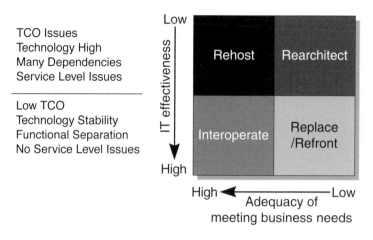

TCO Issues
Technology High
Many Dependencies
Service Level Issues

Low TCO
Technology Stability
Functional Separation
No Service Level Issues

Low

IT effectiveness

High

Rehost    Rearchitect

Interoperate    Replace /Refront

High ◄──────── Low
Adequacy of
meeting business needs

Functionality, Business Growth,
Time to Adapt, Ease of Use

**FIGURE 3-2**  Effectiveness Versus Business Needs

The x axis evaluates how well the application currently fulfills its function in the business process. The y axis rates its IT effectiveness in terms of cost, technological stability, dependencies, and other factors. To determine a migration solution for each of the applications within the enterprise, you should begin by plotting the applications that have the greatest impact on the business process within this framework.

The evaluation of the application can be formal (for example, a complete TCO study), or it can be ad hoc. Typically, the Chief Financial Officer of the enterprise will have to agree with the evaluation before agreeing to a budget to support the migration. By systematically evaluating all applications with the same criteria, a comprehensive migration strategy can be developed that will include a number of different solutions, as illustrated in the example shown in the following figure.

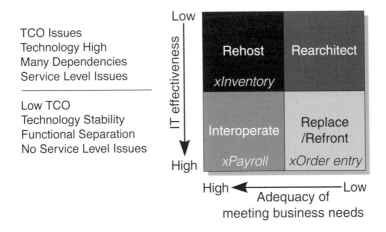

FIGURE 3-3  Example Evaluation of Applications

Applications with the following characteristics should be treated as follows:

- Applications that fall in the lower-left quadrant are meeting business process needs and are highly effective with respect to IT; they probably should be maintained as they are.

- Applications in the lower-right quadrant have high IT effectiveness, but are not meeting business process needs; they should be enhanced, not migrated.

- Applications that fall in the upper quadrants are the best candidates for migration. If they are meeting functional business process needs but are low in IT effectiveness (upper-left quadrant), it is probably time to move them to a new environment. If they exhibit low IT effectiveness and lack functionality (upper-right quadrant), it is probably time for the applications to be rearchitected.

FIGURE 3-3 illustrates how different applications (for example, payroll, inventory, and order entry applications) map to different migration solution spaces. For example:

- Order entry should be refronted because it relies on an antiquated user interface.

- The implementation and deployment of the payroll application is highly effective from an IT perspective and adequately meets business needs. It should remain where it is and be connected to new applications in the environment, as they are implemented, using connectors or adapters.

- The inventory application should be rehosted because the functionality it provides meets business needs, but there are issues with the hardware when it is implemented.

The terms "refront" and "rehost" are defined in detail in the following section.

# Examining Strategies

In the following sections, we examine the various strategies available for a migration effort, including the following:

- Refronting
- Replacement
- Rehosting—technology porting
- Rearchitecting—reverse engineering
- Interoperation
- Retirement

When planning a migration project, consider how your environment could benefit from the strategies described in this section.

# Refronting

Many legacy applications have excellent functionality but are not user friendly. Data entry for the application is accomplished by means of a series of screens that frequently contain cryptic names for fields and unintuitive menus, which result from limited screen space. These interfaces were based on CRT technology that was available 20 to 30 years ago.

Rather than rewriting an entire application, a programmer might be able to change just the data entry portion of the application. *Refronting*, or adding a more aesthetic interface to an existing application without changing the functionality, is an option. Users will have access to the same data but will be able to access it in a more efficient fashion without the use of expensive terminals, cabling, or peripheral interconnects.

When desired and appropriate, a browser-based solution can be developed. In the case of mainframe replacement, 3270 data entry screens can be replicated over a network. Web-enabling an application can provide significant cost reduction. Different approaches for refronting include screen scraping, HTML generation, source code porting, and other techniques.

Modern graphical user interface (GUI) technology can also be integrated into a legacy application to support a clearer representation of the required input. Conversely, for reasons of efficiency, the data entry screens might be replicated in the new technology "as is" to eliminate the need to train the data entry staff.

Some of the user acceptance issues identified by this example might reveal themselves when a rehost strategy is adopted and a COTS product upgrade involves a change to the input form's hosting technology (for example, when ASCII forms are replaced by a web browser).

The refront strategy requires an architectural model so that new components can invoke old, migrated components with minimum change to the migrated components. Such a migration project requires the application of architectural skills.

# Replacement

The refronting strategy is really a variation of the much broader *replacement* strategy. With the replacement approach, the legacy application is decomposed into functional building blocks. Once an application is broken down in this manner, portions of a generic and often complex, custom-written legacy application can be replaced with a COTS application. Of course, the package must be able to run on the target OS.

When evaluating replacement strategies, consider packages that offer better functionality and robustness than do the existing, deployed application components. Make sure the vendor's solution is well tested and accepted in the marketplace, and verify that it is configurable, enhanceable, and well supported by the vendor. Product longevity and backward compatibility must also be taken into account.

One of the key drivers for the applicability of this strategy is the competitive dynamics of the software supply industry. Any custom (or bespoke) applications owned by users are always competing with the market, whether the competitive position is implicitly or explicitly evaluated. The marketplace is also driven by a sedimentation process. ISVs are seeking to maximize the value in business terms of their software products. Sedimentation refers to the moving of supporting functionality from the application implementation space to middleware (or utility software). From there, the functionality moves to the OS and often to hardware. For example, print spoolers and job schedulers are good examples of components that have been extracted from the application space and are now usually provided by utility software suppliers or by infrastructure vendors. Sometimes this moves even further, for example, in the case where web server load balancing functionality moved from the application layer to become an OS feature and is now implemented in networking hardware.

The sedimentation process is an opportunity for migration planners because it enables their state-of-the-art business functionality to become available to the enterprise. This occurs because the ISV developers can outsource the functionality development and maintenance to alternative providers and can concentrate on transactional logic. By migrating some functionality through the use of the replacement strategy, this trend can be copied, and the in-house code maintenance problem can be reduced, albeit through transfer to a third party. For example, cost can be reduced or developer wages can be more focused on benefits, but cost is not eliminated. The replacement strategy enables in-house developers and maintainers of the utility code lines to be redeployed on more business-critical code lines and modules.

When considering replacement as a strategy, you might be attracted to the option to replace the application's code with a new third-party software product. If this approach is chosen, the migration project must do the following:

- Document the current business process and data model.
- Perform a gap analysis between the proposed application and the current state with respect to business process.
- Create a transformational data model, where appropriate.

These steps require traditional systems and business analysis skills.

A more powerful option might be to adopt a new application solution and change the organization's business logic when it no longer yields competitive advantage to match the package's optimum business process. This approach leaves migrators with the problem of identifying the still-used legacy data and migrating it to the new software solution. It also requires the development of a rollout plan that encompasses the enterprise's user community. Such a rollout is likely to be expensive, so the cost/benefit analysis of this approach needs to be solid and substantial. This analysis involves data modeling skills and, potentially, programs for transforming the data into the target data model and populating the new database. The latter approach allows the enterprise to transform applications built to deliver functional competitive advantage to software built to allow the user organization to compete through superior cost advantage. This goal mandates that the replacement product be competitively inexpensive to deploy and run.

Replacement can be a quick, low-risk solution, although the replacement of complete applications will have large implications in terms of business acceptance and rollout. However, replacing a homegrown solution with a COTS package can also take upward of two years. Effort is required to ensure that business processes and logic now conform to the capabilities of the COTS component, rather than the other way around. For some applications, the cost of acquiring custom logic for these software packages can be equivalent to maintaining and modifying a custom code base, depending on the function provided by that package, which is why it might be more appropriate to adopt the COTS vendors' assumed business process. Not all business processes, and hence not all applications, are designed to enable functional competitive advantage. For instance, a customer relationship management (CRM) package deployed to replace a specific business function will require more maintenance than configuring a replacement print spooler. If the proposed source modules for the migration are only a subset of the target package's functionality, it might make more sense to identify additional business processes to encapsulate within the CRM solution. For example, you might replace more code and increase the potential benefits case. This example shows the trade-offs available when replacement strategy-based migrations are being planned.

There are three clear options within the replacement strategy:

- Use a COTS package to replace or retire the source modules.
- Use a COTS/utility package to replace sedimented functionality.
- Use operating system functionality to replace sedimented application functionality.

The last option in the preceding list uses functionality that has been integrated into the existing OS. Examples of this include complicated memory management schemes that have been implemented because of older memory limitations, coarse-grained parallelism that is used instead of threading models, or shared memory that is used as an improved IPC shared memory.

The advantages of moving from a homegrown solution to a COTS-based solution include the following:

- Integration with other internal and third-party external applications
- The release of the budget associated with inflexible development resources
- An improved opportunity to tap skilled resources from established labor markets supporting both the business and IT communities

Replacement can act as a strategy on its own, and it can also be applied to components within an alternative strategy. Interestingly, as a strategy, it potentially yields the highest benefits and involves the highest degree of cost, yet when applied to components within an alternative strategy, it can be a quick and low-risk strategy.

# Rehosting—Technology Porting

*Rehosting* involves moving complete applications from a legacy environment with no change in functionality. There are several ways this can be accomplished for custom-written applications:

- **Recompilation.** As previously mentioned, an application can be ported to the new environment. There are two approaches for doing this. The first approach is primarily associated with developing or acquiring a compatibility library that provides identical functionality to that of the APIs found on the original OS and that supports third-party products. For example, Sun provides compatibility libraries for some of the major competing operating systems such as HP/UX. An alternative approach is to use intelligent code transformation tools to alter the original source code to correctly call the new operating system's APIs. Both approaches have the benefit of capturing the changes required during the migration, although the second might limit backward compatibility.

- **Emulation.** This approach introduces an additional software layer to emulate the instruction set used in the source binaries. While introducing another software layer between the application and the hardware can affect performance, the new layer eliminates the need for recompilation. When adopting this strategy, it is important to understand that the old environment has not really been left behind. The application will be developed and compiled using the old environment and will execute only in the new environment. By their nature, emulation solutions incur additional cost above that of the target platform environment. This results from the need to supplement the OS with the emulator, which is rarely free.

Although emulation is a useful approach, if source code is available, it is more common for an application to be recompiled to the native instruction set because native code runs faster. Emulation is most useful when migrating applications that are written in interpreted languages or when the original execution environment was tightly coupled within the OS. BASIC, PICK, or MUMPS are examples of environments that are suitable for emulation solutions.

Most emulators are for interpreted languages; therefore, the source code is available to the organization. However, source code engineering and reverse engineering rights might not have been granted in the right-to-use license. If you intend to use an emulation solution or reverse engineer a solution, ensure that you are licensed to do so in the environment where it will be used.

- **Technology porting.** Technology porting is a technique that supplements the target environment with the capability to execute code (usually interpreted) that runs natively on the original system. Many applications are developed and written in a superstructure software environment that is installed as a layered product on the source system. The most common types of these applications are created by relational database management system (RDBMS) vendors, many of whom support an array of hardware platforms and guarantee a common API across those platforms. The advantage of this approach is that one common API owner, the software ISV, owns the API on both the source and target systems. While the discovery stages of a migration project are still required, the APIs on the source and target systems remain the same.

  The leveraging of the ISV solution is often an opportunity to upgrade the ISV product version to obtain new functionality or to obtain superior support from the ISV. For instance, the transaction processing system known as CICS relies on a well-understood series of APIs. These APIs and their functionality have been ported or reimplemented on the new target Solaris OS. Applications using these APIs are compiled to run native instructions on the new system.

Rehosting offers the advantage of low development risk and enables familiar legacy applications to be quickly transferred to a more cost-effective platform that exhibits lower TCO and a faster return on investment (ROI). Extensive retraining of users is not needed because the architecture, interface, and functionality do not change. Rehosting is an excellent approach for companies desiring to decrease their maintenance and support costs.

Rehosting is, by definition, a quick fix. Rehosting does not change the application or the architecture. This means that new technology that is available in the target environment might not be properly utilized without some modification of the application. Rehosting is a preferred solution when the current business logic and business process remain competitive in the enterprise's markets and are worth preserving. Rehosting offers the possibility of using cost savings accrued through switching development and runtime environments to fund full rearchitecture projects, when warranted.

# Rearchitecting—Reverse Engineering

*Rearchitecting* is a tailored approach that enables the entire application architecture to migrate to the new OS, possibly using new programming paradigms and languages. Using this approach, applications are developed from scratch on a new platform, enabling organizations to significantly improve functionality and thereby take full advantage of the full potential of a target system.

Applications poor in IT effectiveness and functionality are the best candidates for rearchitecting. This approach is best used when time is not a major factor in the decision. Most rearchitecture projects require a skilled development staff that is well versed in the new technology to be implemented.

The downside to this approach is that it requires new or additional training for users, developers, and technical staff. In addition, rearchitecting requires the most time and is the most error prone of all the possible solutions. Sometimes, business rules can be well hidden in user interface or database management systems. For example, this was the case with DECforms, DEC FMS, and any RDBMS triggers. The ability to extract all the necessary business logic from the application's source can be severely inhibited by poor coding methodology and practice. An example is the hard-coding of business parameters.

Despite these problems, it remains that rearchitecture and reverse engineering are perceived to be the correct strategies and these problems become project risks. These risks can be mitigated by the application of appropriate business acceptance testing with internal and external users.

Rearchitecting does, however, open the opportunity to improve the business logic and processes and to change the developer productivity model.

A technique particularly appropriate to rearchitecture is reverse engineering. It is an axiom that the business logic encapsulated in the source code is the business logic implemented, and thus the source code is the most accurate place to discover the business logic. One of the key problems of software development is that most usability errors in software are introduced by poor business-process documentation and even poorer translation into software idioms. Some software environments have embedded dictionary or repository functionality. Where these exist, they may be supplemented with original author or third-party tools to enable the extraction of business logic and the recreation of that business logic in new environments. With these tools, the process can be reversed, the dictionary can be parsed, the user world view can be generated, and the implementation source code can be generated. A classic example is the RDBMS world in which data definition language scripts for a database implementation can be generated from the database implementation itself. This is tool based, and tools might be proprietary to a single RDBMS or environment, or they might be open, running across multiple environments. Database schema generators are particularly useful for migrating from one RDBMS to another, such as from Microsoft's SQL Server to Oracle or Sybase.

# Interoperation

In certain cases, it might be advantageous to leave an application where it is and surround it with new technology when it is required by an enterprise. *Interoperability* is a strategy that should be considered in the following cases:

- If business requirements are being met and IT effectiveness is high, it might be desirable to leave the application in its current environment, provided that environment is capable of interacting with current technology.

- Unfortunately, business drivers—for example, the existence of a leasing or outsourcing contract—might dictate that an application should stay where it is for some period of time. This is one of the risks of abandoning your IT environment to a third party. Over time, outsourced applications become orphans within the IT infrastructure. They are not fully integrated into the IT environment, most likely do not have a development staff, and run on outdated hardware that is no longer cost effective.

Many ISVs provide technology that enables legacy applications and storage technology to interoperate with newer technology. Intelligent adapters exist that support interactions between the mainframe and modern computing alternatives. It is also possible to compile an older language such as COBOL or PL/1 into Java™ bytecode, enabling it to seamlessly interact with a modern application server and other components of a Java™ 2 Enterprise Edition (J2EE™) environment.

When you choose this strategy, it is important to understand the vendor's commitment to the existing product line, as well as any future maintenance and product licensing costs. In addition, consider the availability of third-party software and current technological trends. When possible, open standards should be favored to allow a wide choice of competitive options.

# Retirement

Changes in technology can obviate the need for specific functionality in an application or an overall solution. As middleware or third-party products mature, they might render the functionality implemented in the application obsolete. In this case, legacy utilities or legacy application functionalities can be retired because they are no longer required or are implemented elsewhere in the solution.

# Choosing a Strategy and Developing Tactics

The ideal migration solution incorporates a number of the strategies listed in this chapter, where appropriate. Each of the strategies identified in the preceding section has a number of closely aligned supporting techniques. The selection of a strategy will define the obvious and most effective technique, but it might need to be supplemented with techniques more appropriate to other strategies.

The following table summarizes the strong alignments of particular migration techniques with the migration strategies.

**TABLE 3-2**    Strategy and Technique Alignment

| Strategy | Complementary Technique |
| --- | --- |
| Refronting | Redeveloping, reverse engineering, source code porting |
| Replacement | Reverse engineering |
| Rehosting | Source code porting, technology porting |
| Rearchitecting | Reverse engineering, redeveloping |
| Interoperation | Technology porting, emulation |
| Retirement | Reverse engineering |

As with the migration decision itself, the tactical approach used to solve a problem or to provide functionality must be evaluated in terms of its effectiveness, its impact on the ability to meet business needs, and its cost. Tactical decisions made to resolve technical issues might impact the overall project, either beneficially or adversely, in terms of systemic qualities, manageability, training, and cost.

As described in the preceding sections, there are a number of migration solutions for you to choose from. Each has its own benefits, as well as its own drawbacks. Selecting the correct solution should realize the associated value proposition.

## Decision Factors

One factor in your decision should be based on your application architecture. Most modern application architectures are now based on n-tier models. This decomposition allows for different strategies to be applied to different tiers, when appropriate. This might mean that more than one strategy will drive your migration.

Conversely, older legacy applications might be monolithic or client-server in design and implementation, which offers the opportunity to rearchitect to an n-tier model. The following table outlines some common (not exclusive) approaches for each tier.

**TABLE 3-3**    n-Tier Migration Strategies

| Tier | Purpose | Common Approaches |
|---|---|---|
| Presentation | Hosts the processing that adapts the display and interaction as appropriate for the accessing client device, be it a desktop computer, a cell phone, a PDA, or any other device. | Refronting, rehosting, interoperating, and replacing |
| Application or Business Logic | Hosts the logic that embodies the rules of the enterprise, irrespective of access device or resource implementation. | Rehosting, interoperating, and replacing |
| Integration | Allows for the connection of disparate applications and data sources. | Rehosting, interoperating, and replacing |
| Resource or Database | Consists of legacy systems, relational databases, data warehouses, or any other back-end or external processing system that accesses and organizes data. | Rehosting and replacing |
| Persistence | Holds the permanent data for the enterprise. In the past, this was considered part of the Resources tier, but with the growth of intelligent storage (SANs, NAS, and intelligent arrays), it has become a tier in itself. | Rehosting and replacing |

Another factor to consider is the relationship between value and effort, as shown in the following figure. Typically, value is proportional to the amount of effort that is expended on a project. In the following paragraphs, we examine each of the proposed migration solutions as they relate to value versus effort.

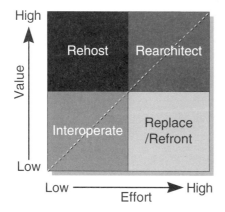

**FIGURE 3-4**  Relationship of Value to Effort

- **Interoperation.** This solution requires the least amount of effort but also provides the least amount of benefit. The existing architecture and infrastructure stay in place and simple connector technology is deployed to support the interaction with new applications or hardware that might be deployed. Because no new functionality is introduced, this effort requires minimal time and expense.

- **Rearchitecting.** This solution occupies the other end of the scale. Rearchitecting the application has great benefits: it supports tailored functionality; modular, tiered design; and a modern implementation language. However, the amount of effort (and associated cost) can be significant. As well as incurring significant expense, time, and effort, this solution can also introduce errors, so it requires a rigorous validation and verification effort.

- **Refronting or replacement.** This solution is targeted toward enhancing an application that has already been deemed to be somewhat unacceptable in meeting business needs. This solution is targeted to applications that are not meeting business needs but that do not have any IT-related problems relating to Service Level Agreements (SLAs), QoS, TCO, and the like. Enhancing the application by adding a presentation layer will add new functionality, but given that the application has already been found to be somewhat unacceptable, this enhancement adds minimal overall benefit compared with the amount of effort that it requires.

- **Rehosting.** As illustrated in FIGURE 3-4, rehosting is the solution that provides the most value for the least effort. Rehosting typically involves modifying the source code and build environment for an application so that it compiles and runs on the new target system. During this process, new features and functionality are not added. Many companies often want to add new features or functionality when they migrate, but these steps should take place after the application has been migrated.

Business logic remains the same when an application is rehosted. The only application changes usually relate to the APIs of the target OS. Over time, standards (SVR4, POSIX, and the like) have converged so that differences between versions of UNIX are minimal; therefore, migrations of applications between different versions of UNIX require minimal effort.

Rehosting applications from proprietary, non-UNIX environments that do not adhere to open standards can prove to be more challenging.

In certain cases, an application must be changed to not only adhere to the APIs of the OS but to interact with third-party product code as well. For example, consider the rehosting of a CICS application from MVS to MTP/MBM application running on the Solaris OS. The application's interaction with the MVS environment must be recoded in such a way that similar calls and functionality are used in the Solaris OS, but the CICS interaction requires minimal conversion because the CICS functionality and APIs have been redeveloped under the Solaris OS by the MTP and MBM product set.

Rehosting has the following characteristics:

- **Least expensive and requires the least effort.** Rehosting requires minimal changes to applications to enable them to run under the new environment. Therefore, the cost and effort involved in this strategy are minimal.

- **Quickest implementation.** Because little or no code is written and no new functionality is added, this solution can be completed in minimal time, compared with the other migration solutions.

- **Business logic remains the same.** Rehosting doesn't typically include the addition of new features or functionality. Consequently, the business logic remains the same, meaning that minimal or no staff training is required and few, if any, changes have to be made to the organizational structure.

# Case Studies

In the last three chapters of this book, we examine three case studies, each of which uses a different migration strategy.

- **Case 1: Small business, Linux.** This example is based on a small software and services development company that is looking to move from Linux to the Solaris OS. Approximately 20 servers are being used: 10 for production, 5 for development and testing, and 5 for office support tasks. Their application is mostly Java-based, but they use MySQL for the database. Significant shell scripting has also been used for utilities in the product.

- **Case 2: Custom application, Tru64.** In this example, we examine the migration of a mythical inventory application implemented in the C programming language. The application is integrated with a Sybase database running under the Tru64 environment. The exercise involves porting the application so that it runs under the Solaris environment and replacing the Sybase database with an Oracle relational database.

- **Case 3: General ledger, HP-UX.** In this example, an insurance company planned to move its accounting, risks, and claims software from HP/UX to the Solaris OS to achieve superior scalability against planned business and system growth. This exercise employs the rehost strategy, in which the technology porting approach is used to minimize risk and cost.

# CHAPTER 4

# Justifying and Planning a Migration Project

Before you can begin addressing the technical aspects of a migration project, you must prove that a business case exists to support a migration effort. In addition, you must begin building an infrastructure for the work that will be done during the architect, implement, and manage phases of the project.

This chapter presents the following sections to address these tasks:

- "Establishing a Business Justification for a Migration Effort" on page 43
- "Planning Your Migration Project" on page 52
- "Closing the Project" on page 64

# Establishing a Business Justification for a Migration Effort

The decision to migrate is never an easy one. There is inherent risk associated with the task, and there are several drawbacks that can make a migration effort appear to be unattractive when you first consider one, including the following:

- The benefits of a migration project, both tangible and intangible, are only achievable and measurable after the migration of the IT infrastructure is complete.
- The costs to the organization in terms of productivity and monetary expenditures can be significant.
- As a result of a migration effort, there is always a chance that people could lose their jobs.

Consequently, the undertaking must be clearly justified by the business benefits it yields. These benefits can be expressed in terms of technological advances as well as financial rewards, which can be related to improved productivity, scalability, availability, and the like. For information about the common benefits that can be achieved through migration, refer to Chapter 1.

In this section, we explain how gaining executive sponsorship and performing due diligence help justify the decision to undertake a migration effort

## Gaining Executive Sponsorship

When undertaking a migration project, ensure that you receive executive approval by someone in a CFO capacity, as well as someone with CTO, CIO, or data center manager responsibilities. The CIO or CTO will be interested in the technical feasibility of the migration solution and will want to ensure that Service Level Agreements (SLAs) will be met and that the systemic qualities (reliability, scalability, availability, and manageability) are achievable. Additionally, a CIO or CTO will position the enterprise so that its technology will be implemented on a modern, extensible platform that will have longevity.

When executive sponsors consider the longevity of a platform, it is critical that they assess the ability of the chosen vendor to provide a technology road map that details the product plans for both hardware and software for some period of time. When working with vendors who are attempting to eradicate or merge existing product lines or environments, it is important to closely examine their offerings to ensure that the new products they are providing actually exist and will be backward compatible with earlier releases. The last thing any enterprise wants is to have to repeatedly migrate their environment and infrastructure to a schedule that is dictated by a third party, such as a hardware or software vendor.

The CFO, on the other hand, will want everything the CTO or CIO looks for, and more. A CFO's concerns relate to the total cost of ownership (TCO) of the new environment, as well as the cost to get there. This includes not only the costs of the new hardware and software, but also the associated costs of training, facilities modification, testing, system transition, hardware amortization costs, and the like.

Regardless of the metric used to justify a migration effort, be it TCO, return on investment (ROI), or some more esoteric construction, the metric must be measurable to ensure that all parties are satisfied. Moreover, as the following sections describe, the establishment of these metrics and the manner in which they are determined will be critical to the justification of the migration effort.

# Performing Due Diligence

*Due diligence* is the act of verifying that a migration opportunity exists. The level of due diligence you perform will vary depending on the amount of risk involved in a migration project. Obviously, risk tends to scale proportionally to the size and complexity of a project. The amount of due diligence required will scale accordingly. For example, it is not unusual to spend considerable amounts of time and effort to perform due diligence for a mission-critical enterprise application. However, you would not expend this effort for a simple application port.

At this early stage of the project, the level of detail required for approval can vary. However, as you proceed through iterations of this phase or later phases, the detail captured during this phase might need to be refined through further assessment and analysis.

To successfully perform due diligence before beginning a migration project, you must perform the following tasks:

- Identify the business case
- Build consensus
- Establish and prioritize objectives
- Define a value proposition
- Identify benefits

## Identify the Business Case

A *business case* is a document that includes an investment appraisal based on cost/benefit analysis. There are several ways to derive an investment appraisal, including leveraging prior experience, applying industry rules of thumb, or performing detailed fact-finding. For example, lines of code might provide a rough estimate for rehosting projects involving source code porting techniques, whereas the number of business rules might be more appropriate for COTS applications in a rearchitecture effort. The business case includes high-level estimates of the cost involved in your project that are based on the duration of the tasks and the level of effort required to perform them; these costs need to be approved by a budget holder. The level of detail captured in this document will vary from project to project. In some cases, the benefits of a project are easily identified. In other cases, further analysis, both technical and financial, must be performed before a business case can be formalized.

After justifying a migration, you will create a *resource plan* that identifies the roles and responsibilities involved in a project, and the level of commitment required to support them. The high-level details that you capture in the business case should be moved forward into the resource plan you develop.

Chapter 3 provides information about the strategies you can use to develop a business case that can be used as an outline for the resource plan. It is possible that candidate architecture plans and artifacts might be required to develop the business case. It is this difficulty of defining justification activities that has led to confusion between these activities and the architect phase.

## Build Consensus

Before beginning a migration that will touch many different components of an organization, you must ensure that everyone who will be affected by the migration is consulted. They do not necessarily have to be in agreement with the plan to migrate, but it is critical that all concerns are brought to the table before you begin the project. This also requires input from all stakeholders. Not all organizations are able to accomplish this. Frequently, upper-level management's decision to migrate is made in a vacuum without consulting other stakeholders. At the opposite end of the spectrum, the IT staff might initiate discussions about a migration without considering the business functionality supported by the application or the long-term technology plans for the organization as a whole.

To better accomplish the task of discovery, you should conduct a migration workshop. This event typically lasts two to three days, and allows all segments of the organization that might be affected by the migration to review the project together. Having everyone in the same room ensures that all viewpoints are heard and, hopefully, understood.

As an example of the types of interactions that occur at these types of events, consider a situation where the IT staff rejects the idea of migrating to a new platform, stating that things work fine as they are currently implemented. Their viewpoint might change when they find that the company is about to double its capacity and therefore double its demand on the current infrastructure. Similarly, the IT staff might say that application X works well, meets the existing SLAs, and is understood by everyone. However, upon finding out that the licensing fees for that technology have increased fivefold, they will understand why the business functionality must be migrated.

The workshop also has an additional advantage: It can be an early gauge of the amount of commitment there is for the migration within the organization. Little or no commitment to the workshop often indicates a lack of commitment to the migration effort itself.

The following figure illustrates the various components of an enterprise architecture. It is critical that participants representing all segments of the architecture are represented in the discussion of a migration.

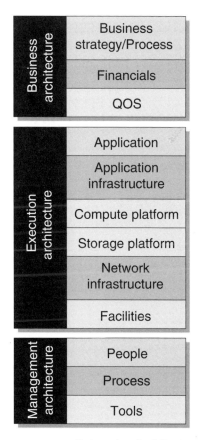

FIGURE 4-1    Enterprise Architecture

The following table identifies who is responsible for the functionality associated with each component of the architecture. Before implementing a migration, consult all of these people (or their representatives), and ensure that they provide input about the impact the migration will have on their area of the enterprise architecture.

**TABLE 4-1**  Architectural Roles and Responsibilities

| Position | Role | Function |
|---|---|---|
| **Business Architecture** | | |
| Process/Strategy | CIO or CTO | Understands and sets the technological direction for the organization as whole, identifying long-term technological trends, and positions the enterprise to take advantage of the trends whenever possible. This person typically attempts to implement technological convergence. |
| Financials | CFO | Understands the financial state of the enterprise as a whole rather than the line of business owner. This person ensures that the migration meets specific financial objectives. |
| Quality of Service (QoS) | Business unit owner | Understands the functionality provided by the application. This person is typically involved with developing SLAs and has the responsibility to ensure that they are met or exceeded. |
| **Execution Architecture** | | |
| Application | Software developer | Supports, maintains, and enhances the application. Understands how it is built, its dependencies, interactions, and third-party products used in the runtime or development environment. |
| Application Infrastructure | System/database administrator | Understands the data requirements of application. They are usually responsible for backup requirements. |
| Compute Platform | Operator/system administrator | Ensures that the platforms remain available. |
| Storage Platform | System administrator | Understands the interaction between the application and the storage platform, be it a SAN, NAS, or directly attached. |
| Network Infrastructure | System/network administrator | Understand the technology used to connect the application to a network. |

**TABLE 4-1**   Architectural Roles and Responsibilities *(Continued)*

| Position | Role | Function |
|---|---|---|
| Facilities | Technician | Ensures that the necessary environmentals (power, air conditioning, ventilation, battery backups, etc.) can support the hardware. |
| **Management Architecture** | | |
| People | IT manager | Defines the required skills for the IT staff. |
| Process | Management architect | Implements the IT management process (change management, trouble ticket reports, etc.). |
| Tools | System administrator | Implements the instrumentation of the IT environment. |

The workshop is structured such that the initial kickoff session is attended by all participants. The perceived business and technological drivers for the migration are put forward for discussion. Having all the players in the same room allows for a quick determination of consensus or the identification of dissent. Remember, for the migration to be successful, everyone must understand why the project is being undertaken and the projected outcome before starting the project. Migrating IT functionality, only to find that the requirements of one group of stakeholders have not been met, is a fruitless, costly, exercise. Conflicts should be identified so that they can be remedied through the development of an alternative approach or by executive decree.

After the initial kickoff, interviews with the stakeholders are conducted to document their requirements and comments. Finally, a report providing an overview of the problems and business drivers is presented to those who attended the kickoff meeting. The purpose of this report is to draw a line in the sand and to identify what has to be done. The purpose of this activity is to define the "what," not the "how," of a project. As you will see, you cannot determine how parts of the project will be executed until you have fully assessed the three levels of architecture, developed a strategy, and evaluated the cost of implementing a solution.

In rare cases, organizations might fully understand what migrations require, both in terms of a solution and in terms of the necessary outcomes. In these cases, the necessary interviews and discussion have already been conducted, the approach identified, and required outcomes documented, so the workshop activity can be eliminated. However, before implementing a proposed solution, the organization might benefit from having its approach evaluated or assessed by an outside consultant as a form of due diligence. A neutral third party can provide an objective evaluation of the problem and recommended solutions.

In all cases, assumptions should be documented and deliverables clearly defined with specified due dates.

## Establish and Prioritize Objectives

With any large or complex undertaking, it is vitally important that you clearly define and document the project's objectives and scope. Addressed too broadly, the project will not complete to the user expectations; defined too narrowly, it might not bring the benefits the organization requires. Balancing the objective and scope with the technical migration strategies is the key to a successful project.

Major objectives will fall into three main categories:

- *Business objectives* focus around process and functionality, assuring that the newly migrated environment provides adequate functionality and integrates smoothly into existing business processes.

- *Financial objectives* center on the cost (or total cost of ownership) differential between the legacy solution and the new solution.

- *Technical objectives* concentrate on ensuring that the delivered solution provides the qualitative factors to fully support the business.

When setting objectives for a migration project, ensure that they are measurable, achievable, and timely. The biggest pitfall when setting migration project objectives is failing to define measurable objectives that can be closely followed by estimating the timeliness of the objectives. Vaguely worded objectives such as "providing similar functionality" or "roughly the same performance" leave the project's success at the mercy of end-user opinion, which might not be kind after a migration has disrupted their routine. Objectives should be more clearly stated—for instance, "meeting the functional tests outlined in the service definition document" or "providing performance that meets or exceeds the performance tests outlined in the service capacity plan."

Once you have identified the high-level objectives for a migration, prioritize them to suit your business case. All project stakeholders should be involved in the prioritization of objectives.

## Define a Value Proposition

The choice of long-term strategies and short-term tactics depends on the drivers that were already in play. For example, if the inability to meet SLAs is a primary driver for a migration project, the migration should produce improved QoS or improved service levels. Addressing the business driver as a value proposition can help you determine which strategies and tactics will best satisfy your business needs.

Some of the value propositions resulting from a migration are tangible and measurable, whereas others are intangible. The tangible benefits are outlined in the following table.

**TABLE 4-2**  Tangible Value Propositions

| Value Proposition | Description |
| --- | --- |
| Faster time to market | Ability to get application to market faster than redevelopment (rehosting) |
| Investment protection (intellectual property) | The same features and functions from the legacy environment (rehosting) |
| Improved service levels | Rearchitect new and improved service levels in the new environment, or architect to deliver on existing service levels |
| Reduction in hardware costs | Migration/consolidation of legacy assets due to performance characteristic of new technology |
| Reduction in software cost | Migration/consolidation of legacy applications resulting in fewer software licenses |
| Reduction in operational cost | Migration/consolidation of legacy assets due to performance characteristic of new technology, architected to support SLA requirements and defined processes and procedures |
| Reduction in facilities costs | Migration/consolidation of legacy assets due to performance characteristic of new technology causing footprint reduction |
| Improved performance | Increased performance characteristic of new technology |

The intangible (or unmeasurable) benefits are outlined in the following table.

**TABLE 4-3**  Intangible Value Propositions

| Value Proposition | Description |
| --- | --- |
| Staff skills retention | In the case of mainframe rehosting, there is no need to retrain the IT staff for new skills. |
| Staff skills improvement | In the case of UNIX/NT, staff retraining would be required; in most cases, it is looked upon as career enhancing. |
| Technological longevity | Sun provides best-of-breed investment protection with the Solaris OS. |
| Simplicity | Typically, when moving from multiple operating systems to a single operating system, all aspects of data center management are simplified. |
| Superior use of software market supply chain | By migrating from legacy solutions based on old hardware or software, the enterprise can rearchitect external support agreements to improve service or reduce cost (replace, rehost). |

## Identify Benefits

A number of migration benefits were defined in Chapter 1. As described in Chapter 3, these benefits create a value proposition for the migration exercise. As a result of migrating to new technology, the enterprise can expect to see an improvement in some metric that is relevant to its business functionality.

Ideally, benefits should be both objective and measurable. These benefits are the key drivers for the migration effort. If the benefits are not realized, it will be difficult to show that the migration effort was successful. Objective, measurable benefits, such as reduced licensing costs, improved throughput, or reduced transaction costs are clearer evidence of improvement than are subjective benefits such as the adoption of a a more modern technology, improved productivity, and reduced vendor dependencies.

## Defining the Project Startup Stage

The justify stage defines a project plan including a project governance model. The business plan is used to obtain executive buy-in and sponsorship. The project governance model should be used to sustain the executive support throughout the project. Project governance includes the definition and nomination of a Project Executive/Project Manager team, together with other key roles to be undertaken during the project.

# Planning Your Migration Project

With a successful project justification and approvals in place, you need to start building a vital infrastructure that will make the migration successful. This section details the tasks involved in planning a migration project. From a high level, building the infrastructure involves the following tasks:

- Defining scope
- Understanding risks and planning contingencies
- Organizing the project team
- Developing a project plan

While the earlier chapters of this book focused on the reasons behind migrations and general technical strategies to approach them, this section starts addressing the logistics involved with turning a migration plan into a reality. It takes you through a detailed implementation of the migration methodology, illustrating key points with a sample migration project plan. In addition, this section presents techniques for identifying and assembling the technical skills necessary to execute the project plan.

# Defining Scope

As with any complex project, scope must be tightly defined and zealously controlled throughout the project. Scope creep is the number one threat to any migration project. Be prepared for people to try to seize upon the project to change some detail of the solution (be it hardware, software, tools, processes, or management) for their own needs. These attempts must be resisted at all costs. Migrations are complex projects when they have a proper scope, and additional challenges can mean the difference between success and failure.

In addition, however, you must ensure that scope is not too tightly defined. Shortcuts and omissions that occur during the architect phase will be uncovered during the implement phase, often resulting in a need to adjust the scope of a project. This flexibility to adjust scope, but only when absolutely required, can be the difference between the overall success or failure of a migration effort. Inflexibly resisting scope creep can affect customer confidence and completion of a project on time, but to try to incomplete specifications is a costly and pointless exercise.

Ideally, any migration project's scope will be the provision of equivalent end-user service or business support by way of a different platform, application, or process. Deviations from a scope should be fully documented with appropriate risks, mitigation procedures, and contingency plans as outlined in the following sections.

# Understanding Risks and Planning Contingencies

Risks are inherent in any IT project. However, migrations tend to be considered the most risky because of the number of interdependencies they involve and the amount of change they produce. To minimize risk in migrations, you should follow a risk management technique. While many different techniques exist, most include the following components:

- Risk identification
- Risk estimation
- Risk evaluation
- Mitigation and contingency plan creation

By choosing a risk management technique that has each of these components, you can actively monitor and control risk.

Because of the risky nature of migration projects, it is especially important to plan for contingencies in case your project runs into trouble. A contingency plan needs to be documented and approved during project planning so that it can be executed as an option should the need arise, not as a panic response that precipitates scores of other emergencies.

The following figure illustrates how risk is decreased with knowledge gained through an assessment of the migration opportunity. At one extreme, if you know absolutely nothing about the application and the associated infrastructure, your risk is high. On the other hand, if you have invested so much time and effort into understanding the environment and implementing proofs of concept that you have already completed the bulk of the project, your risk is nonexistent. The amount of effort expended during an assessment should be directly related to the level of risk the organization is willing to accept and the associated costs it is willing to pay, both in terms of labor and organizational disruption caused by the assessment activity itself.

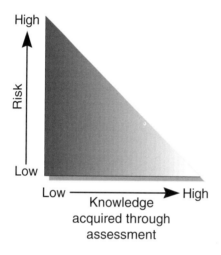

**FIGURE 4-2** Risk Evaluation Rating Graph

This section explains how to identify and estimate risk in a project and how to evaluate that risk. It then presents a common risk management technique and its application to migration projects.

## Identify Risk

All risks need to be stated so that they can be evaluated. There are generally two types of risk: business risk and project risk. Business risks prevent the project's ability to deliver the desired business benefits. Project risks jeopardize the project from delivering its objectives. In Chapter 1, we outlined a number of problems that can occur during a migration project. Any and all of these problems are potential business or project risks. They include the following:

- Business risks
  - Cost
  - Complexity

- Time and effort
- Lack of executive support
- Resistance to change
- Project risks
  - Inappropriate scope
  - Lack of accurate information
  - Poor change control

The risks that you identify for your project should cover most of these, as well as any risks that are specific to your project, situation, or organization. It is not uncommon for complex migration projects to have dozens of risks.

## Estimate Risk

Each identified risk must be assessed. This assessment measures the possible repercussions to the business or project from the identified risk. While there are many ways to perform this estimation, most methodologies use the sums of two numerical indexes to ascertain the total severity of a problem. Often, these numerical indexes relate to impact (the portion of the project the risk might affect), and severity (the level of detriment it might impose).

For example, the inability of your new tape drives to read legacy backup tapes would have a narrow impact (an impact level of one), whereas the inability to secure proper testing facilities would have a broad impact (impact level of five). Expressing the estimate as a numerical index between one and five, we might rate this situation as having an impact of four.

Each identified risk must also be categorized by the severity of its impediment to the success of the project. This too will be a numerical index representing a possible problem. In the example above, if the legacy tape drives were the only source of data and were quite rare, the inability to access them would rate as a high severity. However, because we can simply back up this data to another tape drive or across the network, we rate its severity as one.

## Evaluate Risk

After identifying risks and estimating their impact and severity, you need to evaluate and prioritize the risks to your project. This task allows you to concentrate on risks that pose the greatest threat to your project. Most methodologies prioritize risks according to the product of their numerical impact and severity ratings.

Continuing with our example above, we produce the risk evaluation rating of four by multiplying the impact score of four times the severity score of one. However, if we had to rely on these tape drives and the severity rating was four, our risk evaluation rating would soar to sixteen (4 x 4 = 16). These risk evaluation ratings become very clear when they are graphed.

## Create Mitigation and Contingency Plans

Once all the risks have been identified and prioritized, mitigation and contingency plans must be created. Mitigation plans reduce the risk of the problem occurring; contingency plans outline the project's recourse if the problem occurs. Some of these plans should be built into the best practices of the project itself. For example, a common risk for migration projects will be the failure to successfully port the source code to the new platform. Mitigation steps for this risk include the following:

- Involving appropriate vendors early in the process. Appropriate vendors in this case would be legacy and current platform vendors, as well as any vendor contributing source code (such as libraries).

- Contracting outside experts in this type of porting to mentor the staff involved in the project.

- Reviewing code frequently with the porting team to identify problems early.

- Porting the code "in place" through the use of macros and other programming constructs so that it compiles on both the legacy and new platforms. This allows the code, with any improvements, to be used on either platform.

However, if these mitigation efforts do not lead to a successful port, contingency plans should be available. Contingency plans for this problem might include the following:

- Outsourcing the porting tasks to a vendor skilled in such projects. The impact on the project from this approach would be cost, resources, and time.

- Revaluating strategy for the migration. For example, instead of porting the source code, you could run it under emulation technology. Or, perhaps a complete rewrite is in order. This option has broad effects on all phases of the project.

- Falling back to the legacy solution. As part of this plan, the original source code was backed up to nonwritable media and securely stored in a software library. Fallback has obvious detrimental effects to the project (possibly even ending it) but protects the business.

As you can see, contingency plans are formed at different levels, depending on the magnitude of the risk.

You should refine and update the risk and contingency methodology during each successive phase of the project. It is hoped that active monitoring will show a downward trend of these risks as the project goes forward.

# Organizing the Project Team

The final piece of the migration project plan is the organization of people, their relationships, and reporting structures. While your specific project management framework will dictate many of the specifics of your general project structure, the following tips might help your migration project run smoothly.

The following figure shows a typical project organization.

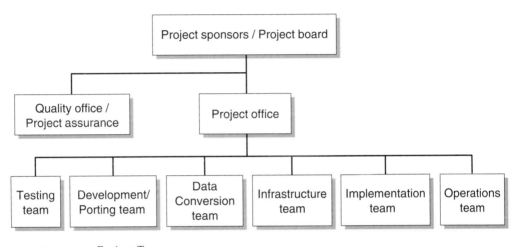

**FIGURE 4-3**  Project Team

Each box within this illustration serves a specific purpose:

- **Project sponsors and Project board.** This group represents the business and provides overall governance to the project through its careful monitoring and evaluation of the project against the business justification and project plan.

- **Project office.** This team usually consists of the project manager, chief architect, and support staff. They are in charge of leading the teams, enforcing the project plan, and reporting status and progress to the project sponsors.

- **Quality office and Project assurance.** This team independently monitors the overall project process and outputs, and reports results to the project sponsors. This monitoring may range from simple project reviews to full-scale audits.

- **Testing team.** A vitally important team will test all produced solutions to ensure they technically meet the project's objectives.

- **Development and Porting team.** This team actually migrates the solution to the new application, process, or platform. The team will vary in size and composition depending on the migration strategy chosen.

- **Data Conversion team.** This team is similar to the Development and Porting team, but is solely concerned with the transformation or conversion of the legacy data for the new environment. While this team can be combined with the Development and Porting team, keeping it separate ensures the different skills and goals are properly represented.

- **Infrastructure team.** This team is responsible for architecting and specifying the infrastructure and platform for the newly migrated solution. As is the case with the Development and Porting team, this team's resources and skills will depend on the migration strategy attempted.

- **Implementation team.** This team builds, deploys, and migrates the consolidated environments. This team is usually a rotating group of subject matter experts with the skills required for the particular consolidation.

- **Operations team.** This team is in charge of scheduled migrations and downtime in the current environment, as well as the eventual day-to-day management of the migrated solution.

## Identify Resources

After detailing tasks and durations in a project plan, you should identify the resource profiles required to complete the tasks. Resource profiles are sets of skills that are required to accomplish groups of tasks within a project plan. For example, assessing the current platform and building the new platform are two separate tasks that require similar skills. To accomplish either task, you must have access to a person who understands the hardware and operating system technologies used in a particular environment. Once you identify all of the resource profiles for a particular project, you can assign people with these profiles to individual tasks, and begin creating a project plan.

---

**Note –** The project manager and implementation team for the project should create the project plan. Although they will work closely with the engagement team to develop a plan and schedule that satisfies the business requirements and timelines, project planning is primarily a technical task and is best left to those who understand the time, skills, and efforts required.

---

# Developing a Project Plan

Now that the project startup and initiation activities have been completed, it is time to construct a realistic project plan for your migration effort. While every migration project will be different in objectives, scope, difficulty, and level of effort, some standard steps and rules of thumb can be applied to any project plan.

This section focuses on the creation of a sample project plan, using the SunTone[SM] Architecture Methodology. Our sample migration will be a small, relatively simple migration that we are rehosting through a technology port of a custom C application that operates in conjunction with an Oracle database. The custom application is composed of about 4000 lines of code. For the sake of this example, imagine that the application was created to run in the HP-UX environment but the organization now wants to run it in the Solaris environment.

## Architect a Migration Solution

Architecture is the first stage of the project that we need to tackle. In the SunTone Architecture Methodology, architecture is divided into three major areas: assessment, design, and prototyping. Each of these areas is aimed at advancing the solution toward a new design.

### Assessment Activities

Assessment activities in this stage are straightforward. We need to investigate each layer of the E-stack within the solution and assess what likely changes are necessary to meet our goals of rehosting this on the Solaris OS. In terms of the project plan, we would create tasks for each layer of the E-stack, making sure that they document all the layer's important systemic requirements, possibly combining adjacent ones when necessary. We would combine layers only when we thought that a single resources could investigate that layer fully.

In our example project, we would construct a task list like the one shown in the following figure.

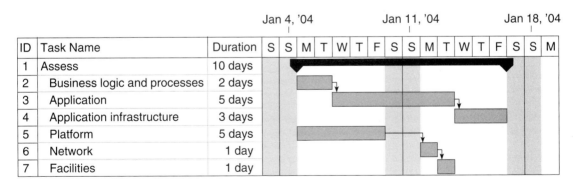

| ID | Task Name | Duration |
|----|-----------|----------|
| 1 | Assess | 10 days |
| 2 | Business logic and processes | 2 days |
| 3 | Application | 5 days |
| 4 | Application infrastructure | 3 days |
| 5 | Platform | 5 days |
| 6 | Network | 1 day |
| 7 | Facilities | 1 day |

**FIGURE 4-4**   Example Task List

There is no set rule for the length of time needed for these assessment activities, but because this is a relatively simple migration with just two servers involved, we give each task one resource and one week to complete it. The output of each of these tasks will be a summary of the current situation, detailed information about key configuration items, and an estimation of the level of effort required to move to a new environment.

In our example project, we have divided the tasks between two roles: an application architect and a system administrator. The application architect investigates the upper levels of the E-stack, and the system administrator documents the current hardware platform.

## Design Activities

With the due diligence of the assessment behind us, we can begin to concentrate on the two major tasks for the design of the new solution:

- **Reviewing the data gathered during the assessment.** This task is a critical part of the design, whereby the raw data is turned into usable information by identification of key requirements within the gathered data. These requirements then drive the initial design of the migrated solution.

- **Developing an initial design.** The initial design takes into account the requirements gleaned in the previous task and matches them with technologies in the key systemic qualities. This combination of technologies becomes the initial design of the migrated solution.

While each company will have different processes, methodologies, and standards for architectural design, the deliverable should be the same: an architectural report detailing the requirements and all components of the solution. The effort to create this deliverable will be much more variable than the preceding assessment because it fundamentally depends on the complexity of the current solution, not necessarily on its size.

For this example, we project three weeks to create the design. One week of that time is set aside for creating the requirements, and two weeks is set aside for the creation of the solution, as shown in the following example architecture schedule.

| ID | Task Name | Duration | Jan 18, '04 | Jan 25, '04 | Feb 1, '04 |
|----|-----------|----------|-------------|-------------|------------|
| | | | S M T W T F S | S M T W T F S | S M T W T F S |
| 8 | Architect | 15 days | | | |
| 9 | Review assessment | 5 days | | | |
| 10 | Design initial solution | 10 days | | | |

FIGURE 4-5  Architecture Schedule

## Prototype Activities

The next activities in the architecture provide a proof of concept for the initial architecture. This is an optional step, depending on the level of risk and the project's mitigation plans. Many migration projects will include this stage, especially if they are migrating to COTS solutions. The prototype will usually take several weeks to develop and will result in the construction of a scaled-down version of the initial solution that can provide the functional validity of the solution.

In our sample project, we decide that a prototype is not necessary since the risks do not warrant the time or efforts. Because of the small scope of the project and our relative confidence in being able to port the code, it simply isn't feasible to spend the time and money necessary to complete this activity.

## Implement the Migration Solution

With the architecture stage completed, it is time for implementation. In the SunTone Architecture Methodology, implementation is divided into many areas:

- Porting
- Data conversion and movement
- Building
- Testing
- Training

Each of these areas is crucial to successfully completing a migration.

## Application Redevelopment and Porting Activities

In migration projects that rely on the porting or redevelopment of applications, this stage receives the most attention. Other migration projects, such as the migration from custom applications to COTS solutions, might not address it at all. These tasks include the process of developing, customizing, or porting applications so that they execute in the new environment. The key activities here include the following:

- Creating the new build environment
- Modifying the application for the new build environment
- Compiling and building the application for the new environment
- Unit testing the new application

Again, these activities vary greatly depending on complexity. However, the key criterion in this level of effort is the application or porting complexity. Some applications will require very little porting assistance; for others, porting will be a massive undertaking. This doesn't directly relate to program size, but rather to the number and difficulty of changes required.

For this example project plan, based on the assessment stage data, we believe that the porting will take a significant amount of time. We budget two months for a team of two developers.

## Data Conversion and Movement Activities

Similar to the developing and porting activities, this set of tasks readies the data for the next environment. However, in addition to the possible conversion of data from one format to another, there may be substantial challenges in actually moving the data from one platform and application to another. This is especially true of databases or any other application that handles data outside the normal UNIX file constructs.

For the purpose of our sample project, we budget only a small amount of time for data conversion and movement. As the data already resides in standard SQL format within the Oracle database, no conversion will be needed, just movement to the new platform. To be on the safe side, we allot two weeks for the planning, implementation, and testing of this movement.

## Build Activities

The build activities of the implementation stage are similar to those of any other project. Infrastructure must be constructed so that the applications can be hosted. Some of the environments that will need to be built include the following:

- Test environment
- Target environment
- Target platform
- Application environment
- Regression environment

In our sample project, this is a fairly simple task because the proposed solution is only one server. We allot three weeks to account for the amount of time that it takes to get onto the production floor.

## Test Activities

One of the more important parts of a migration project is buried here in the middle of the project plan. Testing will make or break a migration project. Several types of tests need to be planned and executed:

- Unit testing
- Integration testing
- Validity testing

- Performance testing
- Transfer testing

We make sure to allow for ample time to test in our sample project. In fact, we give it four weeks, almost as much time as it took for development.

## *Training Activities*

The final activities in the implementation stage address the overlooked human aspect of migration projects: training. Several levels of training will need to conducted to make sure that the newly migrated environment supports the business properly. The following types of training might be necessary:

- Solaris familiarity
- Training classes
- End-user training

Although this activity set is discussed last, it should actually be started before the build tasks within this stage so that administrators have good knowledge of the new environment.

# Manage the Migrated Environment

The final stage of migration is making sure that the migrated solution will meet the previous service level agreements. We do this by addressing the operation and maintenance procedures with the same approach as for the human and technology issues in the project.

These are the key tasks in this phase:

- Evaluating operational procedures and tools
- Redeveloping subpar procedures and tools to meet expected performance
- Implementing new supporting tools

Between each stage of the project, these key project evaluation documents need to be updated and reassessed:

- Risks, mitigation, and contingency plans
- Project actuals compared against the plan
- Review of key benefits and objectives validity

# Closing the Project

After all implementation and management activities have been finished, it is time to disband the team and close the project. However, before this is done, a few key activities must be completed:

- Obtaining the customer's formal acceptance of all deliverables from the project
- Evaluating the delivery of the output and solution against the measurable objectives outlined at the beginning of the project
- Capturing important lessons learned for the next migration project
- Filing all deliverables and documentation so that other parts of the organization can review the project

These activities effectively return control of the environment to the normal operations team, dissolve the project structure, and feed the results of the migration to the project sponsors.

# CHAPTER 5

# Introducing the SunTone Methodology for Migration

Modern project management methodologies have become universal to project and program management. In the software project world, these methodologies need to be supplemented to define the actors, roles, skills, and tasks required to complete an IT project. Modern development methodologies fill this gap and are based on the principles of architecture, prototyping, and iteration.

Sun has been addressing its customers' needs to install current software applications on the Sun operating system (OS) for several years. Sun has helped customers undertake migration projects and has a large body of experience to apply to the problems inherent with these types of projects. Through this experience, Sun has developed a repeatable and systematic methodology for migration that helps ensure predictability and success of migration projects.

This chapter places the ideas expressed in Chapter 3 in the context of a technical planning methodology. Project and program management methodology is addressed later in the book. This chapter defines Sun's high-level methodologies and reviews the roles of the architect, implement, and manage (AIM) phases involved in the methodology.

This chapter contains the following sections:

# SunTone Architecture Methodology

Sun's response to the need for a development methodology is the SunTone Architecture Methodology, which borrows from the best of modern software development methodologies. This approach incorporates the principles of a life-cycle view and incremental development while articulating a cycle of architect, implement, and manage. It provides a common language for defining the nonfunctionality requirements of an applications platform, so Sun can use its knowledge-reuse programs to offer customers access to prototyping, pattern-based architecture, and design reuse in an area that has traditionally not had this advantage.

Following a structured architecture methodology is different from building a solution in an ad hoc fashion in that it requires you to plan upfront for much of the work that needs to be done. In addition, the application of the methodology discussed in this book ensures that you work with all of the stakeholders involved in a migration effort to develop an architecture that will address their needs as well as the business objectives.

Sun's project and life cycle methodology is based on the following stages:

- Architect
- Implement
- Manage

This approach assumes the presence of a business case, a risk log, and a project startup plan, which includes a project governance model. Fundamentally, this is a project methodology, which means that a project justification must have been successful. This methodology should be supplemented with formal project planning activities.

# Architect Phase Defined

Following the principles of the architect, implement, and manage (AIM) methodology, the initial architect phase in a migration project addresses the following technical startup-planning tasks for the project:

- Assessing the environment to ensure that all of the assumptions made during project justification have been proved and that all of the requirements and dependencies for the architecture are documented.

The following types of assessment tasks occur during the architect phase:

- Assessing the technologies used
- Assessing processes used
- Assessing people skills needed

■ Designing and architecting a migration solution, which includes the following types of tasks:

- Identifying the degree of change required
- Identifying service level goals
- Documenting design goals with the SunTone Architecture Methodology
- Creating a component and technique map
- Refining high-level designs
- Creating a transition plan
- Developing a configuration management plan
- Creating a system I/O map
- Creating an acceptance test plan
- Planning test strategies
- Prototyping the process
- Designing a training plan for the new environment

These tasks are detailed in Chapter 6, and the specific deliverables that result from these activities are explored in more detail in the case studies presented in Chapter 9–Chapter 11.

# Implement Phase Defined

The implement phase of a migration project is the active development of a new environment during which the following types of tasks occur:

■ Porting applications to the new operating system, which includes the following types of tasks:

- Creating a target build environment
- Building a new application for the target platform
- Deciding whether to support backward compatibility

■ Migrating data to the new environment by transferring or converting it. This step includes the following types of tasks:

- Transferring data
- Transforming data

■ Creating the production environment, including the following types of tasks:

- Building the production facilities environment
- Building the production platform
- Building the application infrastructure

- Testing the migrated environment, which includes the following types of tasks:
    - Building the test environment
    - Creating the test plan
    - Performing unit testing
    - Performing regression testing
    - Performing integration testing
    - Testing performance
- Refining the migrated solution
- Training end users and staff

The key deliverables of the implement phase include working components and documentation. In addition, the implement phase might possess an iterative structure and might include prototyping. In particular, prototyping is useful for data migration and difficult or risky conversion techniques. If changes are made as a result of the prototyping that occurs during the implement phase, be sure to maintain the outputs from the architect phase.

## Developing Projects Iteratively

The implement phase can be iterated to allow incremental development. This allows a number of drivers to influence staging. You might develop a migration solution incrementally because different management environments are being migrated in different stages, with training done before the quality assurance installation; or it could be that the solution's architecture permits a component-based delivery or that the phasing might be based on project or business resource constraints. You should include phasing in the project plan to allow more effort and testing to be undertaken for the riskier elements of the project. The trial of both conversion and transition process on a training, quality assurance, or user acceptance instance of the application enhances the likelihood of success on a production instance.

An additional architect phase should include a business case review and review of the outputs from the previous architect phase. Implementation should be designed to permit this activity to occur. In particular, data migration timings should be available to validate the transition planning, and the transition plan should be revised in the light of improved knowledge.

# Manage Phase Defined

The manage phase of the SunTone methodology is about supporting systems and applications at runtime. These tasks are out of the scope of the book because migration is fundamentally an implementation exercise. The following management tasks are within the scope of this book and are addressed in the Chapter 8:

- Assessing the current IT management infrastructure
- Addressing the critical gaps
- Extending the infrastructure to account for the migration

Obviously, the management stage starts when migrated code is placed into use. The management regime needs to be designed, or the current management environment needs to be confirmed as being appropriate for use after the migration goes live. This planning and design work should be undertaken during the architecture stage and should be prototyped, built, and tested during the implement stage.

Some issues to address during the manage phase are obvious, but if the proposed target environment is a workload consolidation solution, both a resource management solution, possibly involving Solaris Resource Manager and an applications object namespace solution need to be developed in order to distinguish between instances of the application or applications components.

It is critical to comprehensively define the management problem. This can be done with a service management methodology. The two major methodologies used by Sun are the IT Infrastructure Library (ITIL) and SunTone. SunTone is Sun's service management methodology, which is heavily influenced by ITIL. The activities of systems managers have been defined by the United Kingdom (UK) Office of Government Commerce in the IT Infrastructure Libraries (ITIL). ITIL is broken down into service delivery and service support. Service delivery addresses these issues:

- Service level management
- Financial management
- Capacity management
- Availability management
- IT service continuity management

Service support addresses the following areas:

- Service desk
- Incident management
- Problem management
- Change management
- Release management
- Configuration management

Other methodologies are available and are based on vendor or industry alignment.

The manage phase concerns the operation of processes within the management space. The processes and infrastructure to support management will need to be architected, designed, and implemented. Chapter 8 discusses the details of applying AIM to the manage phase. The architect and implement phases are best undertaken in accordance with a gap analysis methodology as follows: document the current solutions, design a new solution, and document the changes needed to achieve the required improvements. The subsequent chapters in the book illustrate how to do this in more detail. This process might involve leveraging the Solaris OS' implementation of the UNIX utilities, or the provision of third-party software.

# Moving Between Phases

Sun's AIM life-cycle view implies that there is a stately progression from architecture, through implementation, to management, but this is not the case. In practice, migration projects will iterate within phases and reenter preceding phases to improve the deliverables of those preceding phases. Sun considers assessment and technology planning work to be part of the architect phase, and the application of the AIM methodology assumes that a justification activity has already taken place.

For example, during the justification process, a business case will be delivered. Fact finding that occurs during the architect phase might require you to reevaluate the business case. In this case, the methodology requires that the justification activities be repeated. Because architecture includes fact-finding, assessment, and architectural planning activities, these classes of activities can be iterated so that increased fact-finding improves the solutions architecture. Clearly, implementation activities might require you to repeat architect phase activities to maintain the artifacts against changes undertaken during implementation. Project planning and estimation techniques, including product-based planning, time boxing, and variance management, should be used to ensure that plans are delivered on time.

Once a project deliverable goes live, it will require management and production quality change control processes. Any change to production configurations requires a project, and will therefore involve justification, architecture, and implementation activities.

The iteration of activities can occur within and between phases. The phases outlined here should not necessarily be confused with stages within the project plan. The project planning methodology will also mandate certain activities as projects transition between stages.

The following chapters detail the SunTone Architecture Methodology and the AIM life-cycle view. They explain how to apply the methodology and the principles of iteration and refinement to incrementally develop delivery artifacts. They also provide detailed information about the different phases of the methodology.

# CHAPTER 6

# Architecting a Migration

As described in the previous chapter, our methodology consists of three main phases: architect, implement, and manage. This chapter explores the tasks involved in architecting a migration solution. The architect phase involves the following tasks:

- "Assessing the Environment" on page 71
- "Designing and Architecting a Migration Solution" on page 81

While all migration projects should include these tasks, the amount of time spent on them and the level of detail required to successfully complete them will vary according to the size and scope of the migration.

# Assessing the Environment

Before undertaking any migration project, you must understand the environment that will be migrated. Regrettably, this is typically not an easy task. Organizational changes, attrition, and the inexorable passing of time often combine to make it difficult to understand the full scope of the application composition and the associated supporting infrastructure, as well as the various interconnects and dependencies that might exist. Ideally, the enterprise should be able to furnish a document set that contains all the relevant information that will be required, but this is rarely the case. Usually, the best you can hope for is that an individual or small group of people will know or have access to documentation that contains the relevant information.

It is critical that local sources, who are knowledgeable about the application, its component parts, its build environment, third-party products, interconnects, dependencies, and the like be assigned to the migration team. Without this guidance, the migration team might never completely understand the application and its supporting environment.

The goal of assessment is to ensure that all assumptions made during the project justification are proved and that all of the requirements and dependencies for the architecture are documented. This documentation is the deliverable for the project assessment of a migration project.

To provide complete documentation of the current environment, you must address the following major topics:

- Assessing technologies used in the existing environment, during which you perform the following tasks:
    - Assess the requirements of the application
    - Assess the requirements of the existing platform
- Assessing existing and new processes, which involves the following tasks:
    - Assess the new environment's ability to satisfy business requirements
    - Assess the development environment
    - Assess IT operations requirements and existing management capabilities
- Assessing skills and training requirements for the staff to support the migrated environment

When performing assessment tasks, you must be careful that you do not perform too cursory an assessment. Failing to uncover significant dependencies that could jeopardize the project's viability can easily lead to expensive architectural revisions. On the other hand, you must also be careful that you do not perform too detailed an assessment. Wasting time on minutiae that are not relevant to the migration can reduce project momentum and negatively affect the return on investment.

# Assessing Technologies Used

When assessing the technologies used in an existing environment, focus on existing applications, the application infrastructure, and the platforms on which the applications run. The following sections describe how to assess each of these areas.

## Assess Application Requirements

Before determining an appropriate migration strategy, you must determine the exact composition of the application that is to be migrated. Tasks you will usually perform during this part of assessment include the following:

- Interviewing application owners and maintainers
- Describing major software and hardware components used to support the application

- Identifying and documenting API differences between existing and new environments

- Identifying and documenting the effort required to transform source code

These tasks are detailed later in this book when specific case studies and the tasks involved in their development are described.

In addition to the common tasks you perform when assessing application requirements, consider the issues presented in the following sections with respect to the migration of a custom-written application or an off-the-shelf application.

## Custom-Written Applications

For custom-written applications, examine the APIs used by the application that are specific to a particular OS. The fewer dependencies the application has on OS support, the easier it will be to migrate.

After you identify any dependencies that might exist between the application and the OS, develop an issues database that defines the API differences between the OS that currently supports the application and the new target OS. For example, you might find that differences exist in the parameters specified in the function call, the behavior of the function itself (what it does), or the format of the results that it returns. At this point, you can also create compatibility libraries that mimic the behavior of the original system, thereby minimizing the amount of change that has to be made to the application. These libraries usually do not contain solutions for all APIs provided by an OS, just those that are most frequently used. The issues database helps you assess the amount of effort that will be required to transform an application's source code to be compatible with the new OS. The compatibility libraries are used in the transformation process itself.

After you create an issues database, assign weights for each API provided by the source OS to indicate the amount of effort that will be required to change the logic or calling sequence within the application, following these guidelines:

- If the type or ordering of a parameter to the API has to be changed, assign the API a low weight because the change can be easily effected.

- If an existing compatibility library already supports that API, assign it a slightly higher rating to reflect that changes to the source code will include conditional compilation.

- If a solution for the API has yet to be created, assign it a high weighting to reflect that a substantial amount of work will have to be done implement a solution.

- In some cases, there is no way to replicate the functionality of an API because the target OS lacks the hardware to implement the required functionality. Assign these APIs the highest weight in the issues database.

Once the issues database exists, you can develop a tool that scans the source code of the application, looking up the weight of each API it finds. The sum of these weights determines a portability index for that particular application. You can then use the portability index to determine the level of effort (LOE) required to transform the code.

---

**Note –** To migrate code, you should understand how to perform the tasks described in this section. To access the issues database, compatibility libraries, and assessment tools when migrating to the Solaris OS, visit `http://www.sun.com/migration/`

---

Assessing application source code in this fashion provides a quick and objective measure of cost and effort that can be a useful input when you are determining a solution for a migration project.

Sun provides tools to assist your assessments of custom-written applications. The most important of these tools is called the Solaris OE Analyzer for C/C++ and Cobol Source Code. This Java technology-based tool, formerly called Score and then JScore, identifies porting issues with C/C++ or Cobol source codes from other operating systems. In addition to identifying these problems, it estimates their difficulty and suggests possible solutions.

The Solaris OE Analyzer for C/C++ and Cobol Source Code works by comparing the source code against databases of known porting issues. Using a modular approach like the methodology described above, the Solaris OE Analyzer for C/C++ and Cobol Source Code contains databases for the following operating systems:

- Microsoft Windows NT/9x
- Linux
- HP-UX 9.x, 10.x, 11.x
- AIX 3.x, 4.x
- SGI IRIX
- SunOS 4.x
- VMS
- Digital Unix (now called HP Tru64)
- HP MPE Cobol

Because this tool is in continual development, visit `http://www.sun.com/migration/ntmigration/tools/jscoretool.html` for the latest information on the operating systems it supports.

The Solaris OE Analyzer for C/C++ and Cobol Source Code is easily used. Simply execute either the `JScore` (Solaris) or `JScore.bat` (Windows) programs to invoke the GUI shown in the following figure.

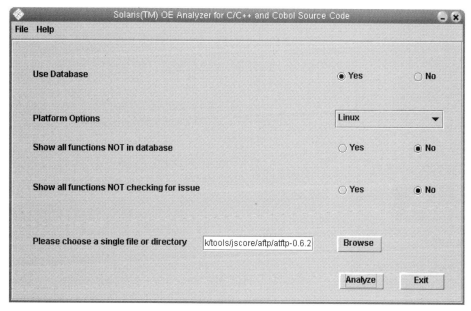

**FIGURE 6-1**   Solaris OE Analyzer for C/C++ and Cobol Source Code GUI

Normally, you will need to adjust options on the Solaris OE Analyzer for C/C++ and Cobol Source Code. First, choose your platform's source code from the Platform Options pull-down menu. Then, click the Browse button next to the Please choose a single file or directory text box. Navigate to your source code top-level directory and click Select. While the tool has other options (all well described within the download help files and release notes), these two options are the only required ones. After the options have been chosen, click the Analyze button. The tools will then run your source code (or source code tree) through the selected platform database and present the migration analysis results, as shown in the following figure.

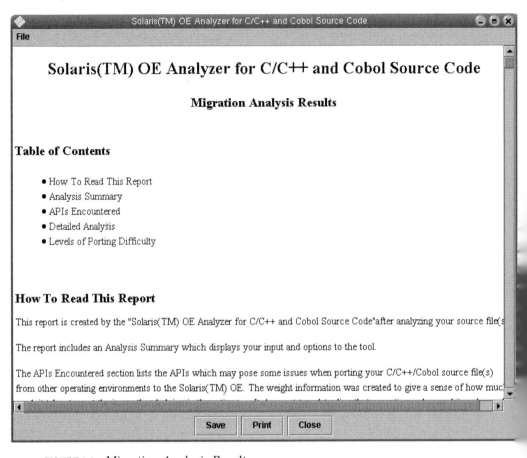

**FIGURE 6-2** Migration Analysis Results

The migration analysis results are divided into the following three sections:

- **Analysis summary.** Details statistics of the source code files analyzed and the too settings selected.

- **APIs encountered.** Lists the APIs found in your source code that are flagged as porting issues within the selected platform database. Each of these API issues is categorized by difficulty from Easy to Toughest.

- **Detailed analysis.** Cites specific source code files and line numbers at which eac problem API was found. In addition to citing each call of these APIs, the report usually provides specific details about the solution to the problem. These detail range from simple syntax solutions to complete reimplementation of the API.

With the results of this report, you should have a good idea of the specific areas th you will need to address in your porting effort, the general difficulty level of the port, and the possible level of effort required.

## Off-the-Shelf Applications

In the case where a COTS product is to be migrated, a version of the product must exist for the new target OS. Although products are quite similar, regardless of the environments in which they are designed to operate, there will be differences in the ways they are implemented. COTS vendors usually provide guides that highlight the differences between versions of differing operating systems. Before choosing a migration strategy, examine the implementation to determine the amount of change required to move from one version of the product to another. The level of effort (LOE) for this activity is a critical input for choosing the migration strategy.

If a version of the COTS product does not exist for the new platform, the migration becomes a rearchitecture effort. Determining the LOE for this form of activity requires significant time and effort and is not as accurate as it is for code transformation.

## Third-Party Products and Locally Developed Scripts

If third-party products are used to support the application, you must also consider the amount of effort required to migrate these products. The first step in this assessment is to determine whether a version of the third-party product exists for the target OS. If one exists, you will also have to determine API differences. Most independent software vendors attempt to keep consistent interfaces between different versions of their products. Differences should be minimal, but they must be evaluated. From this assessment, you should identify the LOE required to transform the code to use the third-party APIs, as discussed above.

If a version of the third-party product does not exist on the new platform, you will have to identify the functionality of the product and find a replacement for it. Differences between the APIs of different products will probably be significant, requiring changes in source code logic within the application. This effort is more like a reengineering effort than simple code transformation. Significantly more risk is involved in this effort because the appropriateness of the new product, as well as the amount of change that must be introduced to the application, might not be well known.

Databases are perhaps the most common form of third-party product used by applications. Some of the considerations involved in migrating databases are described in Chapter 11.

All third-party products must be assessed to determine their licensing costs and the services they provide. Changing third-party vendors might result in reduced licensing costs, but real savings might not be realized when the cost of integrating the new product into the application is taken into account.

Although they are not really third-party products, many applications are surrounded by a host of locally developed scripts that start, stop, or monitor an application. Scripts are also frequently used to age log files, collect and analyze data sets, and prepare input. All of these scripts must be identified in the application infrastructure assessment because they will have to be ported to the new OS.

## Assess Platform Requirements

In addition to assessing applications, you need to assess the existing hardware—usually the compute, storage, and network platforms—to determine suitable replacements. These assets usually are examined in terms of capacity, scalability, price/performance ratio, maintainability, reliability, and availability. Hardware vendors usually provide this service without charge. Keep in mind that the platform assessment should provide an objective analysis of the existing system and its replacement. This analysis will allow for a meaningful comparison of the platforms when you are developing a migration strategy.

From the perspective of a migration, hardware design details must be noted. Differences between platforms might require changes or redesign to the application.

### Big Endian Versus Little Endian

When assessing platform requirements, be sure to consider whether the application you are migrating was created in big endian or little endian format. If the standard APIs are used to access data, the endianness of the platform is usually not an issue, because the layout of the data in the word will be abstracted by the APIs used to access it.

If you are using lower-level languages or legacy coding techniques and an application uses operators such as shifts, or logical or arithmetic ands and ors, then assumptions about the layout of the word and, consequently, the significance of the bits, might become an issue. Application logic might have to be rewritten if it depends on the position of a bit in a word. In the past, when memory limitations were a concern, this was an issue.

Understanding the logic and replicating it using the different model can require significant effort.

### Word Size

Most applications have been written to use a 32-bit data model. Although most 64-bit operating environments support 32-bit applications without modification, you might have to change the application if it interacts with an operating system kernel that uses a 64-bit data model.

Migrating an application to use a 64-bit data model rather than a 32-bit data model requires considerably more effort than the conventional migration between operating environments described above. That type of migration is primarily concerned with modifying APIs to be compatible with the new environment. An understanding of the program logic and the size of the data need not be considered. This is not the case when you are migrating to a new data model. The size of the quantities being manipulated must be considered, and what that manipulation is to accomplish must be understood.

In Chapter 11, we discuss data models and identify dependencies that will require data model conversion in more detail.

### Proprietary Hardware Support

To obtain a competitive advantage, vendors sometimes develop proprietary hardware such as fault-tolerant CPUs or tunable crystal oscillators that minimize the skew in timers. Be sure to note use of such features during the platform assessment. Because software cannot simulate these features, their presence will require you to choose comparable hardware or to reengineer the business process.

In addition, the application itself might require the presence of special hardware to provide its functionality. This is frequently the case in engineering or process control applications. If the application controls a device that either provides a specific input or that can be used to effect a specific change, the availability of the device must be verified for the new hardware platform as well as for the device driver both of which will integrate into the operating system.

# Assessing Processes Used

In addition to assessing the applications and platforms affected by a migration, you must also assess existing and new processes to ensure that the migrated application will integrate into the procedures executed by the enterprise.

## Assess Business Requirements

The application provides functionality for specific business processes. Assess these processes to determine their requirements. When attempting to develop a strategy to migrate the application, always remember that the new environment must support all business-critical functionality. For information about identifying business requirements, refer to Chapter 4.

## Assess Development Requirements

If the application is written in house, the development environment also must be migrated. This development environment must be assessed to ensure that a suitable replacement can be found for use in the new OS.

Tools such as text editors, compilers, and debuggers must be available for the application. Many development environments also use source code repositories that support multiple users modifying the source code at the same time. A development process is used to ensure that all changes are recorded and that people do not overwrite existing versions of source files.

Any changes introduced into the development environment will probably have an initial adverse effect on productivity because there will be a learning curve as people come up to speed. You will also have to determine training costs involved in preparing staff to work in the new development environment.

Test suites and scripts are also used in a development environment to ensure that changes or modifications to the application have not introduced errors or unwanted side effects. The testing process must be assessed to ensure that any tools or products used in testing the application are also available in the new environment.

## Assess IT Operations Requirements

The management architecture will also need to be migrated to the new environment. An assessment of the existing management capabilities should be conducted to determine what will be required in the new environment.

The organization has some level of management capability, as defined in the Capability Maturity Model (CMM). Overall, IT management should conform to some methodology (ITIL, SunTone) and will use a number of products to assist in the collection of data and reporting of problems.

The new IT infrastructure will need to be integrated into this management framework. The existing management architecture will have to be assessed to ensure that products for the new IT infrastructure exist and can be integrated into the existing management architecture.

# Assessing Skills Requirements

A key input into the selection of any migration strategy will be the skills of the existing IT staff. Training on new technologies can be expensive and can affect the overall cost of the migration project. Additionally, introducing new technology might result in decreased availability or productivity as people attempt to come up to speed on the new technology.

The existing skill level of the staff must be assessed, and their abilities should be an input to the migration strategy decision.

The assessment should focus on the skills at all levels in the organization: operators, administrators, and developers. You should develop a skills catalog that captures the abilities of the staff in terms of their familiarity with specific products and activities. You can then use this catalog when deciding on a migration strategy. Having this catalog enables you to identify gaps in skills and to develop a training curriculum to address any shortfalls.

Where appropriate, new hires or outside consultants can be used to fill gaps.

# Designing and Architecting a Migration Solution

When designing the target technology platform, you must understand the degree of change required by the enterprise. Changes might be in business functionality, or more commonly, they might be changes in the service level. Within the context of this book and the methodology presented in it, the design stage addresses issues of platform technology, process, and people. The following tasks are involved in the design and architecture of a migration solution:

- Identifying the degree of change required
- Identifying service level goals
- Documenting design goals with the SunTone Architecture Methodology
- Creating a component and technique map
- Refining high-level designs
- Creating a transition plan
- Developing a configuration management plan
- Creating a system I/O map
- Creating an acceptance test plan
- Planning test strategies
- Prototyping the process
- Designing a training plan for the new environment

## Identifying the Degree of Change Required

One of the key objectives of migration is to preserve an organization's investment in business logic. Therefore, the migration project team will rarely have to exercise business logic design skills except to maintain semantic meaning. Despite this priority, changes are often required. These changes will usually be in the nonfunctional qualities of the system to improve costs or service levels. The likelihood of this being necessary depends on the migration strategy chosen because the primacy of preserving the business logic unchanged depends on this. For example, a refronting strategy might cause the presentation layer to change significantly. If either business usability or business logic is encapsulated in the presentation code modules, the business logic might need to change or might require enhancement.

Earlier in this book, we described the functionality sedimentation process. For example, we explained how when the application of a replacement strategy leads to the decision to move printing from the application code to a utility, the recording of a print date can impact the recording of business-relevant data such as an invoice date. This example illustrates how the proposition that migration projects do not require changes to the business logic ($\Delta L$) is not universally true, and the reliability of this proposal depends on the strategy adopted (S).

$$\Delta L = f(S)$$

The amount of change in the business logic depends on the migration strategy chosen to meet the business requirements. Further, the degree of change in the business logic depends on the requirements (R), and it is the requirements that drive the strategy selection.

$$\Delta L = f(R)$$

Changes in the functional requirement of an application cannot be achieved by platform design alone. The migration project must apply one or more of the migration strategies or techniques to the software components requiring change. Changes in the service level requirements should be achievable either through platform architecture and design or through process design. Change requirements will often form part of the benefits case for a platform transition. For testing designs, a requirements statement is mandatory.

# Identifying Service Level Goals

The SunTone Architecture Methodology defines an application solution's systemic qualities as belonging to one of the following four families:

- **Manifest.** Reflect the user experience of nonfunctionality qualities of the system.
- **Operational.** Reflect the experience of operations managers and operators.
- **Developmental.** Reflect the views of developers or builders.
- **Evolutionary.** Anticipate the future needs of the application.

These systemic qualities define the application community's service level goals for an application. Critically, they exclude the business logic and the implementation of business process or transactional logic.

*Manifest* qualities include usability, performance (response time), reliability, availability, and accessibility. *Operational* qualities include performance (throughput), manageability, security, serviceability, and maintainability. The *developmental* qualities include buildability, budgetability, and planability, and the *evolutionary* qualities include scalability, maintainability, extensibility, reusability, and portability. It should be noted that maintainability occurs in both the operational and evolutionary families. The difference between them is based on the definition of the family, the operational versus the evolutionary requirements and qualities of the system. It is also important to understand that some of these nonfunctionality qualities might need to be modeled and defined in the functional analysis. The obvious examples are response time performance and security as it applies to user authority definition. The decision to implement user privilege management in specific software components (either application code modules or infrastructure products) is made by the application architect.

The following table summarizes these service-level goals.

**TABLE 6-1**    System Qualities for Systemic Quality Families

| Systemic Quality Family | System Quality |
| --- | --- |
| Manifest | Usability, performance (response time), reliability, availability, and accessibility |
| Operational | Performance (throughput), manageability, security, serviceability and maintainability |
| Developmental | Buildability, budgetability, and planability |
| Evolutionary | Scalability, maintainability, extensibility, reusability, and portability |

For information about the SunTone Architecture Methodology, refer to (`http://www.sun.com/service/sunps/jdc/suntoneam_wp_5.2.4.pdf`)

## Identify Manifest Quality Design Goals

The preceding table shows that what might traditionally be seen as performance has spilled over into several areas and, in the case of response time, can also be derived from the functional analysis. The following sections explain how to identify manifest quality design goals for an application.

## Performance and Scalability

Scalability is usually planned by adoption of a strategy to apply when performance thresholds fail to be reached and the failure is caused by a change to the scale of the system that results from an increase in business volumes or the user community. Several scalability strategies are available to platform designers.

Scalability has two dimensions:

- The definition of the change strategy required to meet changes in the business volume or user community size. These change strategies impact deployment decisions and might vary from software component to software component. This means that the target platform needs to account for more than one scalability strategy. An example is designers deciding to apply a vertically scaling design pattern to the database layer and a horizontally scaling pattern to the web servers. Scalability design patterns can also be applied to storage, network, and backup solutions. Diagonally scalable solutions might apply, for instance when vertical and horizontal strategies are applied in an iterative sequence.

- The appropriate change strategy might change as different volume thresholds are met. A good example is an RDBMS. A vertically scaling solution can be planned until a certain volume threshold is reached. At that point, the deployment managers can move to a horizontally scaling solution either with parallel database technology (such as Oracle RAC), or through applications design and implementing multiple databases.

Scalability strategies (an evolutionary quality) have a significant impact on the deployment design. Designers need to design for growth, and business volume predictions are therefore required. These can be hard to discover, but migrators have the advantage that the history should be available because the application, and hence the business process, already exist. Scalability design also needs to account for any predictions that the performance constraint will move as business volumes grow.

System performance management is about understanding whether the application's response time or throughput is constrained by memory, CPU, or I/O. Given the nature of the migrator's problems when the source and target systems have massively different performance ratios across these three dimensions, an application could be CPU bound on the source system and become I/O bound on the target system. This situation can be discovered through prototyping or testing. If you expect this problem to arise, include performance tests as part of the platform integration test plan. If an application's performance can be characterized as hardware bound by a single hardware attribute, scaling performance is relatively easy. Additional resources can be added, although the constraint often will be accepted for cost reasons if the performance is good enough and the additional cost is not justified. In some applications, particularly those implemented on distributed platforms, there might be multiple constraints. Each system is different, and the bottleneck moves as the multiple application's components process the business transaction. This is rarely a problem in user facing online transaction processing

(OLTP) modules because the required and actual response times are relatively low but an overnight batch process or an investment banking risk calculation, might display this sort of behavior.

System performance management is usually reactive but involves identifying the system constraints on meeting the performance requirements and designing them out of the configuration. We have both a performance history and the opportunity to prototype or benchmark and a number of design patterns to deploy.

- **CPU constraint.** SMP, horizontal scaling, CPU clock upgrade (occasionally)

- **Memory constraint.** 64-bit very large memory addressing, horizontal scaling

- **I/O constraint (disk).** Bandwidth scaling, RAID, disk cache1.

- **I/O constraint (network).** Bandwidth scaling (trunking or base technology), with caching implemented

However, applying platform design solutions to the performance and scalability requirements mandates that the code scales within these designs and does not meet a threshold that moves the bottleneck. If it does, and the bottleneck becomes another system constraint, then an additional appropriate pattern can be applied. When considering scalability, consider the possibility that when software is moved from one system to another, new-generation, system, bottlenecks might exist in the application's code, caused by the length of the code path exposed by the new more powerful CPUs. The multiuser concurrency mechanisms might also cause bottlenecks when run on hardware considerably more capable than that for which they were originally designed. This is unlikely for software built recently, but applications undertaking their fourth or fifth migration might suffer from this problem. An additional problem for some RDBMS users is that as their business scales and the demand on the application grows, the ISV-supplied database code lines become contention bound. Scalability constraints are not exclusively hardware based or system based. The only way around software bottlenecks is to recode or redesign.

## Availability and Reliability

In the SunTone architecture requirements methodology, availability is defined in a slightly more complex way than platform designers expect. This ensures that software developers consider all the issues that they need to address so that platform designers can apply their patterns. It is not possible or sensible to improve availability on an application with critical components that fail more frequently than the host platform or that take longer to recover than the host platform. Additionally, issues such as online patching and upgrades need to be designed into the applications environment through software architecture, although protection against failure is an operational quality and online upgrades and patching are evolutionary qualities.

The two key availability patterns are clustering and component replication. Clustering permits the hosted software components to fail fast and restart: software component replication redirects nonfailing client processes to an alternative server process. Sun™ Cluster software and its competitors use a shared disk configuration architecture to ensure that an alternative host system is available to restart a software component that previously existed on a failing hardware node. Software components suitable for clustering must be capable of failing cleanly, and they must be capable of taking their network identities from the cluster configuration, not from the individual host system nodes. RDBMSs are examples of software components that can be clustered, whereas the common name server components usually provide some form of replication (or cache server) functionality and are suitable for replication-based patterns.

Some versions of the Sun ONE Application Server also support clustering, albeit without a shared disk model. The option of using clustering or replication also maps to the decision in clustered-solutions design to leverage a host service (making it cluster aware) or to encapsulate a service within a logical host. By using these two patterns in your designs, the decision of which host to use within a platform design abstracts the location of the service from its physical host system. This is beneficial because the other systemic qualities can be easily incorporated into the design. Abstracting the software component's network identity from the physical platform also leads to greater runtime flexibility and prepares the application for deployment on N1 compute fabrics.

As a systemic quality, reliability is a software design goal that reflects on error condition definition and handling. In a migration project, the project design goal is to minimize code line changes to only those required to leverage the new platform; therefore, improvements in the software's reliability might not be a goal of the project. Platform reliability design is examined further in "Serviceability and Maintainability" on page 90. It is worth repeating that the application's service cannot be more reliable than the software itself. If the application contains fatal failure conditions based on logic paths, the platform designer will have difficulty protecting users against service outages caused by these failures. It is also worth noting that spending high amounts of money on making the platform of an inherently fragile application more rugged is unlikely to be worthwhile, although reductions in the mean time to recover (MTTR) might be worthwhile and the techniques discussed under availability patterns might be worth considering.

## Usability and Accessibility

Usability and accessibility are software design goals. The refronting strategy can have usability implications if, for instance, ASCII or 3270 forms are being ported into a browser or Java solution. Usability qualities need to be examined and the solutions selection might be impacted by these goals. If the project's goals are for zero change, an emulation solution is more appropriate. If changes supported by replacement are required, apply the replacement strategy and rehost the presentation logic in the new infrastructure component.

## Identify Operational Quality Design Goals

Throughput performance is another aspect of scalability. A throughput goal might be defined as part of the acceptance test criteria at transition time, but it will need to be defended against change during operations. The section "Identify Manifest Quality Design Goals" on page 83 provides more detail about designing for performance and scalability. Because throughput can be defined as the product of the number of users (each of whom can conduct only one transaction at a time) and transaction duration (or response time), there is a direct relationship between response time, system throughput, and the number of users.

$T = f(U,rt)$,

U = number of users, rt = response time, T = throughput, which is a rate.

The change in the number of users defines the scalability problem.

The main difference between an operations manager's view of throughput and a user's view is around systems management jobs that need to be applied to relatively large jobs. A user typically undertakes an OLTP transaction and is only interested in a tiny subset of data available, whereas a systems manager is interested in the whole database. The systems manager's jobs are often serial batch jobs that can require relatively long periods of time. These jobs also often require sole use of software components in order to undertake the management activity. Much of the solutions design around this problem is spent in minimizing the exclusive usage time period required by the systems manager. The other batch constraint is the seriality of the process. The seriality factors only become an issue once any hardware constraints have been removed. The key design patterns are as follows:

- **Asynchronous processing.** Planning and configuring to do the work before or after the time it is required.

- **Symmetrization.** The application of multiple workload processors to a job or transaction.

Strictly speaking, these are not design patterns, but classes of patterns. An example of asynchronous processing includes the use of disk image snapshots to allow backups to occur while the original image remains in use. Another example comes from the database design world in which schema denormalization occurs by including total fields as columns in a master table in the master-detail relationship, which can be updated by the application's logic or triggers. This means that the additional logic occurs when the database is updated, not when it is read. This enables you to avoid a table join and its processing overhead. The processing of the total is undertaken at the time the detail record is written or updated. Asynchronous processing is particularly useful when the expected response time is long and users are happy to wait for their replies. Submitting reports into a job queue is an example of asynchronous processing. A call center user or investment banker might not be able to wait, but the call center manager can ask for a member's next calls in advance of needing them.

For an application to use symmetrization techniques, the application's components need to be scalable by the preceding technique. Key patterns in this class include increasing the number of batch job queues, using SMP hardware, designing for or deploying system grids, or using infrastructure software that automatically symmetrizes a serial problem such as a backup solution that uses multiple tape drives, or RDBMS that uses parallel query optimization plans. From these examples, you can see that symmetrization is complex and requires that the objects to which the technique is being applied is appropriate in that it lacks significant seriality. Seriality is an outcome of either the design process, or fundamental properties of the applications problem. At the moment, because of the need to negotiate between more than one user, databases must have a degree of seriality in the lock resolution code lines and the database write-after log. This seriality can be reduced by either good database design or DBMS design. Seriality in batch jobs or third-GL legacy code can also be reviewed to apply optimization techniques. Since infrastructure providers such as Sun spend a lot of research and development money offering platforms for symmetrically scaling software, symmetrization, where appropriate, is cheaper to implement and less likely to conflict with other design goals.

## Manageability

When you are designing for manageability, the key requirement to understand is what operational management transactions need to be undertaken. Some management transactions will be defined by use cases and are therefore application management transactions. The operational management transactions are those undertaken and defined by system managers. System managers' activities also impact the IT service delivery process design. These are examined later in this chapter in the section on management design.

Application management activities are defined by developers. Typically, these include running specific ad hoc or regular jobs as required by the applications process. Examples might include cutting tapes for intercompany communication or setting the logical day clock.

The other major manageability activity is problem and incident handling, which can be IT based or applications based. The solutions designer should seek to create a single incident-handling regime, although when the applications error handling is tightly integrated with the transaction logic, migrating these code lines to infrastructure or utility software might be prohibitively costly.

## Security

The security qualities you can incorporate in your design can be broken into four problem areas:

- Secrecy
- Integrity
- Authentication
- Nonrepudiation

The enforcement of business processing rules based on users authority requires an authentication solution that cannot be compromised, strong and effective privilege definitions, and the assignment of a privilege list. The business rule is a functional requirement, and capturing it requires use-case analysis and actor identification. For example, the business rule might require that payments over a certain amount need to be approved by someone with approval authorization, and larger amounts might need multiple signatories. This implies a sign-off attribute on financial authorities and a signed-off state on a payment, which itself is derived from possessing sufficient sign-offs. This business rule can only be captured with functional design techniques. The decision to use certain technologies to implement the security piece is an architectural design. The option to embed the business rules in the application code exists; however, secrecy and integrity can be provided through infrastructure products, as can authority limits and privileges.

Encryption is the technology that underpins the security design. Secrecy and integrity design goals can be developed in isolation from applications, and thus users approaching the application will have a known level of identity. Most installations will have security and security technology policies, which migration project planners need to read, understand, and conform to.

The application being migrated will place additional constraints on the security solutions design, and where replacement strategies are being applied, functionality might migrate from the application's code to infrastructure products. For example, user privileges can be held in directory servers as additional personal attributes. Clearly, the application would need to be designed to leverage these additional services, and this is an example of recoding to support a replacement strategy. Again, the strategies used in migration strongly influence the design process.

An additional dimension to the security quality is an application's support for multiple economic entities or businesses. At one level, this is just another object in the security model, but because an OS instance is a security delivery object, it is necessary to take this into account while the platform is designed.

## Serviceability and Maintainability

First and foremost, serviceability and maintainability are software design goals. The objects of migration projects are less likely than modern software products to have had effective design solutions to the requirements of these qualities.

Platform solution designers must understand the constraints and strategies designed by application designers, and they need to design a platform that meets these constraints and requirements. Platform designers have a number of tools in the design toolbox.

The Solaris OS has number of software features to support the serviceability and maintainability of the applications runtime file system tree. These include:

- UNIX System V packages
- Solaris Live Upgrade
- UNIX file system semantics
- Solaris library management semantics and utilities

Examine the application being migrated to determine if any of these features can improve the serviceability and maintainability of the application once it is deployed on the target system. Again, you must examine the proposed architecture to understand the capability of the application. It is not cost effective to overachieve on the goals within the platform if the application can't take advantage of the improvements in the platform.

## Identify Developmental Quality Design Goals

Developmental qualities consist of buildability, budgetability, and planability. These qualities derive from a series of design decisions made early in the development cycle. Given that in a migration project, the application already exists, the opportunity to improve these qualities might be limited. However, changes in the platform can lead to improvements in all three areas.

## Buildability

The new generation of hardware can significantly reduce compilation times, allowing a more proactive release cycle, while migration to the Solaris OS allows access to a wide range of development tools, including the Sun ONE development environment and tools.

## Budgetability and Planability

In the context of a migration project in which the application already exists, these qualities reduce to financial scalability. They also affect platform component selection. Horizontally scaling components can be deployed on a just-in-time basis: vertically scaling components can be deployed using financial engineering tools such as lease financing to allow additional system boards to be deployed over time in Sun Fire systems.

Alternatively, a storage design that permits the easy swapping of systems into and out of the configuration permits midrange systems to be swapped for large systems when required. Both designs allow the deployment of additional resources when required, and the financial solution allows an appropriate stable payment schedule.

The following design solutions are available to meet these qualities:

- Horizontal scaling
- Vertical scaling, using platform product features
- Design for upgrade, which impacts storage and network design and enables vertical scaling through replacement

# Identify Evolutionary Quality Design Goals

Evolutionary qualities relate to the ability and ease of changing the application and its platform configuration. Scalability is clearly an evolutionary quality; however, the appropriate strategies to scale an application's component or its platform are manifest qualities. Designing for scalability is covered in "Identify Manifest Quality Design Goals" on page 83.

## Maintainability

The tools and approaches discussed in the operational qualities section must be designed into the software. The design of the platform's use of the maintenance features of the hosted software is an operational quality design problem. Resolving the maintainability requirements through design-impact decisions is related to designing preproduction environments. Most end-user software departments possess a development and production environment, and the majority of them have at least one preproduction environment variously referred to as the "user acceptance test," "integration test," or "quality assurance" environment. The variety of titles strongly implies that these preproduction environments might have different purposes and thus multiple preproduction environments might be required. The number and purpose of these environments is an enterprise management decision, because of their cost. The decision does, however, have technical constraints, and the proposed software release process has a major impact on these decisions.

The key input to decisions about designing for maintainability is the frequency of releases and the number of versions of the application required at any one time. Developers might be working on the next +2 and next +3 release, while integration testing is being undertaken on next +1, the user support team and user training might be working on the next release, and production is, of course, working on the current release. In a service provider environment, additional presales environments might also be required to support the sales process so that customers in transition have facilities to allow them to migrate their business or undertake a "try before you buy" exercise. This latter example might need to be segmented by the customer.

### Extensibility and Reusability

Extensibility and reusability are software design qualities. A refronting strategy might introduce significant changes to these qualities. The goals should be documented and designed against. Extensibility refers to functional extensibility. A migration can be a good opportunity to improve the extensibility and reusability of the application's code.

### Portability

Depending on the source code's implementation technology and the migration strategy adopted, improvements in the portability qualities of an application can be obvious, inexpensive, and required. As you identify which code idioms require change, you might identify existing options to improve the portability of code lines. This can involve changing code to use POSIX library calls, or replacing proprietary SQL calls with open connectivity libraries such as Java™ Database Connectivity (JDBC™) software. Refronting offers new and specific opportunities to improve the portability qualities of an application.

## Documenting Design Goals With the SunTone Architecture Methodology

The SunTone Architecture Methodology's nonfunctionality quality list gives platform and migration designers a framework for documenting their design goals and the extent to which the current system meets the required goals. Designers can then specify the changes required and design against the new goals. These new goals might require you to make no change to the current system, or in cases for which you must make a trade-off design decision, you might have to reduce the quality goal. Given that the primary reason for a migration is the preservation of business logic, changes in goals are more likely to be within the operational qualities family.

Because platform design is aimed at improving service management goals, functional improvements are unusual in migration projects. This will be examined further in the section on management design.

The application of technology patterns to meet requirements is the key to design.

# Creating a Component and Technique Map

Chapter 3 identifies a series of strategies that can be applied to migration projects. Typically, one of these strategies dominates a project. In fact, in the selection of a strategy, it is often obvious which strategy is the best fit for a situation. The choice of the strategy is based on two axioms. The first is that the business logic is worth preserving (except in the case of a replacement project). The second is that the cost/benefit analysis proves the need for a migration project.

While strategy selection is often straightforward, the techniques usually associated with the chosen strategy will need to be augmented with others to complete the project. It is rare that the techniques and tactics used to implement the strategy are sufficient to complete the project. Other techniques and tactics are often required to implement a migration solution. This is where the component/technique map is required. Additionally, the way you apply a technique might vary according to the strategy you are using.

Once you have selected a strategy, you need to identify the techniques you will use to apply this strategy to the components involved in the migration. This information is captured in a document called a *component and technique map*. Be aware that you might need to update this document during the project and that prototyping and iteration might also lead to changes in this document. During an initial architecture stage, this document serves as a first-cut component technique map.

The technique you use to implement a strategy is based on cost and risk criteria and on the extent to which you will be using tools. When source code porting techniques are used, an interim source code control system might be required and the build environment might need to be ported or reverse-engineered. Source code porting also encourages the use of code scanners to identify common known idioms in the source environment and to apply known transformations to them. These techniques can also be applied to data structures, although the data transformations will differ from code transformations.

The techniques you apply to data files are of critical importance to replacement or rehost-technology porting strategies. Data files might be anything from source environment proprietary formats through indexed or ASCII flat files to RDBMS data volumes. Such data migrations might require specific conversion programs to be written or purchased and deployed, and decisions about physical versus logical copy strategies need to be defined, along with the need to transform or augment the source data.

Creating a component/technique map involves creating a component list based on data attributes of the source object and assigning a migration technique to each object class in the component list.

# Refining High-Level Designs

Platform design artifacts that might require further refinement might include the following:

- Required system capability
- Deployment topology (for example, the number of boxes)
- Storage requirements
- Storage connectivity topology
- A network connection topology
- A nonfunctionality requirements compliance statement

This refinement process is iterative in nature. As more information, requirements, constraints, and costs are discovered, changes to the overall design might also be required. These changes must be documented and agreed to by those responsible for managing as well as implementing the migration.

## Refine Platform Design

Earlier in this chapter, we examined a methodology for defining platform design requirements and some of the platform design patterns used to meet differing requirements. The overall assembly framework used by Sun platform designers, called the service-point architecture, is based on the provision of compute pools conforming to a vertical, horizontal, edge role-based organizational nexus. This is supported by a storage architecture that is based on block and file services (SAN and NAS) and a management capability.

Applying platform design patterns to requirements permits the development of a candidate architecture capable of supporting an instance of the application. This candidate design needs to be tested against two additional issues: environments and consolidation.

Most organizations have one or more preproduction environments to support their development and software release processes. They might also have multiple production environments to support differing user communities, which might or might not be from different companies. The least expensive platform design is the replication of the production environment. However, the capital and management costs involved in this approach might prohibit its use, and cost scaling might need to be applied to at least one of the preproduction environments. An environment built for full volume performance or scalability testing needs to be large enough to meet these goals and might, therefore, be larger than the production environment and might also contain a load generation capability. In situations in which a development team has a significant commitment to the Solaris OS and the applications to be migrated are only a small part of the portfolio, Sun's N1 Provisioning Server, currently available only on blades, might offer development communities the opportunity to share hardware on a bookable basis, because hardware resources can be switched between development users by a reprovisioning transaction. For example, if developers need an integration test facility for only one month as they enter the integration test phase, you might provision the environment and release the resources to other users after the tests have been completed. A similar solution could be used for the volume test environment's load generators, and even for some components of the volume test environment.

Infrastructure designers are now looking to increase system utilization through various forms of consolidation solutions, one of the most important being workload sharing. Planning for consolidation is another iteration in the platform design cycle. Cost effectiveness and utilization maximization are the key goals for this design stage. The citizenship factors of an application depend on the degree of exclusivity an application makes on scarce resources. Traditional bad citizenship caused by memory leaks or fork bombs can now be managed by the Solaris OS such that while such applications still fail, they do not jeopardize the OS instance. Although we don't live in a perfect world, applications that exhibit these traits are not production quality and shouldn't be implemented. The majority of scarce resources, where scarce means one resource, are related to the TCP/IP stack: TCP addresses, port addresses, or gethostname replies. CPU, RAM, and I/O bandwidth are never scarce because it is always possible to design more of these resources into a platform by use of the vertical and horizontal scaling design patterns. Defining the citizenship factors of the applications' components, either formally or informally, is a prerequisite for designing the co-host schema in a consolidation solution. Applications with good citizenships can be collocated, a strategy that leads to sharing nonutilized cycles. Abstracting the application from a host instance by means of remote storage patterns and application name services solutions permits flexible and timely job location decisions, such as the development and load generator solutions documented above.

Despite conducting a detailed requirements definition, and iteratively refining the system's and storage platform's architectures, you must tune the design stage depending on the strategies employed.

Refronting, replacement, and interoperation usually introduce new components into the application's runtime environment, and original and new design patterns based on prototyping-based fact-finding might be required. For example, these strategies might be used if the customer organization is able to leverage newer infrastructure components and if the migrated application is sharing resources that are already deployed, such as a message bus infrastructure when the interoperate strategy is employed. This case enables current capacity planning and service level management knowledge to be engineered into the platform design. It also enables the migration project to leverage historic investments. This is often the key justification for the migration. One of the reasons for performing a system I/O architecture review is to determine whether economies in the feed interfaces (if they exist) can be achieved. It is these sorts of economies that can often justify a migration necessitated by the retirement of data propagation code lines and their replacement with publish/subscribe messaging solutions.

Refronting will have required the isolation, extraction, and reimplementation of presentation logic, and this will have host platform redesign issues because of new software components that require hosting. The implementation of the presentation logic in browser-hosted technology raises a simple software distribution problem that is fairly simple to solve because the application will become available through an http URL. It is also likely to raise training issues because the GUI will likely change enough that retraining the user base will be required. Obviously, if refronting is undertaken to extend the user community from within the company to either suppliers or customers, the training effort is likely to be justified. Optionally, you can undertake refronting by provisioning the legacy terminal environment, thereby making training issues are less acute. The definition of the hosting environment as a browser will often mean that system infrastructure is in place to support this requirement.

Replacement strategies that leverage the functionality sedimentation process require the provision of additional infrastructure, and the designer must include these new functional components in the runtime environment catalog.


## Refine the Build Environment Design

The outputs from project planning will determine the list of infrastructure components required of the migration project. These might include the following:

- Document management repository
- Code control systems
- Compilation environment
- Analytic/architecture repositories
- Data dictionaries
- Software release and distribution control system

These necessary resources require system resources to work. A migration workbench is required. The capability and capacity of the migration workbench will depend on the transition plan. If the proposed production resources are available before you transition the production environment, the necessity for additional resources is limited. Software release and distribution is an ITIL function, and thus might logically fall into designing or refining the management solution. In the context of migration, software release and distribution is highly likely to be a significant implementation and transition enabler. Therefore, the solutions design for software release distribution should be considered as part of project architecture.

In addition to a build environment for the target application's execution environment, you might need additional system resources (for example, system and infrastructure software) to develop components of the management solution. These resources can be made available through the sharing of the application's build environment or through the candidate production resource. If the candidate production resource is currently in use for production, as is the case when already existing infrastructure is leveraged, formal change control is required and a separate build environment for the management solutions is needed. It is better to build the proposed software release environment before transition and to use it in the transition process than to implement the management regime after the transition.

## Create a Target Runtime Environment's Inventory

The definition of the target runtime environment might seem obvious, but you should test it against the component and technique map. The purpose of this testing is to ensure completeness of the target environment's functionality to meet the needs of the migrated application. The key requirements are as follows:

- Additional libraries (for example, JVM™ or RogueWave)
- Application servers (for example, the Sun ONE Application Server, WebSphere, or WebLogic)
- Third-party products (such as shell interpreters, RDBMSs, or emulators)
- Deployment or provisioning agents for the build environment (for example, JumpStart™ technology or `rdist`)
- Software agents required for transition (for example, SQL-BackTrack or database replication technology)

Obviously, objects that should be supported in the target environment and that should be captured in the runtime environments catalog include any interpreters or other application development environments required on the target production systems, including both RDBMS and their forms packages.

The runtime environment's inventory needs to be comprehensive and it needs to fit within the budget defined during cost/benefit analysis. For example, if you're migrating from a non-UNIX system to the Solaris environment, it might be best to rehost the job control logic (JCL) within either UNIX shell script or an infrastructure component such as a third-party job scheduler. This technique allows you to reduce the complexity and cost of the target system and maximizes the usefulness of the target system.

# Refine the Application Design

Given that the goal of a migration project is usually the preservation of business logic, application design skills are only required in projects in which the migration strategy introduces significant changes to the code base. For example, if you were migrating business systems by moving from one COTS product to another, the migration problem would be reduced to data transformation and migration. Even in this example, the techniques of reverse engineering minimize the need for application design skills. However, detailed data modeling skills might still be required, and suitable tools might need to be deployed to support the modelers. Additionally, utilities might need to be planned, designed, or acquired to support transformations and to eliminate bugs that are exposed by the migration. This might also be necessary when implementation technology implementations differ, for example, with Cobol packed decimals.

Strategies adopted will determine the amount of applications design skill and infrastructure required to support the migration project, with rehosting requiring the least and rearchitecture requiring the most. The amount of genuine applications design skill that is required within the project will determine the complexity, functionality, and cost of the build environment and its supporting infrastructure.

# Refine the Network Design

Organizations with a strong networking capability believe that network design is a core competence. They frequently have very strong and inflexible policies that are strongly aligned to their business service delivery. Two factors are changing the constraints of solutions network designers:

- Network hardware technology
- Intersystem communication overtaking intersite communication

Network hardware vendors are among the prime beneficiaries of the sedimentation process discussed earlier in this book. The security, virtualization, and routing capabilities of network hardware are significantly more effective than they have been in the past, and this trend will continue. The bandwidth and speed of TCP/IP networks are also on a growth curve, and the costs are also on long-term decline. Like systems, the supply industry is offering improved price performance as a long term trend, and this must impact network designers.

The deepening reality behind Sun's tagline "The Computer is the Network" is introducing new requirements to network design within the data center. These requirements are different from traditional design criteria in that they emphasize intersystem communication, as opposed to geographical or inter-site communication. This could mean that your data center design might vary from your overall enterprise network design. Mass consumer portals such as vodafone.net are examples of these new Internet data centers. It is clear that the needs of intersystem communication are beginning to influence the principles and patterns of network design and are becoming as important as the physical network. For example, geographic distribution models have traditionally driven much of the intellectual property involved in current network design efforts, and therefore they have driven network design standards.

Applications designers will have provided an intercomponent data communication model. This is also a critical input to the network design process.

Most data networks are owned by a networking group, and the network design rules are often a constraint to migration project designers. Negotiation with the network's standards owner need to be based on sound requirements to solutions. The business requirements are not negotiable by the networks team, and if the requirements mandate a standards or policy change, this change should be achievable. Changes proposed for non-essential reasons, such as the personal comfort of the platform designer, are not justifiable.

Another key area of network design is the need to supply name services. The design rules and responsibilities between IP-address distribution architecture and host-name resolution is well understood. Distributed applications require name services solution designers to supply a name service for the application's components. Many infrastructure providers mandate enhancements or additions to the traditional name service applications to allow intercomponent communication. For instance, Oracle implements a name services solution (SQL*Net) to allow clients, servers, and replication nodes to talk to each other. Sybase also implements a name services solution, using files or Lightweight Directory Access Protocol (LDAP).

The needs of management also place demands on the network designer. The usual design is to separate management traffic from business traffic because they have different demand profiles and routing requirements, and applying quality of service criteria to business traffic is easier when separate network segments are used.

Parts of security solutions design can be delegated to network hardware. Sun consultants recommend an in-depth security strategy that leverages an architecture with network hardware and system hosts playing specific cooperative roles.

## Develop a Management Services Design

Sun's current management vision is driven by SunTone and the IT Infrastructure Libraries (ITIL). ITIL defines runtime systems management as consisting of service delivery and service support, as follows:

- **ITIL service delivery.** Service level management, financial management, capacity management, availability management, and IT service continuity management
- **ITIL service support.** Service desk, incident management, problem management, change management, release management, and configuration management.

While business logic needs to be preserved, the management regime is often where improvement is expected, although these improvements can be specified as improvements in the SunTone Architectural Method's nonfunctionality requirements. As a UNIX implementation, the Solaris OS has rich functionality. It is also one of the most popular operating systems for ISV offerings. Management solution designers have many choices about how to implement management solutions. They can choose whether to use Solaris OE-based functionality, to use Solaris third-party layered software products (including those that emulate the behavior of the source environment such as DEC control language (DCL) shells for ex-VMS users), or to use elements of BMC Software Inc. or Computer Associates (CA) product sets often available on both IBM mainframe operating systems and the Solaris OS.

Service improvements can be based on either improved quality or reduced cost. Where cost improvement changes are sought, reviewing how to implement Solaris environment-bundled functionality should be considered. This functionality will already have been paid for, and support is included in Sun's standard support offerings. In a number of cases, some functionality can be suboptimal and the cost/ benefit case should be carefully considered. For instance, the UNIX clock daemon, cron, and its various interfaces will run jobs at specific times. On request, they will implement a primitive security (privilege) model, but they do not support a job contingency semantic or language. Invoking applications jobs within a distributed deployment also requires that you leverage name servers and use the remote execution capabilities of the Solaris OS (UNIX). The cron utility can be suboptimal and lack some functionality, but it might also meet all the business requirements and is free in that it is bundled with the Solaris OS.

The good thing is that these features do exist, although the developer productivity for job control might be less than is required, jeopardizing both time to market goals and the cost of the new job deployment if you decide to implement job control in the UNIX shell. In this case, applying a "no worse than before" rule might help you make decisions. Reviewing the preceding example, if the job control in the source system is based on a proprietary job control language such as REXX or DCL, then the decision to port the job control scripts to a UNIX shell will lead to a "no worse than before" deployment and cost solution, which will improve the portability of the job control solution. Other key areas in which the UNIX market, and hence the Solaris market, offer cheaper layered software solutions include service continuity, capacity planning, incident management, and release management. A decision to migrate functionality from one third-party supplier to a more cost-effective software provider can offer both functional and cost advantages, and in the case of migration from IBM proprietary mainframes, this can add significantly to the benefits case.

In summary, migration management tools from either proprietary or bespoke technologies to either cheaper third-party or base OS functionality can save money.

We can now examine the process piece. The preservation of business logic is a key requirement. Applications are tightly bound to business processes, and process redesign opportunities are, therefore, likely to be restricted to the IT department.

The development of a process and the selection and implementation of tools are iterative and are driven by requirements. To maximize financial efficiency, adopt a principle of minimal compliance, and evaluate the evolutionary qualities of the management solution to determine the level of investment protection that is required and the changes that are expected to be paid for as part of the project.

The big rule is this: "Don't design for tomorrow's problem unless the customer wants to pay for it today." The corollary is that the business case owner will want to pay for some of tomorrow's problems today.

Examine each of the ITIL disciplines and determine the service level, process definition, and technology infrastructure supporting the process. Determine the service level changes required, both improvements and reductions. Because these changes might require a design that will impact the system, storage, and network solutions design, be sure to obtain sign-off for the changes before implementing them. In addition, leverage the current infrastructure. For instance, if the migration is from a proprietary environment to the Solaris environment and the organization has a significant Solaris estate, many of the ITIL disciplines will be in place and an infrastructure and process will already be defined. In this case, the design will be about including the new targets within a solution that already exists.

It is also likely that differing ITIL disciplines will be implemented to different levels of effectiveness. The platform design and the management process design need to go through an iterative, cooperative design review to ensure that design features of the platform and application can be used by the service support/delivery functions of the organization. This way, process change can be identified and the design can be simplified to meet the required IT process. An example of where design drives process is the definition of backup operations within the IT service continuity function. The actual backup processes are defined by the solutions designer, and the design needs to be reflected in the operational instructions that include how to manage backup source systems and backup media. The availability management function goals include an additional requirement statement for the platform designer, and the design needs to be tested for both compliance and potential over-supply and complexity.

In summary, designing for management services involves the following tasks:

- Identifying management requirements, using the operational qualities and ITIL
- Identifying where changes must occur as a result of the platform changes
- Identifying where changes must occur to implement the benefits case
- Testing the platform design against the management requirements
- Testing the management process against the solutions design

# Creating a Transition Plan

After developing a component and technique map, develop a first-pass transition plan that explains the business acceptability of downtime windows. Transition planning is the process of planning for the transition of the production environment from the legacy environment to your new production-ready target environment. Planning the transition tasks involves the following activities:

- Determining the transition window
- Extending the downtime window (for example, with database replication)
- Identifying and planning transition activities

It is significantly easier to develop a transition plan if limited downtime windows are available to permit the final data copying to occur while an application is not running. It is necessary to design alternative transition plans, leveraging additional infrastructure such as replication or messaging software, when limited downtime is required. This plan also needs to take into account the final acceptance plan, which might need to consider the downtime window that is available. The transition plan needs to take the system I/O architecture into account. Any system that feeds from other systems within the enterprise needs to be repointed at the new production solution. Documenting the time at which this occurs is an essential part of the transition plan.

The process involved in performing this task is described in Chapter 7.

# Developing a Configuration Management Plan

Configuration management is frequently more complex in a migration project than in other deployments, because additional tools are required to act as configuration management repositories. Both reverse engineering and source code porting place unique demands on the configuration management discipline, and the proposed approach and tool set must be planned and documented in a configuration management plan. The installation of any required tools on the development support systems should be undertaken before their use, and the additional hardware requirements of the migration project also need to be defined (for example, the tool hosts and disk to be used).

# Creating a System I/O Map

The scope of a project implicitly defines a series of system objects that will not be migrated to a new technology. This is especially the case when you are applying the refronting and interoperation strategies. For platform architects, system I/O normally applies to network, serial port, or disk I/O. However, in this case, we are talking about a software system.

Some of the classic I/O sources are likely to be ported and should be identified in a system I/O map. These include the following:

- I/O using forms packages
- Other data feeds
- Interfaces that might need to be redesigned to ensure that legacy (or heritage) functionality remains available to the migrated system
- Batch feeds from other systems
- Value-added network (VAN) connections such as credit checking transactions

Batch feeds might be implemented in nonbatch technologies such as a message bus. These system interfaces need to be identified, and both migration and transition plans need to be designed.

## Creating an Acceptance Test Plan

One of the first things to plan for in any project is the mutually acceptable definition of an end point for the project. The mutuality might be between the business and the IT department, or it might be between the IT department and their suppliers. The definition you establish to identify the successful completion of a project should be captured in a document called an acceptance test plan.

Two key inputs to designing an acceptance test plan are necessary:

- An acceptable definition of the required functionality
- The definition of the improvement goals as defined in the project scope

Testing costs include money and time. The downtime window available for transition is also a factor to be considered during the development of the acceptance test plan. The runtime durations of the final acceptance test need to take into account the downtime window (for example, don't design an acceptance test that jeopardizes production transition). The critical tests to include in an acceptance test should focus on the business to ensure that business logic on the target systems will meet the migration requirements. This usually tests that all the requirements are addressed and that the migration solution remains an accurate and usable representation of the state of the business.

## Planning Test Strategies

The usual principles of unit testing should be applied to designated components and work packages. These need to be supplemented by integration tests that involve members of the user community and by a user acceptance testing infrastructure. Some organizations will release test scripts. When appropriate, these should be used during unit testing. The tests you perform might or might not be the final acceptance tests, or they might be prefinal test. The purpose of the unit tests is to ensure that the planned inputs and outputs are consumed and produced correctly. These tests should be designed to ensure that the components interact correctly with each other and that any application's input and outputs are correctly handled. The application's system I/Os include screens, forms, reports, and any batch or real-time feeds. The application and its components need to be tested against any mandatory systemic qualities.

In addition, any software or process designed to support the transition requires testing. Again, the usual principles of unit and integration testing need to be applied. However, specific instrumentation can and should be designed into the transition harness to reduce the post-transition testing. If the transition process can reliably report on its success, or degrees of success, testing for the completeness and accuracy of the transition can be avoided after the transition and the only testing required becomes the final acceptance tests.

The acceptance test must be business focused. A degree of pretesting is required to ensure that the acceptance test is performed in an acceptable time frame and the copy process will require some instrumentation so that the acceptance testers have confidence that they are testing the correct bill of materials.

# Prototyping the Process

One dimension of the design problem in migration projects that has not yet been explored is that of multiple environments. The word environment as used here describes an instance of the application to which different purposes and management goals are applied. Most applications posses multiple environments, if only a development and a production environment. Usually, at least one test environment will exist, which is usually called User Acceptance Testing (UAT), Training, Volume Test, Quality Assurance, or something similar. The variety of titles illustrates that it is possible to have more than one test environment. Additionally, instances of the application might exist to allow certain states of the business to be represented over a longer period of time than they would be in reality. The end-of-month position can be copied into an instance of an application to allow read-intensive "as at end of month" reports to be run over the succeeding month. This can be done to help minimize contention between the users of historic data and the new business workers, or because the application cannot support "as at" reporting. Other environments can be created to support business continuity. In the case study in Chapter 11, the organization had development, training, user acceptance, production, and MIS instances of the application's environment. The MIS instance held an "as at" end-of-previous-month state.

Separate environments are likely to have different downtime criteria and different acceptability as to failure of the transition, in that a training instance may be able t cope with remediation time on a partially successful copy. Additionally, the regression from an unsuccessful migration is likely to be simpler. These difference in manageability of the separate instances should be used in the migration planning process. One of the key advantages multiple environments deliver is a prototyping/benchmarking resource.

Prototyping and benchmarking can be used to test delivered manifest qualities and the manifest qualities of the transition process. The need to instrument the transition process has already been discussed, but the existence of separate environments allows the instrumentation to be developed iteratively. The existence of reduced-size integral data sets also allows rapid prototyping and the use of extrapolation for predicting the performance of the transition harness. If the transition harness's logic needs testing, this can be done on a subset. The performance of the transition process is a key factor in the transition, and if a full-size data set can be obtained in a nonintrusive way, test transitions should be undertaken to provide the following benefits:

- To assure users and migrators of the accuracy and acceptability of the transition process
- To train the transition team in the transition process to minimize the chance of process failure

Prototyping can be of an iterative or throwaway nature. Because the transition harness is only to be used for a short period of time while the various environments are migrated, throwaway techniques can be appropriate for the harness. However, the development of the test plans and any transition code to be inherited by either the development team or operations staff is best developed iteratively and documented appropriately.

# Designing a Training Plan for the New Environment

At this point, you need to consider the impact of implementing the new solution for the users or administrators and develop a training plan that addresses them. This plan will reflect the strategies and techniques used in the migration and will also fall into the IT/business divide. We have already argued that process redesign should be minimal in the context of migration projects. However, user interfaces might vary dramatically, such as in the case of a COTS version upgrade that changes the middleware infrastructure, moving from ASCII forms to web browser/server presentation solutions.

The rest of the training plan should concentrate on the IT department and the process and technology changes implemented within the context of a migration project.

Training falls into two areas: skills and process. Training potentially has two target communities: business and IT. The amount of training required will depend on the strategies you have adopted. A review of the project-benefits case will reinforce where business logic within the application will remain unchanged and where both business skills and business process should require minimal enhancement. The three strategies that contradict this statement are:

- Refronting
- Rearchitecting
- Replacing

Refronting might require you to retrain users in the use of the GUI. Rearchitecture and replacing might have significant user impact because the migration of a business from a legacy ledger solution to an up-to-date COTS solution is likely to have a massive impact on both business processes and the individual use of the system. Retirement strategies might mean that certain operations are no longer to be conducted, and therefore process changes are required.

Another factor influencing the amount of change and, therefore, the amount of training that will potentially be required is the change in technologies used by the business and IT. Migrations from non-UNIX platforms will mandate that the enterprise conduct a skills audit to ensure that it has sufficient skills in its IT department to run the new platform. The likelihood of this occurring depends on the degree of heterogeneity in the IT department before the migration. If the migration has led to the enterprise's first Solaris systems, then a training and transition plan needs to be implemented. The impact on an organization's IT process of a migration also varies depending on the maturity and coverage of the process—for example, how many ITIL functions are implemented and how well. The final factor is the degree of change implemented in the process, which might depend on the technologies deployed during the migration.

# CHAPTER 7

# Implementing a Migration

With a successful prototype of the target environment in place, you are ready to implement the migration. This chapter describes the steps involved in migrating the current environment to the target environment. The majority of this chapter focuses on porting, moving, and testing activities of the migration methodology introduced earlier in the book.

This chapter contains the following sections:

# Porting an Application to a New Operating System

As previously discussed, porting is an activity of moving a custom application, written in one or more programming languages, to a new operating system (OS). This activity relates primarily to creating a new executable that is compatible with the new OS. This is accomplished by modifying the application programming interfaces (APIs) used by the software so that they conform to or match the APIs offered by the new OS while maintaining similar functionality.

A detailed understanding of the application logic is not necessary for this task. Instead, familiarity with the development tools and the linkers and library technology that exist for the target environment is required because the porting effort is primarily one of modifying, compiling, and linking the application to the new OS.

The first step in porting an application is to identify which APIs are incompatible with the new OS and need to be rebuilt. Once you flag an API as being incompatible, you must develop a solution for a compatibility library that you can use to replicate the functionality that existed on the old platform. You can then modify the source code of the application to use the new API, as defined in the compatibility library, wherever the older incompatible version occurs.

In the following sections, we describe how to create a build environment on the target system. In addition, we explore some of the issues associated with creating the new application executable and discuss nondestructive methods of transforming the code.

# Creating a Target Build Environment

The development environment is composed of the development tools, the source code for the application, and any third-party products that are required to create the application. It also includes the hardware to support the developers who will use the tools to create the application executable and the supporting application infrastructure.

When migrating custom-written applications, you must also migrate the development environment to the new target environment. To migrate the build environment, perform the following tasks:

- Prepare the hardware environments, including backup and restore facilities.
- Identify the software to use in the new environment.
- Acquire a recent reference build log.
- Plan to acquire and install tools and utilities.

## Prepare the Hardware Environments

The development environment is usually created on nonproduction hardware. Although the development hardware can be purchased with the production hardware, it will almost certainly be required before the production hardware. Arrangements must be made to ensure that the hardware used in the development environment is delivered in a timely manner. However, keep in mind that large production environments require significant installation and verification efforts. Because of this, they must be acquired long before they are actually scheduled for use. The vendor's sales representatives can assist you in determining the lead time required for the acquiring and installing both the development and production hardware environments.

Although the porting process can involve significant effort that uses numerous resources, the development environment should be sized to support steady-state development and maintenance rather than the loads created by the one-time-only migration effort. It might be possible to lease equipment to support the migration activity, but care must be taken to ensure that the following items are sufficient for your project:

- Desktops are available for the migration engineers.
- Licenses have been acquired for the software, where appropriate.
- Compute capacity exists to support the migration effort.
- Storage capacity exists to support the migration effort.

## Identify the Software to Use in the New Environment

The target build software environment generally consists of the following items, which you should identify before beginning the porting exercise:

- **Development tools.** The utilities and tools used to create application binaries in the new environment. Typically, these consist of things like the following items:
  - Compilers
  - Debuggers
  - Linker-loaders
  - Libraries
  - Preprocessors/precompilers

  These tools are frequently incorporated into an Integrated Development Environment (IDE) that might or might not support the sharing of software among a number of different development teams. The IDE allows developers to edit, compile, execute, and debug the application executable in an environment that supports tracing the execution of the application at the source level, inserts compiler errors into the source code in-line, and allows for recompilation at the click of a button.

  Custom-written applications usually use a utility to build or make the application executable. This utility will usually be controlled by a configuration file that defines the following items:
  - The tool used to process the source code file (for example, a C compiler, a C++ compiler, a FORTRAN compiler, or a C preprocessor)
  - The compiler options that must be used
  - The order in which libraries should be referenced for symbol resolution
  - The location at which to look for header files
  - The location at which to install the compiled binary

  The most popular version of this tool is the make utility. There are different variants of the tool with similar names and functionality (for example, nmake and gmake). Another key tool used in the build environment is the source code repository that supports version control.

These tools enable developers to create and retrieve snapshots of specific versions of the source code, allowing them to label a specific version of the code. For example, a release with specific features might be labeled REL_2.3. Later, when release 3.1 is in production, the developers might want to fix a bug in the 2.3 release of the product. Using the version control tool, they can retrieve a snapshot of the source as it was when the 2.3 release was created by requesting copies of all files as they were when they were labeled REL_2.3. These tools also allow developers to record a history of the changes that have been made to a file along with who made them.

Source code version control systems usually require some training to use. The choice of which system to use is best left to the team that will support the development and maintenance of the application after it has been migrated. Common version control systems include the Source Code Control System (SCCS), Revision Control System (RCS), and Code Version System (CVS).

- **Application source code.** Normally, the application source code will have been acquired before you begin the porting process so that it could be assessed when you estimated the level of effort required to implement the migration. During porting, the code must be transferred to the target environment and imported into the source code revision control system that the client will use in the new development environment.

- **Third-party products used to develop the application.** These are additional libraries, classes, or templates that are not distributed with the OS or the development environment. They typically provide some functionality for the application in a supporting capacity or simplify the development of applications that rely on an object-oriented methodology.

## Acquire a Recent Reference Build Log

The best way to ensure that you fully understand the build environment is to acquire a build log that was created when the application source that you are going to port was last compiled. There are two main reasons for acquiring a build log of the source that you are transforming:

- The log will verify that the source builds without errors.
- The log will capture the specifics of the build process, including the following:
  - Which libraries are used
  - Which tools are used
  - The order in which symbols are resolved
  - The switches and options used by the compiler and in the linking processes
  - The location of header files

## Plan to Acquire and Install Tools and Utilities

For the purposes of creating the build environment, the build log is useful in that it specifies all the tools and utilities that are required to create the application executable. You will have to acquire new versions of these products that will run under the new target OS from the various software vendors. Lead times for acquiring products can vary, so some effort must be put into ensuring that the required hardware and software products are available before the porting effort is begun. Training might also be required for any new tools that are going to be used and should be arranged and delivered so that training does not impact the migration schedule.

When installing the new software, examine the `make` files and the build logs that were used or created on the old platform. Installing the new products in the same location under the new environment might reduce or minimize changes that have to be made to hard-coded paths in scripts or `make` files.

Access to documentation that describes the tools and APIs of the old environment is essential because the behavior of the old tools must be well understood. Although it is not a necessity, it can be useful to have access to the old environment if you need to verify how things were done on the old system.

Once the development environment is installed, create and compile several test examples to ensure that executables perform as required.

It is now time to install the source code control system and populate it with the source that is to be transformed. Mark or label the source in the repository to ensure that you can quickly go backwards if you need to compare a modified version of the source to the original code. In addition, ensure that you have tools like Perl, the `sed` commands, and shells to automate source code transformation.

# Building a New Application for the Target Platform

Once you've verified that the development environment is functioning correctly, you can start to build the application. Ideally, the process used to build an application should be well documented. However, frequently, this is not the case. If build documentation does exist, it might not be current or reflect the latest changes that have been implemented to the code or to the build process. The advantage of having a reference build of the application is the understanding that you will be porting the application as it is configured in that reference snapshot of the code.

As mentioned previously, much of the information about how an application should be built can be obtained from the `make` files and the reference build log that were created when the application was built on the old system.

Building the application results in the creation of an application executable. The functionality provided by the application can depend on a number of different elements of the build process. The output of the build process usually depends on one or more of the following items:

- Header files
- Compiler options
- Symbol resolution
- Variable initialization
- Conditional compilation
- Precompilation

The following paragraphs explain possible dependencies that exist for the preceding items:

- **Header files.** These are also referred to as *include files* because of the language construct used to make their contents available to the source code. Header files can exist anywhere in the file system. They usually provide definitions for both constants and types, as well as prototypes for library functions that are relevant to the OS. The header files provided by the system are usually located under the directory /usr/include and its subdirectories. Header files for third-party products can be placed anywhere, but you must tell the compiler where to look for them. Consult the old make files and build logs to determine which include file paths were specified in the old environment.

- **Compiler options.** To build correctly, applications might require the use of specific compiler options. Although the compilation options will be readily available from the old make files and build logs, these options might not map directly to the new environment. You will have to consult documentation (man pages and manuals) from the old system to determine why these options were used. Once you have identified the required functionality, consult the documentation for the new compiler, determine the appropriate option to use, and modify the make files to use the new options. Note that some options might not be available in the new environment.

- **Symbol resolution.** Multiple definitions might exist for a symbol within the code base of an application. Symbols are typically resolved against the first definition they encounter. By specifying which library to use, as well as the order in which libraries should be examined for a symbol, you can control which definition will be assigned a symbol. Examine the make file and build log to determine which libraries should be used and the order in which they should be examined.

- **Variable initialization.** Variables can be initialized when the application executable is created. The make file and build log should specify whether any initialization is required and what values should be used. There are differences in how variables are initialized between compilers and languages. Ensure that the behavior is well understood and faithfully replicated. (For example, some compilers default uninitialized variables to 0, others use –32768, and still others use random numbers.)

- **Conditional compilation.** Over time, the business functionality required from an application can change. New requirements will require changes to the application's source code base. When new functionality is needed for only a short period of time or in specific locations, different versions of the application will be required. Rather than creating a new copy of the existing source base and adding the new functionality to that code, developers typically add the new functionality to the same code base and make its inclusion dependent on an option that is passed to the compiler. For example, in the following conditional compilation code sample, function `foo()` will return 1 if `BAR` is defined; otherwise, the value is 0.

**TABLE 7-1**    Conditional Compilation Code Sample

```
foo()
{
#ifdef  BAR
    return (1);
#else
    return (0);
#endif
}
Fragment 7.1- Conditional Compilation
```

BAR is defined outside the code base when the executable is created, by specifying a switch to the compiler, using the syntax `-DBAR`. It will be difficult to figure this out without a copy of the old `make` file, build log, or accurate documentation.

Using a single source base reduces the amount of maintenance that must be expended to keep all of the different versions up to date with new features or bug fixes.

The knowledge of which switches to use during compilation must be provided by local domain experts from within a company.

- **Precompilation.** In certain cases, the source code must be precompiled or preprocessed by a utility or scripts before the application is built. Unlike conditional compilation, preprocessing or precompilation results in a new source base that has been modified by the utility. This modified or preconfigured code is then used in the build process.

Again, the knowledge of which options to pass to these precompilation utilities and the rationale for their use must come from the local domain experts within the organization.

# Create a Compatibility Library

You should use a compatibility library to replicate the functionality of the old environment. Doing so will minimize the amount of change that will have to be made to the source code base. A compatibility library might be available from the vendor of the new system, or it can be created by the migration team that is transforming the code.

When migrating to the Solaris OS, consider using the tools and migration kits found at http://www.sun.com/migration. The following example shows how to create a function to minimize the change to an application to an application that was written for an HP-UX environment that is being ported to the Solaris environment.

**TABLE 7-2**    Compatibility Library Sample

```
/*
 *   This call is available on HP-UX 10.x (tm) only.
 *   ltostr( )- converts long integers to strings
 */
#include <errno.h>
#include <stdlib.h>

char *ltostr(long a,int base) {
        static char buf[34];
        char *theChar;
        char sign=' ';
        int tmp;

        if(base > 32 || base < 2) {
                errno=ERANGE;
                return NULL;
        }
        theChar=buf+sizeof(buf);
        *theChar=0;

        if(a < 0) {
                sign='-';
                a=labs(a);
        }
        do{
                tmp=a%base;
                *--theChar = tmp>9 ? tmp+'a'-10 : tmp+'0';
                a=a/b;
        }while(a);
        if(sign=='-')
                *--theChar=sign;
        return theChar;
        }
```

APIs can vary among operating systems in a number of different ways:

- The function name might not exist under the new application. The preceding example illustrates this situation. Before engineering a solution, determine whether the functionality exists under a different name.

- The function might have a different prototype as well as a different functionality than it had in the original OS. These types of differences are rare and are becoming rarer. Over time, standards are minimizing the differences between UNIX implementations. Should the prototype and the functionality of an API differ between platforms, a new function will have to be created to provide the same functionality and footprint.

- The function might have the same prototype as it had in the original OS, but different functionality. Again, this situation does not frequently arise. If only the return value is different, it might make sense to modify the code base of the application and use the function provided by the new system. If there are significant differences, a new version of the function, matching the function found on the old system, will have to be engineered.

- Perhaps the most common case is that of the target OS having a different function prototype than that of the original OS, but similar functionality. There are three ways this can happen:

  - The type of the returned value is different than it was in the original OS. In this case, change the type to match that of the new OS, and change the source code for the application.

  - The number of arguments for the new OS is different than it was for the old OS. In this case, create a wrappered version of the function in the new OS.

  - The types of the arguments for the new OS are different than they were for the old OS. In this case, change the type of the variable in the source code to match that of the new OS.

Again, when attempting to port or transform code, attempt to minimize the changes that have to be made to the application logic, and use compatible functions whenever possible to minimize implementation errors.

Sun has created a set of compatibility libraries to assist developers port from some common operating systems. An example is the Solaris OE Implementation for HP-UX API. It implements a set of commonly used HP-UX functions for Solaris/SPARC™ or Solaris/x86. It is available at http://www.sun.com/migration/hp_ux/tools/hpuxapi.html. To use these libraries, simply download the file and unzip it in your directory. The following content will be created under the directory:

- include: Contains all the header files for the library

- src: Contains the compilation script compileapi.sh and all the source files for the library (*.c)

- lib: Contains the binary code of the library (*.o) and the archive file hp2sunmig.a

- example: Contains examples of how to use and test the library on the Solaris 9 OE

- `test_plans`: Contains the test-case documents

- README: Overview of Solaris OE Implementation for HP-UX API contents; also contains the list of supported APIs

For a complete list of included functions, visit `http://www.sun.com/migration/hp_ux/tools/emulation.html`.

## Modify the Make Environment

Complex applications can contain millions of lines of code. Well-written applications are usually implemented as a number of modules that are broken down along functional lines. Each module is usually contained in its own subdirectory. The code in each subdirectory might be dependent on another subdirectory within the application, as well as on libraries or header files provided by the system.

Building the application should be a monolithic activity that is performed at a high level within the source tree. Rather than starting at the bottom of the tree (the leaf nodes) and building each component from the bottom up, the structure of the build environment should be such that the application can be built from the root node of the source code tree.

Although a little more work will have to go into coordinating the `make` files at a lower level with those higher up in the tree, the effort will be worthwhile because the location of include files, compiler options, and so forth can be assigned at one higher level and inherited through the use of `include` directives by those at a lower level in the source hierarchy. This minimizes the opportunity for errors to creep into the build process, because all definitions are created at a high level.

## Understand the Application Configuration

Applications frequently require configuration information. They might read this data from a configuration file, or they might obtain it dynamically from the environment by using a `getenv()` call. In addition, configuration files might contain data that is environmentally dependent, meaning that it will have to change when you change platforms or operating systems. Be sure to review the data within the configuration file with experts on the current environment who are knowledgeable about the application on the new environment. For example, Oracle configuration options differ depending on whether you implement your solution on the Solaris OS or HP/UX. Attempting to determine the correct configuration data for an application requires a detailed understanding of the application logic, which the porting team might not have. Remember, relying on individuals who are knowledgeable in the application and its configuration ensures the most productive use of resources.

# Deciding Whether to Support Backward Compatibility

When modifying the code base for an application during a migration, you must decide whether the new code base will be able to function in the old environment. This is known as backward compatibility. After the migration, the same source code could be used in the old build environment to produce an application executable targeted for the old platform, or the same source base could be used in the new build environment to support the new platform.

In the source code base, backward compatibility is accomplished by nondestructive source code modification, usually implemented through the use of conditional compilation, as illustrated in the following code fragment. _sun is predefined by the Solaris compiler.

**TABLE 7-3**    Backward Compatibility Example

```
#ifdef _sun
    newFunction()
#else
    originalFunction()
#endif
```

Backward compatibility within a source code base can reduce the amount of work that has to be done by the development staff. If a single source code base is created that can support both the old and the new environments, changes resulting from new requirements or changing business logic only have to be implemented once in the source code.

While code that is heavily modified to include conditional compilation directives can be hard to read and maintain, the benefits of using conditional compilation directives far outweigh the cost. In fact, migrating to the Solaris OS does not usually require significant code modification.

# Migrating Data

With the applications taken care of, it is now time to turn your attention to handling the most delicate part of the migration implementation: data transfer or conversion. While most organizations don't realize it, data migration is one of the most important parts of the migration exercise. After all, what good are most applications on any platform if they don't have data to operate on? Depending on the application that you are using and your outage window, this activity can range in difficulty and effort from trivial to extremely laborious. On the trivial end of the scale, you might be simply copying files over the network or restoring them from magnetic tape. However, at the other end of the scale, you might use exotic networking technologies and complicated utilities requiring several intermediate steps before getting data onto the target platform in the correct format for your application. Whichever end of the spectrum your migration is located on, it is good to understand the range of tools and techniques that are available for moving data.

# Transferring Data

Let's start by looking at the shallow end of the pool: data transfers. The goal here is to get data from the legacy server onto the new target environment. While the physical format of the data might change, the logical (application) format of the data will stay the same. The difficulty of transferring data is determined by three factors: size, transfer window, and rate of change. Looking at all these factors, you should be able to develop a strategy for getting data to your desired location.

The size of data is the most obvious factor in data transfers. Size, in itself, is not a problem, but size and a small transfer window can create one. For example, transferring 10 gigabytes worth of files overnight is not problematic for most networks. However, if you needed to transfer 10 gigabytes of data within 10 minutes, there certainly might be a problem. Problems caused by size are not limited to bandwidth. Staging and backing up data in a timely fashion can also be problematic.

The other variable involved in determining the difficulty of a transfer involves the data's rate of change. Static data can make your transfer much easier by allowing you to segment activities. For example, configuration files that do not frequently change can probably be transferred to a new system at any time by a simple copy. This is also the case for read-only application data. However, data that constantly change, such as transactional databases or real-time data acquisitions, might be very difficult to transfer.

Regardless of the level of difficulty involved in your data transfer process, there are a number of decisions you need to make. The most important of these is the general strategy for transferring the data. In the following sections, we describe two methods for transferring data: network data transfers and media data transfers. Following these sections, we detail the steps involved in this process.

## Network Data Transfers

Network transfers are the preferred technique for data transfers. Because almost every UNIX has TCP/IP networking and Ethernet connectivity, there are few cases where this method won't be the fastest and easiest way to transfer your data. Adding to this convenience, most network transfer applications will automatically encode data transformations, as needed.

Two primary tools transfer large amounts of data over the network: File Transfer Protocol (FTP) and Network File System (NFS). Both tools allow you to move files over the network quickly. Either tool is acceptable, depending on where the data currently reside. Both tools will be limited by the speed of the network or the disks. However, remember to pull the data off the legacy server when using NFS. NFS provides more efficient reading than writing.

FTP and NFS can be automated with Expect (http://expect.nist.gov/), Perl, or shell scripts. This automation can be difficult, but as you can see by the process described in the preceding paragraphs, you will be doing this transfer many times, so the investment should be worthwhile.

Remember to include at least some rudimentary integrity testing with your scripts. For file-based transfers, using some form of the UNIX chksum command should be sufficient.

## Media Data Transfers

If you cannot use the network, perhaps in wide area network (WAN) migrations where the link is too slow, you will be forced to use some kind of media transfer. Traditionally, this has meant restoring streaming tape backups, but today you might also be able to use optical media like CD-ROMs or DVDs. Either way, this transfer requires a temporary storage space where data can be restored on the media, then reassembled before being copied to its final place.

A new type of media transfer is the use of storage area network (SAN) volumes. In this case, a temporary volume is created on the SAN-attached legacy system, unmounted, and remounted in the new environment. While this method can be quite efficient for large data sets, it requires that both systems be connected to the SAN and share a common file system type (UFS, EXT3, and the like). Because this is rarely the case in most migrations, SAN volumes are not commonly used in migration projects.

Regardless of the method you choose for transferring data, there is a basic methodology you should follow. In general, this process includes the following tasks:

- Plan the transfer process
- Perform functional testing
- Conduct performance testing
- Implement the transfer process

Following this process should ensure a successful data transfer. In the following sections, we explore each of these tasks in detail.

# ▼ To Plan the Transfer Process

Before you can start transferring data, you need to make a number of decisions. The most important of these is the general strategy for transferring the data. A number of methods for this are described in the following sections. When planning the transfer process, address the following tasks:

1. **Schedule downtime.**

   Most large transfers require two to three tests before the actual production transfer, so make sure that your downtime windows have been requested.

2. **Create a staging area.**

3. **Plan for the target server.**

4. **Develop backout strategies.**

5. **Create, automate, and test the process.**

   Using a subset of data in the prototype environment, create and unit test the transfer process. When you get something you like, start to automate it. Because you will be doing quite a few transfer tests (and perhaps quite a few transfers), take the time to script the transfer with enough robustness that you can restart failed transfers.

# ▼ To Test Functionality

After you establish a plan for effectively transferring data, you need to test the plan to ensure that it functions as you expect it to and that all of the transferred data run on the production environment.

1. **Schedule downtime for functional testing of the process.**

2. **Back up the data.**

   Take the first full backup of the data you are going to transfer and use it to conduct functional testing of the transfer process. This is often called a *dry run*. This dry run should use the entire data set on the production equipment.

3. **Set up monitoring.**

   Start gathering performance data that you can use to tune the process later.

4. **Evaluate the results.**

   Once you have results from the functional test, evaluate them, and tune your process in preparation for performance testing.

## ▼ To Test Performance

When you are confident that the transfer process is functioning as it should, performance testing needs to be conducted. Performance testing will ensure that the transfer process will perform within the allotted downtime window.

1. **Schedule downtime for the performance test.**

2. **Back up the data again.**

3. **Test the performance of the transfer, monitoring the results.**

   This should result in an accurate estimate of the total transfer time. If the amount of time required to perform the test doesn't fit the downtime window, repeat this step until you achieve the desired results.

## ▼ To Implement the Transfer Process

When you reach a point at which the transfer process functions the way you expect it to, within the allotted amount of time, you are ready to transfer the data.

1. **Schedule the production transfer.**

   Ensure that you allot an appropriate amount of downtime, as determined from the performance tests.

2. **Back up the data again.**

   Make sure the test completely restores the original from this backup.

3. **Begin the transfer.**

   This should be the smoothest part of the process because it has been practiced and timed several times now.

4. **Perform data testing on the transferred data.**

   Conduct tests on the data as described in the master test plan.

5. **Go live.**

   Following this process should ensure a successful data transfer. In the following sections, we explore specific tools and techniques to perform the data transfer.

# Transforming Data

Sometimes you have to contend with even more than just the physical transportation of the data from one platform to another. Data may need to be converted or transformed in some way to work with the new platform, application, or both. Because data transformations deal with both the physical and logical conversion of data, they are much more difficult and expensive.

Data transformations will follow much the same process as the data transfers above; however, extra steps will be needed to process the data. These extra steps, usually called staging, can range from simple mapping to complete rekeying. While they can be automated with commercial tools and scripting languages, the cost of tools or time invested for scripting tends to be expensive.

Data transformation tend to fall into three categories: encoded data transformations, application transformations, and database transformations.

## Transform Encoded Data

Encoded data transformations occur because data has been stored in different or incompatible file formats. While most UNIX files are stored in ASCII encoding, many other file formats are in use on other platforms. For example, mainframes use the older EBCDIC standard, and non-English systems use double-byte character sets or Unicode. Another example would be the difference in text file formatting (CRLF/CR) between DOS and UNIX text files.

Encoded data will require specialized transformation applications. However, most UNIX systems (Solaris included) have a general-purpose utility, called dd, that can do some basic transformations from EBCDIC to ASCII. The following example shows its use to convert between EBCDIC and ASCII while forcing all the resulting text to lower case:

```
# dd if=test.ebcdic of=test.ascii conv=ascii,lcase
```

More difficult encoding transformation, such as the Unicode or double-byte character set described above, will require more specialized tools.

## Transform Application Data

Application data transformations are more demanding than encoding data transformations. Because they are specific to each application, most applications will come with some utility to convert standard data interchange formats like comma-separated value (CSV) or tab-delimited text files into their format.

A specialized, but common subset of application transformations are databases. In fact, these transformations are so common that a class of applications, called extract, transform, and load (ETL), have been created to address them. ETL utilities take a wide array of formats (both standard interchange and proprietary application formats) to convert them into Structured Query Language (SQL) for relational database management system (RDBMS). Most RDBMSs come with a basic set of these utilities to convert SQL or standard interchange formats into their data storage format.

The most basic ETL utilities will be provided by the RDBMS vendors as their logical copy utilities. Examples of these include Oracle's export and import commands, MySQL's dump command, and Sybase's bulkcopy program (bcp command). These commands use the APIs of the RDBMSs to take the proprietary storage format and dump the output in standard (or close to standard) SQL text. For example, the following session uses the MySQL mysqldump command for that purpose:

```
# mysqldump -uroot -p e107 > e107.sql
Enter password:
# more e107.sql
-- MySQL dump 8.22
--
-- Host: localhost     Database: e107
---------------------------------------------------------
-- Server version       3.23.56


--
-- Table structure for table 'e107_core'
--

CREATE TABLE e107_core (
  e107_name varchar(20) NOT NULL default '',
  e107_value text NOT NULL,
  PRIMARY KEY  (e107_name)
) TYPE=MyISAM;


--
-- Dumping data for table 'e107_core'
--


INSERT INTO e107_core VALUES ('e107','a:5:{s:11:\"e107_author\";s:22:\"Steve Dun
stan (jalist)\";s:8:\"e107_url\";s:15:\"http://e107.org\";s:12:\"e107_version\";
s:5:\"0.555\";s:10:\"e107_build\";s:4:\"beta\";s:14:\"e107_datestamp\";i:1055552
502;}');
(CONTINUED)
```

As you can see from the example, the mysqldump utility includes the database schema as well as the actual application data. While this is fine if you are moving from MySQL to MySQL (for instance, from Linux to Solaris), it might not correctly import into other RDBMSs. In that case, you will need to find a slightly more sophisticated tool that understands the differences between RDBMS implementations. One such tool is Oracle Migration Workbench, available for free from Oracle's TechNet Web site (http://technet.oracle.com). This tool allows you to extract data from MySQL, Sybase, DB2, and other RDBMSes, manipulate the data, and import it into Oracle 8 or 9. Most RDBMS vendors will provide tools that allow the migration of database objects and data to their own RDBMS implementations. Additionally, third parties have built tools with heterogeneous capability.

However, if you are considering taking non-SQL or interchange formats into an RDBMS, you will need to look for a commercial utility or write your own. Non-SQL data types commonly include hierarchical database outputs and XML files. Commercial utilities commonly employ mapping technologies that map database fields into the new format (such as objects).

# Creating the Production Environment

The term "migration" implies that we are moving from one environment to a different environment. The environment to which you are moving is referred to as the *target* environment. As illustrated by the E-stack in Chapter 3, the application is only one component of the target environment.

In this section, we explain how you prepare the facilities to support the new compute, network, and storage platforms. In addition, we explain how to install and configure these platforms and how to create the application infrastructure that will support the application.

All of these activities are distinct and separate from the migration of the application. They all require unique, disparate skill sets, and all have differing timelines. We strongly recommend that these activities proceed in a parallel fashion with the migration of the application, to reduce the amount of time required for the migration effort.

## Building the Production Facilities Environment

Modifying a building or the data center is a significant task. Depending on the changes required, this can take a great deal of time. Care must be taken to minimize the disruption to the existing IT operation when bringing in new power, knocking down a wall, or increasing air conditioning efficiencies.

Inspections and building permits might have to be arranged for and acquired in order to make structural modifications to real estate. In addition, new facilities might have to be created or leased to support the new environment. Heating and ventilation additions might not be feasible in some older environments, and building design might limit the amount of heat that can be dissipated. You should also consider any limitations on the generating capacity of the local power utility.

Facilities modification should be executed according to the plan that was created as a result of the facilities assessment that was described earlier in this book.

# Building the Production Platform

Once the facilities are in place, you can deploy the compute platform. This platform might be integrated with existing storage and networking components, or it might require its own storage and networking subsystems.

If existing storage is to be used, ensure that it integrates with the new environment at both the hardware level (fiber channel, SCSI, and the like) and at the software level (file system type, volume management, and so on.) When using existing storage, be extremely careful to ensure that no data on the existing storage is lost or corrupted.

We recommend that experts in the storage technology and the compute platform be hired to configure storage because these systems are typically complex. In the case of NAS and SAN implementations, firmware patches and OS upgrades are frequently required.

If the platform is to use a new storage platform and networking gear, the impact on the existing environment can be minimized, although specialized skills will still be required.

Once the storage platform has been configured, ensure that extensive testing is conducted to verify that the system is performing correctly. These tests should be conducted with utilities supplied by the compute platform or storage vendor, not the application. We provide more information about the testing process later, but it is critical that the newly installed storage be validated before you install the data.

Network infrastructure is usually easier to test and configure than are storage platforms. Ensure that all switches, routers, hubs, and load balancers have been correctly installed and configured. Ensure that you generate sufficient loads for these components to verify that they are performing as intended. When appropriate, use external consultants to generate representative loads for systems before placing them into production.

If a larger, enterprise-class machine is used as the compute platform, the compute platform itself might require extensive configuration. Frequently, large enterprise-class machines can be chosen for the new production platform because of their availability, scalability, dynamic reconfiguration, and hot swap capabilities. Optimal configuration and testing of these complex platforms takes planning and time. In addition, training might be required to understand, design, and administer this state-of-the-art technology. In certain cases, you can reduce TCO and improve ROI by partitioning a large symmetric multiprocessor machine into smaller virtual machines. This can simplify administration, reduce floor space, and improve availability, but might require the deployment of resource management software to ensure that service level agreements can be maintained across all virtual machines. Configuring and sizing this infrastructure will require some experimentation and testing.

These activities can and should take place while the application is being migrated. The production platform build is independent of the migration activity and requires a completely different skill set.

## Building the Application Infrastructure

Once the platform is installed and the OS is up and running, you can start configuring the infrastructure for the application. All the software used to support the enterprise and the application should be available in the new environment, including the following items:

- Directory name services
- Identity services
- Accounting packages
- Management infrastructure
- Backup facilities
- Third-party runtime products required by the application
- Databases

As we discuss in the following sections, these products should be tested as standalone utilities whenever possible before the installation of the migrated application.

# Testing the Migrated Environment

Testing is perhaps the least appreciated component of a successful migration project. It is frequently overlooked, leading to costly deployment delays, incompatible data streams, and incorrect results. Of all the activities associated with a migration project, testing is the "black sheep" of the family. Often thought of as adding little value and being boring and repetitive in nature, this critical activity is often given short shrift in favor of more high-profile activities such as code transformation, database conversion, or third-party product integration. Nothing is further from the truth. Unless the new application and new environment can be verified as fulfilling the requirement specifications, it cannot be deployed.

It is critical that the value of testing or quality assurance (QA) be well understood by the organization. Typically, QA is the last part of a migration activity or product-release cycle. After all the hard work required to migrate an application or to develop a product, the last part of the project is to test and verify that the system does what it is supposed to do. At this time, all eyes are on the QA staff. While the rigorous tests QA teams perform frequently result in the perception that they are holding up the transition to the new solution or the release of a new product, thorough and complete testing is critical to the successful implementation of a migration solution.

In the following sections, we identify the various types of testing that can be performed. We also describe how the testing methodology can be extended so that it is not an activity that is taken on at the end of the project, but one that is integrated into the project from the onset. The development of a test environment and the associated test suites is key to an effective testing strategy.

# Building the Test Environment

In addition to creating development and production environments, a testing environment is also required to support the activity of verifying that the migrated application functions as planned. Testing is rarely permitted in a production environment, and the development environment is usually reserved for the software developers who are producing the new application and may not have all the tools or the capacity to support the tests required before an application is put into production.

As with product development, migration activities must conclude with testing to ensure that the application meets its requirements. Initially, the production environment can and should be used to test the application, because it will also help verify that the hardware platform is functioning correctly. However, this arrangement will no longer work when what was serving as the test environment becomes the production environment. It is important that you carefully plan for the acquisition of additional hardware and software to test the application once the new solution is put into production.

The test environment requires all the same supporting software that is required in the production environment. One approach used to increase availability calls for the purchase of an identical system that might or might not be in a clustered environment. This additional system can be used as a test platform to shake out problems introduced with the addition of new features or functionality during product development, and it can be switched to a production role should the production system have problems or require regularly scheduled maintenance. Always ensure that the test and production platforms are running identical versions of the OS and support software, and ensure that they have the same patches applied.

Of course, cost consideration might influence the way you choose to build a test environment. It might be possible to execute regression, unit, or correctness testing on a smaller machine with limited capacity.

# Creating the Test Plan

The types of testing that should be performed vary depending on the environment that is being migrated. There are two possible scenarios:

- The application was frequently modified in the old environment to include new features or to adapt to changing business requirements, or it hadn't been changed in some time. If the application being migrated has evolved over time and has had new features frequently added or is modified to reflect new business requirements, test cases are probably already available. When new features are added to an application, developers usually verify that an application still meets certain existing requirements. In this case, a test plan can be created that leverages the existing testing methodology used under the old environment.

- The application had not been modified, and test cases will probably have to be developed for the application. This can be a costly proposition in terms of time and effort, as well as impact on the organization. As we have mentioned, a detailed understanding of the business or application logic is not required to migrate the application. Creating a test plan and test cases requires an in-depth understanding of the application, its inputs, and its outputs. This information will have to be provided by members of the organization.

As with all migration requirements that require application-specific knowledge from members of the organization's IT staff, the impact of this interaction will have to be taken into account in terms of the disruption it might cost to ongoing operational or development efforts. The organization must understand that the creation of a test plan requires significant input from the IT staff, and the organization must be willing to provide the local resources as they are required.

As needed, use external consultants to assist in the generation of the test plan and the testing effort itself. A senior tester who is skilled in testing methodology can guide the development of a comprehensive test plan. Once the test plan and test cases have been defined, the execution of the tests can be performed by other external resources. Again, if the testing procedure is very complicated or domain specific, it might be more cost effective to have local resources execute the test cases.

If you use external consultants to create test plans and test cases, the cost and duration of the effort increases because detailed knowledge of the domain will have to be acquired. When developing a test plan, use the following resources:

- Old test cases
- Requirements documents
- Functional specifications
- Business process flows or definitions
- Change documents (customizations/enhancement/patch levels)
- Training documents
- Consultations with users of the application

# Performing Unit Testing

Unit tests are typically small tests that verify the functionality of a class or function used during the creation of a larger application. These tests should be written before the implementation starts to be coded. Unit tests can be run in a batch mode and frequently have automated results analysis, meaning that the tester is informed of exactly what case failed, thereby enabling rapid verification of changes.

When they exist, use unit tests. However, if they do not exist, there is no requirement that they be created. As previously mentioned, unit tests should be created before an application starts to be coded. Any attempt to create them after an application has been written would more accurately reflect the logic implemented in the code, which might or might not be what the author intended. Local environment semantics or "features" might result in the correct result or answer, but for the wrong reasons.

Of course, if the migration activity requires the creation of new technology, using unit tests for these implementations would be entirely appropriate.

# Performing Regression Testing

Regression testing ensures that an application's functionality has not changed (other than as intended) after modifications or updates have been made to the environment. This is usually thought of as end-to-end testing. Regression tests require significant time and effort, and extra care must be given to ensure that all the application's functionality is verified as being correct.

Typically, when software is tested, regression tests are optimized to examine only those components that have been changed. In the case of a migration, there can be no such optimization because significant changes will have been introduced to the entire environment.

Many IT organizations like to run the old and new systems in parallel as a form of regression testing. The generation of identical results produces a feeling of comfort and confidence that the migration was successfully implemented. While there are great benefits and significant cost to running systems in parallel, care must be taken in choosing the length of the parallel tests. For example, running the systems in parallel for several weeks might not test month-end or year-end processing procedures. All aspects of the business process should be tested in a regression test.

A regression test must not only ensure that the correct results are achieved but also that the operational documentation (run books) is still accurate.

# Performing Integration Testing

Integration testing must be performed on hardware and software. For hardware testing, connecting computers with their peripherals can be a complicated task, involving multiple vendors. The cabling alone can present a significant problem. When the hardware has been installed, you must ensure that it is functioning optimally. Storage, in particular, can be problematic. We recommend that tests be conducted on the individual components (compute platform, storage platform, and network facilities) to verify their operation and limitations. For software testing, the integration of different software components can produce erroneous results. Wherever possible, interaction with third-party products and packages should be verified during the migration effort.

# Testing Performance

Once you have verified that the migrated system is producing the correct results, test to verify that it is performing optimally in the new environment and verify that the new environment can support the SLAs required by the enterprise. This will involve stress-testing the application by applying differing workloads and measuring how the application responds in terms of throughput, latency, memory utilization, and processor loads. Care must be taken to ensure that these loads are representative of the real-world operational conditions. When possible, the migrated environment should be tested in parallel with the old implementation to ensure the veracity of the new implementation. However, one of the reasons for the migration might have been the anticipation of increased loads. In this scenario, test cases that provide loads greater than existing real-world conditions will have to be developed

Custom applications will have been ported with little or no knowledge of the application logic. Differences in hardware architecture and supporting software design can result in performance bottlenecks. The application might function correctly, but not efficiently. This can happen for a number of reasons:

- Differences in threading models
- Differences in memory management policies
- User space implementation of constructs that are now supported in the kernel
- Hardware support, the ability to disable interrupts or bind a process to a processor
- Hardware configuration, improperly configured storage

Whenever possible, record and compare measurements of performance on the old system in terms of system metrics, as well as application metrics, with similar metrics in the new system.

A performance tester requires a different skill set than that of the migration engineer. Performance testers usually have a detailed knowledge of the hardware platform and OS, as well as of tools that can be used to trace, profile, or measure application performance metrics.

In addition to the benefits of running systems in parallel described earlier in this chapter, this activity allows for the easy generation and comparison of performance metrics.

# Refining and Documenting Your Migration Methodology

A migration project is not the end of the line for your migration methodology. You need to carefully record the lessons you have learned, the tools you have created, and the best practices you have established so that the next migration can be even more successful than this one.

The following list outlines some of the areas for which you should catalog your triumphs and pitfalls for future projects:

- Tools and techniques
- Testing plans and test harnesses
- Porting libraries
- Porting techniques and standards
- Catalog of lessons learned
- Architectural standards

In addition to the preceding topics, you should document the architecture of the migrated software. Remember when you were trying to assess the existing deployment and infrastructure? How much documentation was available? How much would you have liked to have had? Use the migration assessment and the implementation plan to document the following:

- Overall application structure
- Interconnects and dependencies
- Test cases
- Third-party tools
- Management architecture

This documentation should be stored and used in the planning of your next migration project.

# Training End Users and Staff

Although we have listed training as the last task of the implement phase, it should be addressed throughout the entire implementation, if not earlier. Training, whether in the form of informal on-the-job training and knowledge transfer or formal classroom lectures, is a vital ingredient for the successful completion of a migration project and the future service levels of the environment. It should be treated with the same level of assessment and planning as the code porting or data transformation. Make sure to address the following strategic areas of learning to ensure your successful migration project:

- **Awareness.** IT should prepare an awareness campaign to inform end users, executives, and technical staff about the coming migration. This is especially true if the migration employs a re-engineering strategy. The awareness campaign should start early and provide details about the goals, schedule, and training for the new environment. This awareness campaign is usually a key part of the project's risk mitigation strategy against users' resistance to change.

- **End-user training.** Just as end users need to be informed about the migration process and results, they will need to be trained on any new features or changes within their application or business process. While this training is not necessarily the responsibility of the IT department, it should be part of the project plan. A migration without adequate end-user training is doomed to failure, either in its implementation or in the eyes of its users.

- **Platform training.** This training takes two forms: general familiarity training for the entire IT staff and in-depth functional training for staff intimately involved with the migration. Sun's Educational Services offers a variety of this training options, some courses even specially targeted at administrators and developers migrating to competing platforms.

- **Process training.** As an inevitable result of your migration, some of your internal IT processes will change. This might be in the area of monitoring, change management, or something else. Training for these changes will need to be taken care of, even if it can't be performed before the implementation phase of the project.

# CHAPTER 8

# Managing a Migrated Environment

Before delving into topics specific to managing a migrated environment, we describe the architecture that was developed at Sun to manage open systems in the context of the E-stack. Because of the focus of this book, these architectures are described at a fairly high level.

After this context is set, we develop more detailed information about management considerations during migration to a Solaris environment.

This chapter contains the following sections:

- "Extending the E-Stack" on page 133
- "Defining Migration-Specific Management Tasks" on page 146

# Extending the E-Stack

In Chapter 3, we introduced an abbreviated version of the E-stack. The E-stack construct shown in the following figure is extended to illustrate all the components and interactions that must be addressed when an organization delivers IT-based services to internal or external customers. The architecture process is a complex, high-level set of tasks that considers the inputs, outputs, and dependencies of an IT service on the existing IT environment, along with the definition and mapping of requirements to technology. Sun Professional Services (SunPS℠) developed the E-stack to help organize these considerations and to ensure that they are addressed during the course of solutions architecture development.

The need to address the components of the E-stack drives three separate but related architectural disciplines. The following figure illustrates this mapping and is followed by a brief overview of the business and execution architectures. Details about the management architecture are provided in later sections.

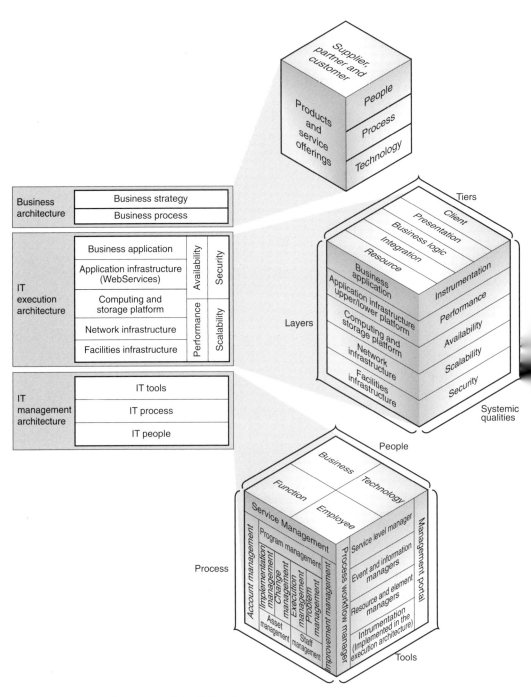

**FIGURE 8-1** Structure of the E-Stack

# Business Architecture

The business architecture captures the activities and requirements that drive the IT architecture process and IT management environment. It consists of the various products and services that are core to the organization's business, the relationships with the organization's key external stakeholders (suppliers, partners, customers), and the people, processes, and technologies required to support the production and distribution of the organization's products and services.

# Execution Architecture

The execution architecture hosts the pieces of business applications and their supporting infrastructure (for example, hardware, software, and networks). The layers of the execution architecture describe the various technology components that make up a business application, system, and the supporting environment. They include the following:

- The business logic that captures the process being implemented
- The software container within which this logic executes
- The supporting operations systems, hardware, and other components that run the software
- The network that allows various distributed systems to communicate
- The facilities required to run the hardware and software (heat, light, power, and so on)

The tiers of the execution architecture describe the logical partitioning of functions within a distributed application. References to *n-tier* applications are, in effect, describing this face of the execution architecture. Systemic qualities serve to capture the various non functionality requirements that must be considered during the architectural process. These considerations will not impact how an application will work, but rather how well it will work. Their position as the third face of the IT execution architecture means that these requirements are considerations at each intersection of the tiers and layers faces.

The use of layers and tiers serves to communicate and enforce common best practices of architecture development, such as separation of concerns and the use of well-defined interfaces. The result is a construct that allows the architect to decompose an application and evaluate its components at the intersection of the three faces.

Special attention should be paid to the instrumentation component of the execution architecture (systemic quality). Instrumentation is the interface between the management architecture and execution architectures. The degree to which this quality is considered and implemented will determine how much visibility into the execution architecture is provided to external entities represented by the management architecture tools face.

# SunTone Management Architecture

The following figure illustrates the SunTone Management Architecture, sometimes referred to as the *management cube*. As seen below, the SunTone Management Architecture consists of three different axes or faces, each detailing a portion of an organization's IT management infrastructure. The following sections describe this construct in detail.

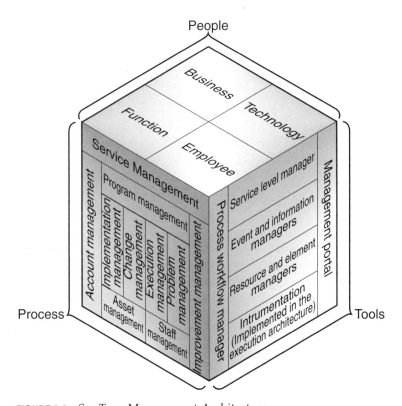

**FIGURE 8-2** SunTone Management Architecture

# People

The people face of the SunTone Management Architecture represents the human aspects of the IT management environment. It describes all best practices in this area. These practices are based on the people capability maturity model (P-CMM) developed by the Carnegie Mellon Software Engineering Institute, and include the following main categories:

- Resourcing
- Skills development
- IT organization
- Knowledge management

# Process

This section describes the IT management processes, as defined in the SunTone Management Architecture. These processes are autonomous, to an extent, so they can be implemented independently. The main requirement to link any related process to another process is that you provide the appropriate input and create the appropriate output for the next process. FIGURE 8-3 on page 138 illustrates this interaction.

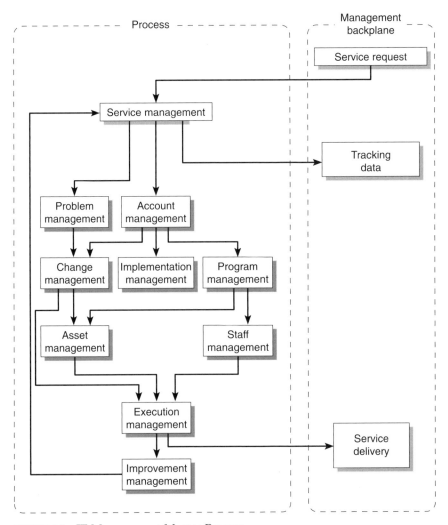

**FIGURE 8-3**  IT Management Master Process

The three major management components in the SunTone Management Architectur
include the following:

- **Service management.** The service management process involves the overall
  management of the following tasks: envisioning, strategizing, architecting,
  standardizing, productizing, marketing, and advertising IT service products to
  support business goals and directions.

During this process, you facilitate the management of the services delivered by the IT environment. This is the first entry point of a service request. It is where you initiate and maintain the status of service requests, enforce progress on existing requests, and close these requests. The following areas should be addressed:

- Account management
- Problem management
- Implementation management
- Program management
- Change management
- Staff management
- Asset management

- **Execution management.** The execution management process addresses all aspects necessary to deliver IT services. These include the management of the production environment, facilitation of monitoring, production control, and resource administration. During this process, you ensure that the compute resources (and any other required resources) are available when they are needed, and you plan and schedule work and personnel. During this process, you also address when and how services are recovered in the event of a failure, ensure that a quality service is delivered, and determine whether improvement is needed or possible.

- **Improvement management.** The improvement management process ensures that continuous improvement is part of IT operations. You can do this by reporting against key performance indicators (KPIs) and by ensuring that all stakeholders are involved in identifying the root causes of performance issues and in suggesting possible solutions.

We have organized the process definitions assessed during this process to follow Sun's best practices as defined in the SunTone methodology. Two other widely adopted management methodologies are ITIL and FCAPS. For information about the relationship between the SunTone methodology and ITIL standards, refer to the SunBlue Prints OnLine article by Edward Wustenhoff on this subject published in the Fall/Winter of 2003.

# Tools

The tools portion of the SunTone Management Framework (STMF) is a functional taxonomy of the technology that facilitates control of the IT environment. This tools solutions model is described in a product-neutral fashion and should not be confused with technology-specific frameworks offered by various software vendors. The intent of this model is to quantify the scope of the technology solution, define the high-level components required, specify the necessary integration of components, and assist in mapping available technology to specific functional areas. Realization of a complete technology infrastructure for management of the IT environment requires use of the solutions model as the basis of an architecture effort that defines the requirements and associated solutions at a level of detail sufficient for implementation. The following figure shows the STMF tools solutions model.

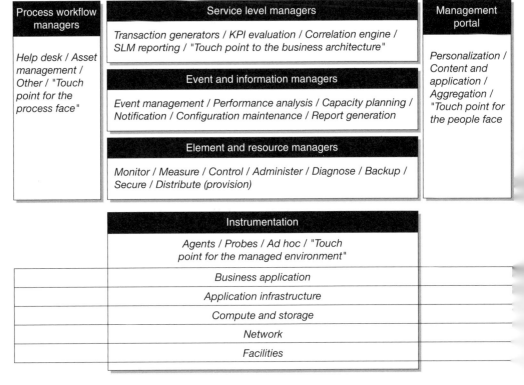

**FIGURE 8-4**   STMF Tools Solution Model

As shown in the preceding figure, the solutions model is a layered set of functional components. As we move up the model, the focus of the components shifts from low-level interactions with the managed environment, to the management of information about the environment, to a focus on the services that support the organization's business. The process workflow and portal components enable the integration of the different components, the automation of IT business processes, and the presentation of management information, as shown in the following figure.

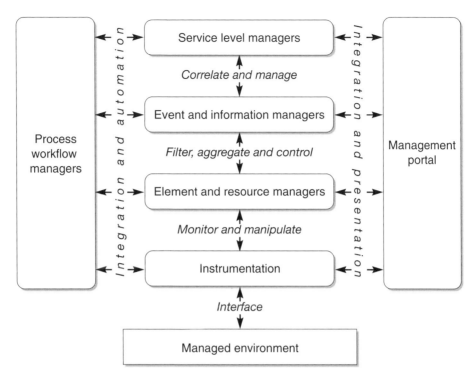

**FIGURE 8-5** Tasks Enabled by Process Workflow and Portal Components

Note that the various components of the tools solutions model are categorized by function as opposed to process. A common error is to attempt to categorize management technology along the process face of the framework—for example, attempting to obtain a "problem management" tool or "performance management" package. This quickly becomes confusing because certain tools can support multiple processes, and each process will rely on the application of more than one tool. The following sections briefly describe each layer and component of the tools solutions model.

## Instrumentation

The instrumentation layer consists of all management elements that allow the various management tools to gain access to managed resources. Instrumentation is generally implemented within the context of the environment in which managed resources reside. Note that the entire managed stack is a candidate for instrumentation. The focus should not just be on the hardware and operating systems layers, but should also address the following items:

- **Agents.** Software entities within the execution framework that communicate with management applications in the management framework, using a defined protocol and naming scheme for managed objects.

- **Probes.** Special-purpose management entities (hardware and software) that operate in the execution environment to perform specific management functions on behalf of management applications. Probes are standalone devices, in which agents are generally installed on a component with another purpose.

- **Ad hoc solutions.** Scripts and executables that operate in an autonomous fashion on components within the execution framework. These components generally do not communicate with or act on behalf of a management application.

Instrumentation components may or may not be provided as part of a management component in another layer. Certain management tools include agent technology as part of the product. By contrast, hardware and software vendors might provide with their product an agent with their product that can communicate with other vendors' management tools through a defined protocol such as SNMP.

## Element and Resource Management Layer

This layer of the model consists of management applications, like those listed below, that directly interact with the managed environment to query or modify managed resources. Management applications perform one or more of the following functions shown in FIGURE 8-5 on page 141:

- **Monitoring applications.** Applications that sample the values of specific managed objects and compare these values to a predefined threshold. In most cases, threshold violations result in some type of notification (alarm) being generated.

- **Measuring applications.** Applications that sample the values associated with specific managed objects and store these values for later review and analysis by other applications within the framework.

- **Control applications.** Applications that modify the execution state of a managed resource. Examples include startup, shutdown, modification of priority, restart, and the like. Applications that manage the use and allocation of system resources (for example, CPU and bandwidth) are also categorized as control applications.

- **Administration applications.** Applications that maintain the runtime configuration of managed resources. Examples include applications used to change host resolution tables, user identification, and entitlement databases or runtime parameters for an application.

- **Backup applications.** Applications that collect images of specific managed resources (data) for use in the event that recovery of this data is required because of system failure or user error.

- **Diagnostic tools.** Applications that facilitate data collection and test execution to identify the root cause of an error condition.

- **Security applications.** Applications that monitor the environment for indications of unauthorized activity by internal or external entities.

- **Distribution applications.** Applications that provide the mechanisms needed to transfer and install software within the managed environment.

## Event and Information Managers

This layer of the model consists of applications that manage events and information generated by the lower layers of the model. The focus of the applications at this layer shifts from dealing with the measurement and modifications of technical metrics to the management of data and alarms. The functional components at this layer are as follows:

- **Event processing applications.** Applications that manage notifications generated by the lower layers (for example, alarms and warnings). Specific activities include event filtering (discarding of unneeded events), event consolidation (combination of like events), event mapping (transformation of event attributes to a standard scheme), and event correlation (parallel processing of events to make inferences concerning the root cause).

- **Performance analysis applications.** Applications that process and analyze performance data collected by measuring applications for the purpose of identifying performance bottlenecks.

- **Capacity analysis applications.** Applications that process and analyze performance data, along with knowledge or application workload drivers, to predict the impact of changes on performance.

- **Notification applications.** Applications that facilitate the process of passing information (for example, alarms and warnings) to external entities including people and other applications. An example would be an application that generates pager messages when critical alarm notifications are received.

- **Configuration maintenance applications.** Applications that maintain information about the configuration of elements within the execution environment and their relationships to each other. This layer includes applications to manage the configuration management database (CMDB), the definitive hardware store (DHS), and the definitive software library (DSL). The CMDB is a virtual database that has asset and configuration information. The DHS is the storage for field-replaceable hardware components. The DSL is the repository of all software master copies.

- **Report generation applications.** Applications that process and format performance and event information for use in management review and decision-making activities. Reporting at this layer is internally focused towards the IT organization.

# Service Level Managers

Service level managers (SLMs) are applications that provide the tie-in between business requirements as defined by SLAs and the technical status of the execution environment as determined by the lower layers of the framework. The functional components of service level managers include the following:

- **Transaction generator applications.** Applications that introduce a workload on a specific service and evaluate the level of response received. These synthetic transactions are used to evaluate the service from the perspective of the end user.

- **Key performance indicator evaluations.** Applications that evaluate KPIs and that can be used as alternative transaction generators or in conjunction with them to assess the availability and performance of a service.

- **Correlation engines.** Applications that analyze management information and make inferences about the impact of given event or group of events on a specific service and the business functions it supports.

- **SLM reporting applications.** Applications that provide both real-time and historical reporting on the organization's compliance with published service levels. SLM reporting is externally focused towards the organization's business.

# Process Workflow Managers

We use workflow technology to automate the management processes described on the process face of the management framework cube. Examples of this type of technology include a trouble ticket system that supports the problem management process, or the automation of a change approval system that supports the change management process. Although we maintain a loose coupling between the process and tools portions of the framework, it is important to realize that process is one of the methods used to integrate the various components of the management architecture.

# Management Portal

The management portal is a collection of applications that enable external entities to access selected portions of the management framework. Examples of this type of application include a web interface for reviewing SLM reports, web or other types of user interfaces for the various tools, and an application used by end users to submit requests for service. It should also be possible, and it is even desirable, to use this portal to expose management information and facilities to people outside the IT organization. A fully realized portal implementation would provide standard portal functionality to include application and content aggregation, and personalization.

# Operational Capability and Maturity

Given the three architectures and the complexity associated with them, there is a tendency to address issues or provide capabilities with the wrong architecture. Systems analysts used to have an axiom that said when you automate a poorly designed business process, you wind up with a poorly designed system. That would be one example of attempting to solve a business architecture issue using the IT execution architecture. Problems must be solved and solutions must be provided within the correct architecture. Attempts to solve business process issues by applying just technology (execution architecture), or attempts to address architectural shortcomings of an application by using IT management architecture components are, at best, inefficient, and in many cases will not work.

## Operational Capability

In addition, it is important to realize what an existing IT environment's management capabilities are. Operational capability is considered to be the ability to deliver IT services to an agreed-on service level in a predictable fashion with acceptable risk and cost. The level of implementation of the SunTone management architecture creates the level of operational capability. The following figure shows the interaction of the faces and the formal definition of operational capability.

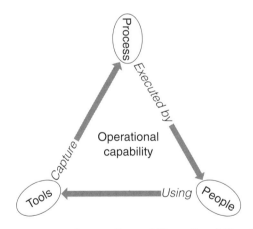

**FIGURE 8-6**  Interactions of Operational Capability

## Maturity

Our definition of organizational maturity is based on industry experience and the notion that capabilities increase over time as IT organizations mature. Identifying the level of maturity that applies to your environment enables you to make decisions about how to best manage the environment and how to plan for its evolution. There are many models for categorizing the maturity of the organization, including those provided by Carnegie Mellon, Gartner Group, and IDC.

# Defining Migration-Specific Management Tasks

The new IT environment components must be integrated into the existing IT management infrastructure. The approach you take and the degree of effort involved with it will depend on the current degree of operational capability the organization possesses. An IT organization with a well-defined set of management processes, supported by an appropriate tools infrastructure, will be able to integrate the migrated environment with a reasonable degree of effort. A less mature organization will need to consider using the migration effort as the catalyst to improving its operational capability, which will require significantly more effort. In this case, the organization might consider improving operational capabilities in a separate project.

It has been our experience that very few organizations will be able to address operational readiness issues by taking a "green field" approach. Even immature organizations will have some existing practices and technology that must be accounted for. A generalized strategy for addressing operational readiness should include the following steps:

- Assessing the current IT management infrastructure
- Addressing the critical gaps
- Extending the infrastructure to account for the migration

The following sections describe each of these steps in more detail. These steps should be focused on the requirements and benefits case defined during the justification activities and the architect phase.

## Assessing the Current IT Management Infrastructure

As a first step to ensuring that they can support the migrated environment, organizations undertaking a migration must develop a realistic understanding of their operational capability. You can begin this process by reviewing the available standards and frameworks, looking for opportunities to leverage them as much as possible. You should adopt a management framework and a maturity model as the basis for both the assessment effort and subsequent improvement activities. A management framework describes what needs to be in place. A maturity model defines the evolutionary path for realizing the framework.

In previous sections, we described both a management framework (the STMF) and a maturity model for operational capability. Other models are available, including the capabilities maturity model and its derivatives from the Software Engineering Institute (`http://www.sei.cmu.edu`), the IT Infrastructure Library or ITIL (`http://www.itsmf.com`), and Control Objectives for Information Related Technology or COBIT (`http://www.isaca.org`).

## Assess People Requirements

When assessing the human aspects of a management solution, focus on the skills that will need to be developed and exploited to manage and control the new environment. Obviously, new skills will need to be adopted and absorbed, which puts a focus on training and development processes that will enable the development of the appropriate competences to successfully control the new environment.

Additionally, the introduction of new migrated technology will require the evaluation of the current workforce and a determination of what is immediately needed to provide the appropriate staffing levels. In addition, to promote the desired behavior of personnel, compensation plans and employee performance management might need to be aligned to include the right measures for success.

When significant changes are introduced, it is essential that you emphasize communication and coordination between workgroups to limit the resistance to change and to increase the chances for success.

## Assess Processes

To be proactive, evaluate the following processes and bring them to an appropriate level of maturity:

- Change management
- Problem management
- Implementation management
- Execution management

Obviously, the ability to introduce changes into the environment with minimal risk and at an acceptable cost is key to the successful migration of any technology. If the change management process is implemented successfully, this can be achieved. The following diagram describes how such a process can be defined. It is ITIL based and incorporated into the STMF.

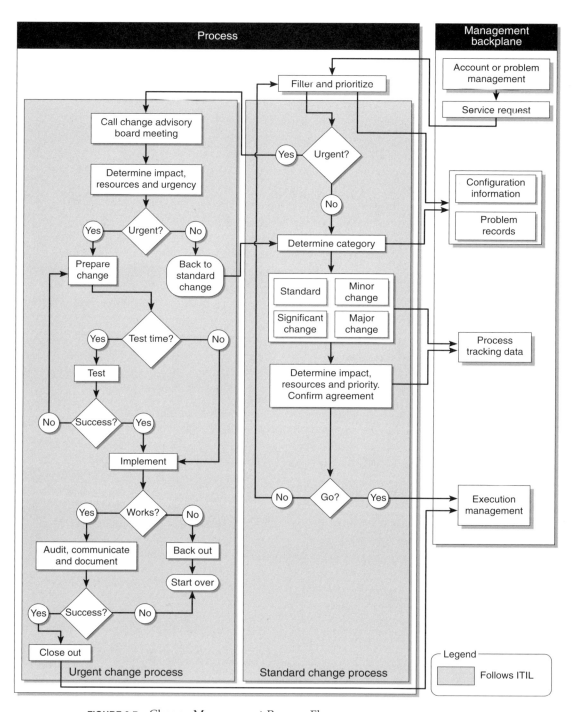

**FIGURE 8-7** Change Management Process Flow

Naturally, implementation management has close ties with change management because projects of this size typically introduce significant change. A solid development and deployment process is key to a smooth transition into production.

For execution management (often referred to as operations management) to become more proactive in accepting and introducing changes, you will need to start addressing the following key areas:

- **Production control.** Ensure that jobs are scheduled appropriately, to avoid exceeding system resource levels.

- **Resource administration.** Enable the quick and safe introduction of new and different technologies while ensuring that minor and daily activities are performed in a secure and nondisruptive way.

- **Resource planning.** Look at the available resources and try to predict future needs or changes to production control activities. By doing this, you will significantly reduce unplanned outages that result from insufficient resources.

- **Service recovery.** Introduce technologies and procedures to limit the impact of an unexpected outage. Think of Sun Cluster software as an example to facilitate automatic failover or disaster recovery procedures to limit the downtime resulting from a major outage.

The ability to manage problems and incidents quickly and consistently is essential to avoid solving the same issue more than once. The focus of problem management, when shifting from reactive to proactive, must move to root cause analysis to enable the most effective solutions for existing issues. The SunTone Management Framework has leveraged many of the ITIL best practices here. The following figure shows how such a process could look.

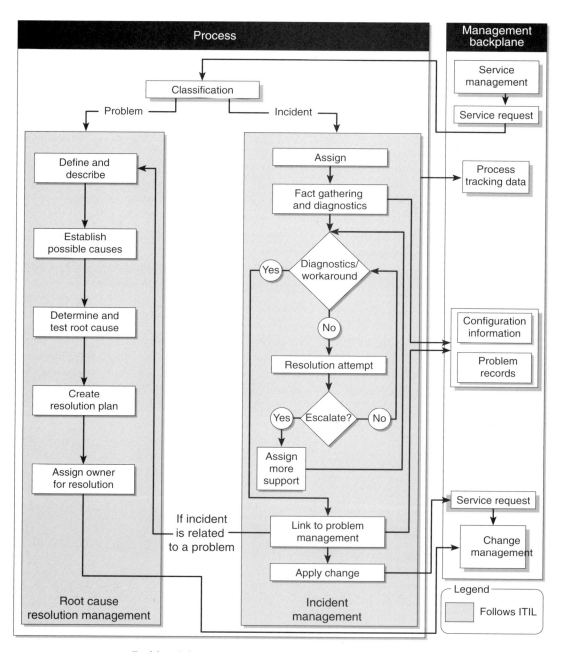

**FIGURE 8-8**   Problem Management Process Flow

# Assess Tools

In moving to a more mature level of operational capability, an organization shifts from technology that is focused on monitoring the lower portions of the E-stack to technology that extends the monitoring coverage and facilitates proactive management of the IT environment. In applying the tools solutions model described previously, we would focus on the following items at each layer:

- **Element and resource management.** Both monitoring and measurement capability for the application infrastructure should be in place. This enables organizations to collect performance data and proactively monitor for critical conditions in all portions of the E-stack, from the facilities to the application infrastructure. Additionally, a robust security and backup capability should be deployed, and basic mechanisms for provisioning new systems and distributing simple packages (such as patches) should be available.

- **Event and information management.** In most organizations, the low level of the management tools architecture will be constructed along silos of expertise. For example, the systems, database, and network expertise centers will each have its own sets of tools to monitor and measure their portions of the environment. As the organization moves to a more mature level of operational capability, it becomes necessary to consolidate and correlate information across silos of expertise. This function is performed at the event and information layer. A common event management console and an associated event model for the organization are key components of this effort. This common event management platform serves as a key integration point in the management tools architecture. With the common event management platform, technology to support the analysis of performance data and IT management reporting should also be in place.

- **Service level managers.** Although systems with this level of operational maturity do not focus on service management, the tool assessment phase is when organizations need to consider managing the end-user experience. To this end, technology to assess the availability and performance of applications and supporting services should be applied. Synthetic transaction generators can test how the user of a web-based application is being served, or can test the availability of common network services such as DNS or IMAP.

- **Process workflow managers.** Other points of integration and cross-domain correlation are the tools used to manage the execution of IT management processes. At this level, the process workflow technology is expanded from providing simple trouble ticket functionality to supporting the automation of problem (incident and root cause), change, and asset management. Additionally, integration of these systems with other portions of the management tools infrastructure is realized.

## Perform Audits

To determine the current state of IT operational capability, you should conduct some type of audit. Audits generally fall into one of two categories:

- **Compliance audits.** These audits determine the degree to which the process, tools, and skills implementations meet the needs of the organization. Part of a compliance audit would be the identification of critical processes, tools, and staff to support management of the IT environment.

- **Effectiveness audits.** These audits assess how well the organization is executing its management processes.

Compliance and effectiveness audits should be conducted as part of any assessment activity. Our experience has been that the existence of a well-documented process does not always mean that the process actually meets the needs of the organization or that it is being followed by the organization. Depending on the expertise and enthusiasm of the staff members involved in such an effort, organizations might want to consider using an external agency to conduct the assessment.

# Addressing Critical Gaps

Detailing the means to address all possible shortcomings in the management infrastructure is beyond the scope of this book. However, we provide the following important rules to help you understand the scope of this task.

- **Improving operational capability is an organization-wide effort.**
  Moving up the maturity scale requires the application of resources (time, skills, and money) and the cooperation of the entire organization. Efforts to improve operational capability require senior management commitment.

- **Improving operational capability is an evolutionary, not revolutionary, activity.**
  Various maturity models for IT operations can communicate the goals of capability improvement activities and define an incremental approach to realizing those goals. Experience has shown that few, if any, organizations are capable of realizing the entire management framework in one big effort. Organizations should focus on incremental activities with a quick return that are conducted within the context of a well-defined strategy. The "big bang" approach to building operational capability is strongly discouraged.

- **IT management is a process-driven activity.**
  Often, organizations react to issues of IT management by acquiring technology to manage the environment without considering the processes needed to operate the environment. It is our experience that focusing on the tools portion of the framework results in poorly executed implementations that do not meet the needs of the organization. The initial focus of efforts associated with improving

operational capability should be on the definition and implementation of the processes to be used in managing the environment. The process architecture should drive the tools and skills architectures.

- **To be successful, organizations must measure progress.**
  We saw that improving operational capability requires organization-wide commitment. As part of meeting that commitment, you must use meaningful metrics to measure baseline capability before starting improvement efforts. Then, periodically evaluate the effect of the improvement efforts. Examples of metrics include cost data, availability data, ratio of supported systems to head count, and mean time to repair (MTTR). Investments in operational capability should be justified by corresponding improvements in key performance metrics.

Established continuous improvement methodologies (like Six-Sigma and Sun-Sigma) are great tools for enabling these projects of change.

# Selecting Tools for Managing the Migrated Environment

The tools solutions model described above implies the application of sound systems-design principles to include modular design, separation of function, and well-defined interfaces. As a result, the management tools architecture should be loosely coupled with the corresponding managed environment. The degree of dependency between the two architectures decreases the farther up the management framework you go. In a properly architected management infrastructure, most of the impact resulting from the introduction of Sun technology will be seen in the instrumentation and element management layers. Most of the Sun technology that is available for managing migrated platforms is focused on these two layers of the tools model. Sun works with a number of industry partners to provide solutions for other portions of the tools framework. The following figure shows some of these tools and how they map to the SunTone Management Framework. This sample is not exhaustive; however, it provides a good overview of the available solutions. The sections that follow briefly explain each of these tools. You are encouraged to consult available vendor documentation for specific information about the tools mentioned.

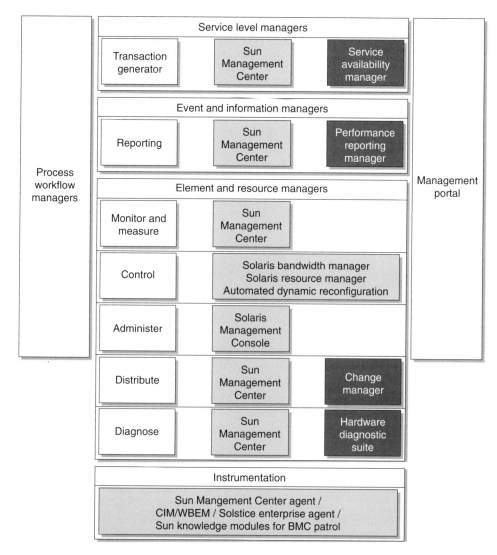

**FIGURE 8-9** Tools Mapped to the SunTone Management Framework

## Instrumentation

The following tools can be used to manage various aspects of the newly migrated environment:

- **Solstice Enterprise Agents™ (SEA) software.** Software that provides basic SNMPv1 functionality for the Solaris OS. The agent uses a master–subagent architecture that supports both MIB II and additional subagents. Other SNMP agents can be installed and run on a Solaris system as subagents. SEA controllers access the SNMP UDP ports and direct SNMP requests to the proper subagent. A desktop management interface (DMI) is also provided.

- **Solaris Web-Based Enterprise Management Services.** Sun also provides an implementation of the Distributed Management Task Force (DMTF) Web-Based Enterprise Management (WBEM) standard. This standard defines a common information model (CIM) that provides a consistent, vendor-independent way to identify managed objects. FIGURE 8-10 on page 156 shows the architecture of Solaris WBEM. For more information, visit the DMTF Web site at `http://www.dmtf.org` or refer to Sun documentation.

- **Sun knowledge modules for BMC Patrol.** BMC Software is a provider of systems management technology and is a Sun partner. Sun has developed extensions to the BMC Patrol agent that allow Patrol customers to manage the Sun environment. These extensions use standard Patrol Knowledge Module (KM) design, which enables them to plug into the Patrol agent. KMs are available for a variety of Sun platforms and software including enterprise class servers, Sun Cluster software, the Sun™ ONE Messaging Server, the Sun™ ONE Portal Server, and the Sun™ ONE Application Server. For more information, visit the BMC Software Web site at `http://www.bmc.com`

## Sun Management Center

Sun™ Management Center (SunMC) is the primary technology platform for the management of Sun products. As seen in FIGURE 8-9 on page 154, SunMC provides functionality in a number of different areas within the framework.

As shown in FIGURE 8-10 on page 156, SunMC has a three-tier architecture consisting of the following components:

- A console layer that is the user interface for the system.

- A server layer that provides core management services to management applications.

- An intelligent agent layer that resides on the managed systems and executes management actions on behalf of the server.

  This agent is considered intelligent because many of the management functions such as sampling, threshold comparison, and alarm generation are carried out by the agent. The agent is extensible, using the APIs and developer facilities for creation of additional agent management modules.

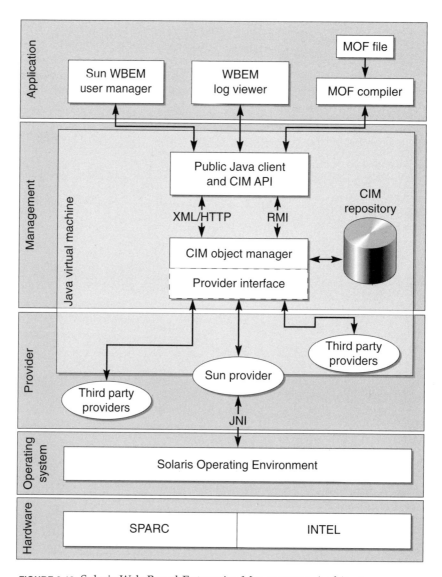

**FIGURE 8-10** Solaris Web-Based Enterprise Management Architecture

The core SunMC functionality includes monitoring Solaris hardware and software components. The visibility SunMC provides into the hardware layer of the Sun environment is a key element of this structure. The Sun Management Center's core functionality can be extended using available product add-ons as shown in FIGURE 8-11 on page 157. Examples include the following:

- **SunMC Change Manager.** SunMC Change Manager software supports the deployment of integrated software stacks to managed systems. It uses Flash archives as the basis of a deployable package and allows for the provisioning of multiple systems.

- **Performance Reporting Manager.** This package manages collected performance data and provides tools to analyze and generate reports using this data.

- **Service Availability Manager.** This package provides service level monitoring through test transactions that are generated against core network services. Supported protocols include HTTP, LDAP, DNS, IMAP, and SMTP.

- **Hardware Diagnostic Suite (HDS).** HDS provides a facility to automate the testing of SPARC hardware. HDS tests and reports on field-replaceable units (FRUs).

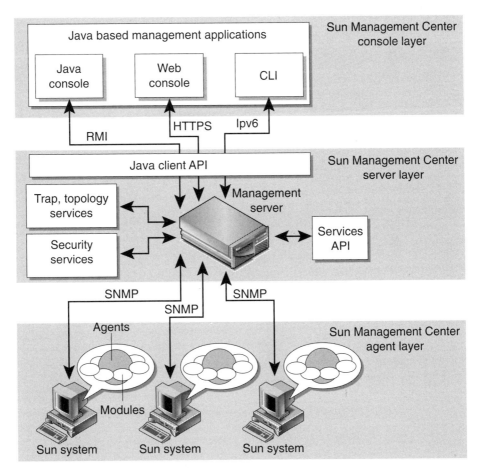

**FIGURE 8-11** Layers of SunMC

Additional management functionality to monitor other Sun and non-Sun software is available from third-party vendors that have extended SunMC capabilities. For example, Halcyon Monitoring Solutions offers the PrimeAlert product line, which extends the management capabilities of SunMC. PrimeAlert modules are also available for a variety of applications including Oracle, Sybase, VERITAS, BEA WebLogic, and the Sun ONE software stack. For more information, visit the Halcyon Web site at http://www.halcyoninc.com

SunMC is designed to coexist with the major system's management framework. Integration facilities are available for CA Unicenter, Tivoli, and BMC. A probe to integrate SunMC with Microm by using Omnibus is also available.

## Solaris Management Console GUI

Solaris™ Management Console is a container-based GUI for administration tools used in the Solaris environment. It provides a common look and feel, access control, and application launch points for a variety of applications used to managed Sun systems. Administrative functions that are supported include systems status, account management, storage management, and management of projects and tasks for Solaris™ Resource Manager software. Solaris Management Console is a two-tier application with a Java client and a server layer. This application is the primary replacement for the AdminSuite tool set.

## Solaris Resource Manager Software

Solaris Resource Manager software is an example of a control application that enables system resources like CPU, memory, and network bandwidth to be allocated among applications. Solaris Resource Manager software supports the definition of resource usage groups, constraints of resource use, and accounting of use. Use of this tool enables multiple applications to coexist on a single instance of the Solaris OS, with each application being able to count on the availability of specific levels of CPU, memory, and network resource availability. Solaris Resource Manager software was offered as an add-on application before the release of version 9 of the Solaris OS. Starting with version 9, the software is bundled with the operating system. This enhanced version of the product also includes functionality from Solaris™ Bandwidth Manager.

## Solaris Bandwidth Manager Software

Solaris Bandwidth Manager software is another control application that enables the management of available network resources. The application enables the allocation of IP traffic to specific traffic classes. These allocation schemes can be based on a number of factors, including IP address, source or destination port, protocol, and type of service (TOS). Incoming and outgoing IP packets are assigned to specific classes. Classes have a guaranteed and maximum bandwidth assigned. Solaris Bandwidth Manager also provides a number of interfaces that can be used to export collected performance information for processing by accounting and billing applications.

## Automated Dynamic Reconfiguration

Solaris Resource Manager and Solaris Bandwidth Manager software allocate resources within a single instance of the Solaris OS. Automated dynamic reconfiguration (ADR) allows hardware resources to be allocated between multiple OS images on platforms running more than one Solaris domain. The idea is to reallocate system boards with CPU or memory from domains that are of a lower priority or not under heavy load to a higher-priority domain under a heavy workload. ADR provides a high-level command set for dynamic reconfiguration that can be used within scripts. Additionally, this functionality is exposed through a CIM/WBEM interface in the Sun Fire 15K/12K servers. In addition to using scripting to control reallocation of systems boards, you can also use agent technology from the framework vendors to integrate this functionality into the management framework. BMC provides this, using the Patrol for Sun ADR product. Patrol for ADR is a KM that uses the exposed ADR interfaces (CLI on the Sun Enterprise™ 10000 server, CIM/WBEM on the Sun Enterprise 12000 server and the Sun Enterprise 15000) to control allocation of systems boards according to CPU use. FIGURE 8-12 on page 160 shows the use of the Patrol ADR KM.

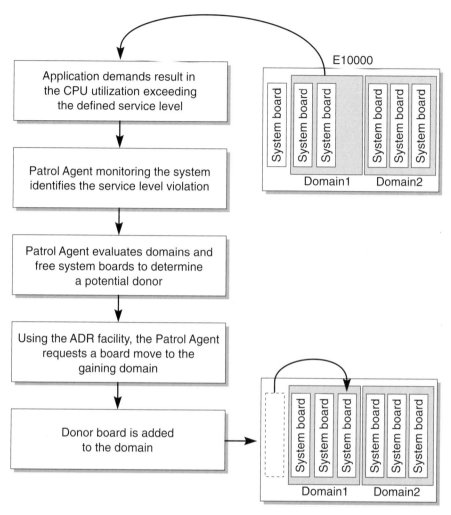

**FIGURE 8-12** Patrol Automated Dynamic Reconfiguration Knowledge Module

# CHAPTER 9

# Migrating From Red Hat Linux

To illustrate the methodology, tools, and best practices discussed earlier in this book, this chapter presents an example of the process using a Linux-to-Solaris migration. The example environment is based on a small company of about 40 people, developing Internet software and services. They initially standardized on the Linux platform for the entire company because of its low acquisition cost, but were recently bought by a larger company that had standardized on Solaris systems. The acquired company was already looking into alternative platforms for their commercial production environment to handle the flood of customers who access their services, but in light of the acquisition, they decided to widen their scope to include all of their information technology systems.

In our example, we follow this migration project through the entire methodology, detailing key activities and decisions along the way. We begin the chapter with information about the initial business case and the high-level decisions about which platform to migrate to, and then detail the assessment of the current environment following the previous sections' methodology and tools. From there, we work through the architecture until we get to a design to prototype. The chapter concludes with the implementation and management of the environment.

This chapter contains the following sections:

## Overview of Linux

Before we jump into the actual activities of the example migration, let's review some information about the Linux operating system and how it compares to the Solaris Operating System (Solaris OS).

Linux has grown from its early beginning as Linus Torvald's attempt to create a freely available operating system running on 80386 hardware to its use today as a general-purpose environment that rivals commercial UNIX implementations. Along the way, Linux has taken cues from many commercial UNIX implementations and has constructed application program interfaces (APIs) and a kernel along similar lines. In addition, Linux has gained application support from the open source community, with alternatives for many of the commercial packages available. Because of these facts, migrating from Linux to Solaris is a relatively painless affair in most environments.

In this example, we focus on the migration from a particular Linux distribution, Red Hat Linux. Red Hat Linux is the best-selling Linux distribution today, capturing over 50 percent of the server market. Other major Linux distributions include SuSE, Debian, and Mandrake. These distributions differ not in core functionality or kernel code, but in marketing focus and utilities. For example, each of the distributions listed above has different installation method and software packaging utilities. While we specifically talk about Red Hat Linux's features and utilities, we also point out features that might be different from some of the other major Linux distributions.

# Differences Between the Linux and Solaris Environments

While many people think of Solaris and Linux as being two separate environments, they have many external similarities. However, because Solaris has been in constant development over the past 20 years, it has obtained a level of maturity that is not present in today's implementations of Linux. This directly translates into some additional features in the enterprise space that Linux lacks. Most Linux developers, administrators, and architects will feel right at home with the Solaris environment, especially when they see the additional features it offers.

In the following sections, we compare some key differences between Linux (focusing on Red Hat) and Solaris. We compare these two environments in the following areas

- Booting process
- Software packaging and installation
- Kernel configuration
- APIs
- Device configuration
- Administration and monitoring
- Networking
- Storage
- Security

This is not an exhaustive list, but it focuses on differences that will affect your migration to the Solaris OS.

# Booting Process

The local disk boot process for Red Hat Linux varies depending on the boot loader you decide to use: Linux Loader (LILO) or Grand Unified Boot (GRUB) loader. GRUB is the newer of the two boot loaders and has some advantages over LILO, especially the ability to read EXT2 and EXT3 file systems. GRUB is the default boot loader, but many people still use LILO because of their familiarity with it. GRUB uses the following booting sequence:

1. The BIOS self-tests the system and launches the first-stage boot loader by reading the master boot record (MBR) of the hard drive.

2. The first-stage boot loader loads into memory and launches the second-stage boot loader. On some non-x86 architectures, there can be an intervening step here that displays the GRUB menu and environment. This allows you to check system parameters as well as pass some variables onto the kernel before booting.

3. The second-stage boot loader loads the kernel into memory and mounts the root partition.

4. The kernel transfers control of the boot process to the `/sbin/init` program.

5. The `/sbin/init` program loads all services and user-space tools, and mounts all partitions listed in `/etc/fstab`. The `/sbin/init` process starts the run control (rc) scripts, which execute a series of other scripts. These scripts (stored in `/etc/init.d/`) check and mount file systems, start various processes, and perform system maintenance tasks.

Solaris on SPARC boots in a similar way, with different programs. For example, Solaris uses a program called `monitor` to do its boot loading. Solaris/SPARC's boot process is as follows:

1. The PROM displays system identification and then runs self-test diagnostics to verify the system's hardware and memory.

2. The PROM loads the primary boot program, `bootblk`, whose purpose is to load the secondary boot program (located in the `ufs` file system) from the default boot device.

3. The `bootblk` program finds and executes the secondary boot program, `ufsboot`, and loads it into memory.

4. The `ufsboot` program loads the kernel.

5. The kernel initializes itself and begins loading modules, using `ufsboot` to read the files. When the kernel has loaded enough modules to mount the root (/) file system, the kernel unmaps the `ufsboot` program and continues, using its own resources.

6. The kernel creates a user process and starts the `/sbin/init` process, which starts other processes by reading the `/etc/inittab` file.

7. The `/sbin/init` process starts the run control (`rc`) scripts, which execute a series of other scripts. These scripts (`/sbin/rc*`) check and mount file systems, start various processes, and perform system maintenance tasks.

Both systems use a process of symbolic linking scripts to control the order of startup and shutdown of processes. However, Red Hat Linux's use of the `chkconfig` command to automate this control is not implemented on Solaris.

## Software Packaging and Installation

Both Solaris and Red Hat Linux provide facilities for the management of software installation and packaging. Red Hat Linux's software installation facilities, called RPM for the RPM Package Manager, enable the easy installation and packaging of both binary and source software. Red Hat Linux also manages patches through this facility. This RPM technology separates Red Hat Linux from most other Linux distributions. For example, Debian Linux uses the Debian package management system to install, upgrade, remove, and verify software. While the specific commands are different, the Debian package management system supports many of the same concepts and features as RPM. Red Hat Linux provides both command-line interface (CLI) and graphical user interface (GUI) tools to manipulate RPMs.

Solaris uses a standard package management system, commonly referred to as `pkgadd` (after the software installation command). With the `pkgadd` family of commands you can manipulate packages, collections of files, and directories in a defined format, according to the System V Interface Definition. Beginning in the Solaris 8 Operating Environment (Solaris OE), Sun started to augment these commands with new GUI tools and a more powerful registry. The following table compares the Red Hat Linux and Solaris packaging commands:

**TABLE 9-1**   Red Hat Linux and Solaris Packaging Commands

|  | **Red Hat Linux** | **Solaris** |
|---|---|---|
| Install package | `#rpm -i <package file>` | `#pkgadd <package file>` |
| Remove package | `#rpm -e <package file>` | `#pkgrm <package file>` |
| Upgrade package | `#rpm -U <package file>` | `#pkgadd <package file>` |
| List package | `#rpm -qa` | `#pkginfo <package file>` |
| Verify package | `#rpm -V <package file>` | `#pkgchk <package file>` |
| GUI | `# gnorpm` | `#prodreg` |

Creating Solaris packages or converting RPMs is beyond the scope of this book. However, these procedures require largely the same components: software, directory structures, control files, and preinstall and postinstall scripts. For more information on creating Solaris packages, consult your Solaris documentation or visit http://docs.sun.com/.

In addition to the manual software installation utilities, the Solaris OS also includes automated installation facilities through the JumpStart technology framework. JumpStart, similar to Red Hat's Kickstart for installation, can be used to automatically install or upgrade servers. For more information on using the JumpStart technology, consult *JumpStart Technology: Effective Use in the Solaris Operating Environment.*

Solaris patches are handled separately from software packages, with more powerful commands specifically suited for patches. More notably, these commands allow for the "backing out" of patches. They include the CLI `patchadd` / `patchrm` commands as well as a GUI and web tool called PatchPro (available at http:// www.sun.com/PatchPro). There are also advanced facilities for upgrading or patching the operating system while it is running so that the patch becomes effective on the next reboot. This feature is called Live Upgrade and can significantly reduce planned downtime.

Just as open source and shareware Linux RPMs are available on Web sites such as http://www.rpmfind.org, you can find Solaris open source packages at the http://www.sunfreeware.com/ Web site. These packages are maintained by third parties but are compiled and packaged in the Solaris `pkgadd` format.

# Kernel Configuration

Kernel configuration under Linux can be a complicated task for the uninitiated. Most major kernel variables require the administrator to change kernel variables, recompile the kernel from its source, reconfigure the boot loader to point to the new kernel, and reboot the server. Luckily, this is only necessary when moving to different kernels such as symmetrical multiprocessing (SMP) or big memory (for 686 systems with over 4 gigabytes of RAM). Most lesser kernel changes can be handled through loadable modules, the `proc` file system, or the `/etc/sysctl.conf` file.

Solaris takes a different approach for configuring kernels than Red Hat Linux does. Only one Solaris kernel has been compiled and optimized for each different hardware platform (depending on the system architecture). Any kernel configuration is taken care of through the `/etc/system` file or the `proc` file system. The `/etc/ system` file acts much like Red Hat Linux's `/etc/sysctl.conf` file, in which kernel parameters are set in a "variable = value" format. However, the variables and values used for the Solaris OS are quite different, even for similar variables such as shared memory. Never use the Red Hat Linux kernel variable values on a Solaris system. One exception to the `/etc/system` convention are TCP/IP parameters, which are usually set with the `ndd(1)` utility.

# Application Programming Interfaces

Because Solaris and Linux are both POSIX-compliant operating systems, they share many of the same APIs. However, Solaris APIs differ from Linux APIs in two key areas: threading and 64-bit support. Luckily, both of these APIs are enhancements, so the initial porting activities from Linux should not be affected.

The Solaris OS implements two threading models: Solaris threads and POSIX threads. Threading allows a single process to take advantage of multiple processors by spawning threads. The Solaris POSIX threads APIs follow the standard implementation and are compatible with the Linux implementation. Solaris proprietary threads predate the POSIX threading standard, but provide higher threading performance on the Solaris OS. Linux-threaded programs can be ported to the Solaris OS by means of POSIX threading APIs, with conversion to Solaris threading if greater performance is necessary.

Solaris 64-bit support is also an enhancement to UNIX that is not currently available on Red Hat Linux. The 64-bit support enables access to larger files, physical memory and process space than is currently available on 32-bit processors or operating systems. Linux programs will need to be converted for 64-bit support on the Solaris OS. Solaris 64-bit support and porting are described in more detail in Chapter 10.

Below the API level, source code for the Solaris OS and Linux might differ because of their hardware platforms. Linux typically runs on x86 processors, while the Solaris OS can run on either x86 or SPARC processors. SPARC processors are "big endian" processors, whereas x86 CPUs are "little endian." Be sure to review your source code for this change, because it can introduce errors that are difficult to troubleshoot.

# Device Configuration

Both the Solaris and Linux operating systems manage their devices through symbolic links in the device tree. Linux manages this device tree through the /etc sysconf/hwconf file that is either manually edited or discovered during the booting process. The Solaris OS handles it in a similar way, but with different commands.

In addition, the Solaris OS can configure hardware in the operating kernel, through a process called dynamic reconfiguration (DR). This feature, offered on supported Sun hardware, allows operators to add or remove processors, memory, storage, or peripheral cards to or from the OS without rebooting.

The following table highlights the differences in functionality between Red Hat Linux and the Solaris OS.

**TABLE 9-2**   Solaris OS Device Management

| Functionality | Solaris |
|---|---|
| Reconfigure hardware during reboot | # devfs<br># reboot -r -or-<br># boot -r  (at boot prom) |
| Reconfigure device links | # devlinks |
| Reconfigure disk drives | # drvconfig |

## Administration and Monitoring

Linux administration tools are specific to each vendor, with the exception of the linuxconf utility. The management functions for the Solaris OS are concentrated in two applications: Sun Management Console (SMC) and Sun Management Center (SunMC). SMC provides server administration functionality, and SunMC remotely monitors groups of servers. Like linuxconf, SMC allows for the remote GUI administration of servers.

## Networking

Networking implementations on the Linux and Solaris operating systems are remarkably similar. Both operating systems use the same basic commands and files for configuring interfaces, default routes, static routes, name servers, and name services (/etc/nsswitch.conf). In addition, Solaris boasts some unique redundancy and management networking features. One of these features is IP multipathing, which allows multiple IP interfaces on a single network. The Solaris OS supports this by load balancing among the interfaces. IP quality of service (IPQoS) to prioritize IP traffic by application according to service levels is also supported by the Solaris OS.

## Storage

The Solaris OS uses the UNIX file system (UFS) as its default file system. Like EXT3, Red Hat Linux's default file system, UFS is a popular and robust block-based file system that supports journalling for faster recovery times. However, unlike EXT3, UFS supports larger file systems and maximum file sizes. UFS is also tightly integrated with Sun™ Volume Manager (SVM), which allows GUI creation and manipulation of redundant array of independent disk (RAID) volumes.

UFS is just one of the file systems supported on the Solaris OS. Common file systems such as PCFS (MS-DOS, or VFAT on Linux), HSFS (iso9960 on Linux), and NFS are also supported on the Solaris OS. Commercially available file systems, including Sun's QFS, and SAM-FS or VERITAS's VxFS (and the complementary VERITAS Volume Manager [VxVM]), are also quite commonly used on the Solaris OS.

## Security

The Solaris and Linux operating systems differ significantly in the security tools they support. Linux uses `iptables` as its default firewalling tool; the Solaris OS uses SunScreen™ software, which provides advanced firewall features such as stealth mode, whereby the server operates without any visible IP address. The software also offers more conventional stateful firewall features like network address translation (NAT), ordered firewall rules, and a GUI management application. SunScreen is bundled with the Solaris 8 Operating Environment and above.

Sun also provides a toolkit called JumpStart™ Architecture and Security Scripts (JASS) to minimize, harden, and secure the Solaris OS. JASS automates and standardizes the process of securing installations of the Solaris OS by leveraging JumpStart software to run scripts on groups of servers. It is an invaluable aid in securing and maintaining security on Sun servers. More information and documentation about JASS is available at the Sun BluePrints OnLine Web site at `http://www.sun.com/solutions/blueprints/online.html`.

In addition to the security tools we've already mentioned, Sun also offers a high-security version of the Solaris OS called Trusted Solaris™. Trusted Solaris implements much more robust auditing, privacy, and user controls than do traditional UNIX operating systems. For example, through more robust user contro facilities, Trusted Solaris implements role-based access control to provide greater granularity than the single `root` user account.

# Justifying the Migration

The initial steps of our migration will be to justify the project by outlining its objectives, scope, and benefits. As we discussed in Chapter 5, it is best to start by defining objectives based on the problems in the current environment. Our sample organization was facing several problems with their current environment.

One of the most significant of these problems was their support of a nonstandard platform. Because their new corporate parent embraced Solaris as their standard operating system, the acquired company's Linux environment did not allow the organization to reap the benefits of combined purchasing, maintenance agreements, tools, or support processes. This could have prevented the parent company from achieving economies of scale within their IT environment.

In addition to this lack of alignment with the corporate IT standards, the Linux environment itself lacks standardization because of kernel recompilation. While most of the servers have Red Hat's stock kernel, some developers have needed new or experimental features and have recompiled the kernels to enable them. This has created a support problem because Red Hat does not support custom kernels.

The rapidly expanding customer base is causing growth pains, both technically and economically. Currently, the Red Hat OS does not effectively scale beyond 4 or 8 processors, locking the organization into a massively horizontal deployment of dozens of servers. Because system administrators can effectively support only a limited number of operating system instances or servers, this scaling is creating the need for more staff. In addition, the organization might need larger facilities and better management tools to accommodate the growth in servers. All these growing pains lead to higher support costs.

For the scope of this project, the company decided to concentrate just on the server environment (they were already in line with the corporate desktop standards). However, instead of just looking at their production environment, they also decided to look at their internal systems. They reasoned that since they developed software and services, it would be good to gain experience in their own environment as well as those of their customers.

To address these problems, this company has decided to set their objectives as follows:

- Align with corporate standard by adopting the Solaris OS for all servers when it is not cost prohibitive.
- Vertically scale high-growth servers to avoid costs associated with massive horizontal scaling.
- Implement better configuration and change management to prevent support problems experienced in the old environment.

Metrics were set for each of these objectives so that the organization could quantify their success on the project. Some of these metrics included cost savings and cost avoidance that will result from the migration, the number of servers managed, changes within the environment, and out-of-configuration servers. These metrics would be measured now and evaluated later to gauge the project's success.

# Architecting the Target Solaris Environment

The architect phase involves two essential tasks: assessing the current environment and designing a migration solution for moving to the new environment. In this section, we describe the assessment and design tasks for an example migration from Red Hat Linux to the Solaris OS.

## Assessing the Current Linux Environment

Assessing our case study's environment is a straightforward process. At the acquired company, approximately 20 servers were being used: 10 production machines, 5 development and test boxes, and 5 standard office servers. The production application was mostly Java based, with an Oracle database. Significant shell scripting has also been used as utilities in the product, and a few Linux open source tools were also deployed. For internal IT services, the company supported file sharing and printing through the open source Samba package, intranet web applications built on PHP, and MySQL database as well extensive use of email (based on the venerable Sendmail).

We start this assessment by inventorying the hardware and software on each server. Because the acquired company standardized on RPM package management and one Linux vendor, there is a single process for assessing each server. The process consists of a few RPM and Linux utility commands that are scripted and executed on each server. This provides a high-level baseline of the configuration of each server.

From this baseline, we start to delve into the configuration of each server. For the production servers, this means identifying the actual programs and scripts that provide service to their customers. While most of the scripts are simple shell or Perl scripts, most of the open source tools are C coded. The shell scripts will need to be run through ScriptTrans for verification of their portability to Solaris, and the C code will be analyzed with the JScore tool. A sample JScore report and analysis is provided in Appendix A.

Along with this hardware and software analysis, we also assess the data. The majority of the production system's data is held in an Oracle database (several hundred gigabytes), and the internal systems have data in a MySQL database and files on the file servers. There is also the matter of the precious source code that is being held on the development servers. The source code resides in a file-based concurrent versioning system (CVS) repository.

Before the assessment is completed, skills and process factors are assessed for the proposed migration. This assessment primarily entails surveying the technical staff for the skills required to work on the Solaris OS (or the lack therefore). However, we also make sure that we look at some of the configuration and change management processes because improving them is one of our objectives.

# Designing a Migration Solution

With the assessment completed, it is now time to choose migration strategies appropriate to each of our applications and apply them in a holistic way to create our new environment. This will involve decomposing each of the current server's needs separately, but creating a solution that integrates their needs in total. While this sounds difficult, it is really the same process used to architect any environment.

Analyzing the data collected in our assessment activities, we start to formulate a strategy for our migration to the Solaris environment. Because most of the applications that we are currently using internally and externally exist on the Solaris platform, we believe that we can use a straight rehosting strategy for most of our migrations. It is the least expensive and least time-consuming strategy. Because it also fulfills the primary aim of this project (to migrate to and standardize on the Solaris OS) and we are satisfied with our current applications functionality and performance, we decide that we will follow this strategy whenever possible. We will follow this strategy for the applications listed in the following table.

**TABLE 9-3**   Actions Required to Support Specific Applications

| Application | Rehosting Action |
| --- | --- |
| Samba | Recompile open source code or obtain compiled package. Eventually, migrate to PCNetlink (another project). |
| MySQL | Recompile open source code or obtain compiled package. Eventually, migrate to Oracle (another project). |
| PHP | Recompiled version included in Solaris. |
| PHP code | Run under newly recompiled PHP interpreter. |
| Oracle | Purchase and install new Oracle for Solaris binaries. |
| GCC (compiler) | Either recompile open source code or obtain a compiled package. Eventually migrate to Forte™ (a different project). |
| Apache | Recompiled version included in Solaris. |
| Sendmail | Recompiled version included in Solaris. Eventually, migrate to Sun ONE Mail Server. |
| Production java applications | Run under a virtual machine for the Java platform (Java™ Virtual Machine) on the Solaris OS. |

Now that we have decided on a rehosting strategy for most of the applications, we still have another decision: Do we rehost the applications on Solaris/x86 or Solaris/SPARC? Solaris/x86 will run on the organization's current hardware (with possibly a few modifications and upgrades), whereas Solaris/SPARC will require the purchase of new hardware. However, Solaris/SPARC will allow us to purchase much more powerful equipment that enables us to scale our production environment vertically. After weighing the costs of buying new hardware versus the benefits of scaling, we decided to upgrade the production environment to Solaris/SPARC while reusing the internal server's hardware for Solaris/x86.

The final decision to make about our rehosting strategy is to choose which build environment we will use. In this scenario, we could use the current GCC compiler (recompiled for Solaris) or move to Sun's Forte compiler. Sun's compiler is tuned for the Solaris environment, building more optimized binaries for the UltraSPARC™ processors. However, it might require changes to the source code, make files, and build environment to use. For this reason, we choose the GNU C/C++/Fortran/Objective C-to-C converter (commonly called GCC2CC). It takes source code written for GCC (our default build environment on Linux), and outputs equivalent C code, which can then be fed into the target ANSI C compiler, like Sun's Forte compiler. (For more information about this free tool, visit `http://www.sun.com/migration/linux/gcc2c_tool.html`.) In this particular scenario, we decide to use GCC to ease our maintenance tasks for the open-source applications that we will be using. However, this option will be investigated for our in-house written applications. This creates the matrix shown in the following table.

**TABLE 9-4**   Platform Selected to Support Specific Applications

| Application | Rehosting Action | Platform |
| --- | --- | --- |
| Samba | Recompile open source code or obtain compiled package. Eventually, migrate to PCNetlink (another project). | Solaris/x86 |
| MySQL | Recompile open source code or obtain compiled package. Eventually, migrate to Oracle (another project). | Solaris/x86 |
| PHP | Recompiled version included with the Solaris OS. | Solaris/x86 |
| PHP code | Run under newly recompiled PHP interpreter. | Solaris/x86 |
| Oracle | Purchase and install new Oracle for Solaris binaries. | Solaris/SPARC |
| GCC (compiler) | Either recompile open source code, obtain compiled package. Eventually migrate to Forte (a different project). | Solaris/SPARC |
| Apache | Recompiled version included with the Solaris OS. | Solaris/x86 |
| Sendmail | Recompiled version included with the Solaris OS. Eventually, migrate to Sun ONE Mail Server. | Solaris/x86 |
| Production Java applications | Run under Java virtual machine (JVM) on the Solaris OS. | Solaris/SPARC |

We have identified that at least one C program does not compile on the Solaris OS. This will require a bit more analysis before we can decide on a migration strategy. We have several options to explore on this application:

- Run the Linux binaries under `lxrun` emulation on Solaris/x86. While this seems like the simplest solution, it will require some configuration on the server, restricts the platform to Solaris/x86, and might cause performance problems stemming from the emulation.

- Search for a replacement application with similar features and performance. Although this seems like a good choice, it will require substantial integration with the current service and extensive regression testing to prove that it will perform.

- Port the code to Solaris and run it under Solaris/x86 or Solaris/SPARC. By examining our JScore output for this application, we see that the report estimates that the porting complexity for this application will be average. Only three system calls will need to be implemented. The rest of the changes will be mostly syntax changes in existing calls. This will also require extensive testing, but little integration work.

- Port the code to Java and run it on either platform with the appropriate Java virtual machine (JVM). This is a very attractive and strategic option but will require substantial work in redeveloping the application from the ground up. Because the application was not designed in an object-oriented model, it will need to be completely rewritten.

After looking at the options and weighing the risks of each option, we decide to port this application to the Solaris OS. This option provides us with many strategic benefits without much of the risk of involved in redeveloping the application in the Java programming language. We expect that this porting work can be accomplished by our developers in about two weeks; however, we make sure and plan for the contingency that they cannot achieve this goal. In this case, our contingency plan is to outsource this activity if we fail to port the code (assuming that this can be done within budget) or to use the `lxrun` rehosting (emulation) strategy.

After the strategy has been determined, we start the real work of the architect phase by breaking down the component technologies for all of our servers. At this point, we also decide on the target platform's technology components. Each component in the Red Hat Linux stack is complemented by a Solaris technology component that provides similar or better functionality.

This architecture achieves most of our objectives for the project. However, some careful capacity planning will be needed to size the new servers to realize our goal of vertically scaling the production servers.

# Implementing the Migration to the Solaris Environment

With all the technical designs and migration plans in place, it is time to execute our migration. Following the project plan, we will minimize risk by using our tested processes and having our contingency plans at the ready. In the best of projects, this phase is anticlimactic because everything operates according to tested plans.

## Building the New Environment

The first step in implementing our migration is building the new environment. This is a tedious job that involves manually paging through the /etc files on the old server and replicating the configuration on the new Solaris environment. Ideally, this will be done through JumpStart configurations; however, it can be done by hand. The important trick here is not to blindly copy files from the old environment to the new environment. Slight differences in syntax and meaning still exist between the two operating systems. In fact, scripting should be used as much as possible to enact the exact commands used in Solaris to create the configuration files. While this is not always possible, especially when we might not be able to obtain user account passwords to recreate the accounts, it is preferable in many cases.

Once the servers are configured, we will need to provision them with applications and data. Because only a few servers are being migrated, this is a straightforward process whereby we manually install applications on the servers. In larger migrations, we might choose to use JumpStart software to deploy applications and the OS to provide a standard, repeatable process. JumpStart should also be considered in complex migrations that might, for testing purposes, require several installations.

Data transfer is also relatively straightforward. All file-based data are copied by NFS from the old servers to the new servers. Database data is exported from the old platform database (with full schema) and reimported onto the new platform database. Database tuning and index creation are handled after this conversion.

## Testing the New Environment

Testing for this example migration is not as difficult as it could be for many migrations. Because we have ported a minimum amount of source code and have kept much of our data intact, we will not have the testing complexity many migrations require. However, that does not excuse our team from following the appropriate testing best practices.

At a minimum, the following tests need to be performed:

- Database integrity
- Application functionality
- File copying
- Business acceptance
- Performance acceptance

Our team has performed a number of application upgrades over the years, so they have already created a number of test plans. These are reviewed and slightly modified for their new purpose by addition of some Solaris OS-specific tests.

## Documenting the Migration Project

With the implementation phase of the project almost complete, we take some time to document our successes and failures. Because we have already planned several more migration projects, it is important to preserve what we have learned. To this set of best practices, we also add the project plan. This will give us a head start for planning the next migration project we undertake.

# Managing the New Solaris Environment

With the migrated environment in place, it is time to turn our full attention to making sure that the "process" part of our skills, process, and technology migration project is successful. While this is a very broad category, we will focus our attention on three key areas: system monitoring, change management, and release management.

To rectify the system monitoring deficiencies, we decide to implement a collection of monitoring solutions aimed at specific components. In a larger environment, we would probably need a more integrated solution. We decide to use Sun Management Center (SunMC). Other tools will be added to augment specific management needs (such as database, backups and storage).

Implementing change and release management will be much more difficult. Changing human behavior is difficult, especially in a dynamic software development environment. However, we will implement the process flows described in this book through a standard process that includes the following tasks:

- Appoint points of contact who will lead the change and release management processes. These people will become the change manager and release manager.
- Produce a mission statement on the purpose of the processes.
- Define roles and responsibilities for key players in the processes.
- Establish scope and purpose of the implementation project.
- Quantify resources and tools needed for the process. This will be an important decision: the correct tool will enhance compliance with the new process, but a poor tool choice will kill it.
- Promote awareness of the new process with all staff and management.

As with any process, these processes will be gradually phased into production and refined along the way.

# Migrating From Tru64 UNIX

Using a fictional case study, this chapter illustrates the methodology, tools, and best practices used to migrate a Tru64 environment to the Solaris environment.

In this study, we examine a simple, custom-written application that uses a Sybase database to store information about the company's inventory, as well as client-specific data. This application is converted to run under the Solaris Operating System (Solaris OS) and is integrated with directory services. Additionally, the database vendor is changed from Sybase to Oracle.

This chapter contains the following sections:

- "Overview of Tru64" on page 177
- "64-Bit Computing" on page 178
- "Clustering" on page 180
- "Justifying the Migration" on page 182
- "Architecting the Migration" on page 185
- "Implementing the Migration to the Solaris Environment" on page 195
- "Managing the New Solaris Environment" on page 203

# Overview of Tru64

Tru64 was the first commercially available UNIX environment that supported a 64-bit data model and computing environment. Originally released to support the Alpha hardware platform from the Digital Equipment Corporation (DEC), this operating environment and hardware combination formed a powerful computing environment that overcame the barriers associated with 32-bit computing.

The Tru64 kernel architecture is based on Carnegie-Mellon University's Mach V2.5 kernel design, with components from Berkeley Software Distribution (BSD) 4.3 and 4.4, UNIX System V, and other sources. Tru64 implements the Open Software Foundation (OSF) OSF/1 R1.0, R1.1, and R1.2 technology. The Tru64 UNIX operating system complies with numerous other standards and industry specifications, including the X/Open XPG4 and XTI, POSIX, and the System V Interface Definition (SVID). Additionally, Tru64 UNIX is compatible with Berkeley 4.3 and System V programming interfaces and conforms to the OSF application environment specifications (AES), the last which specifies an interface for developing portable applications.

As described in Chapter 2, Tru64 and the Solaris OS share a common ancestry. In addition, the development of standards and the willingness of vendors to faithfully implement them ensures that porting an application from Tru64 to the Solaris OS should not prove to be too daunting.

In the following sections, we examine the benefits and drawbacks of 64-bit computing and explore the data models supported by Tru64 and the Solaris OS. Then, we provide a little background on workarounds that were in place before the advent of 64-bit operating environments that permitted us to use files larger than 2 gigabytes.

# 64-Bit Computing

As the complexity and functionality of applications increase, their data sets and address space requirements increase as well. Many applications (databases, web caches, simulation and modeling software, and the like) run more effectively if they are not subject to the 4-gigabyte address space limitation imposed by a 32-bit architecture.

The ability to support larger amounts of primary memory allows the 64-bit architecture to afford performance benefits to a broad class of applications, including the following:

- A greater proportion of a database can be held in primary memory.
- Larger CAD/CAE models and simulations can fit in primary memory.
- Larger scientific computing problems can fit in primary memory.
- Web caches hold more data in memory, reducing latency.

The following are also compelling reasons for creating 64-bit applications:

- To improve performance by performing several computations on 64-bit integer quantities, using the wider data paths of a 64-bit processor

- To improve efficiency with arithmetic and logical operations on 64-bit quantities

- To enable operations to use full-register widths, the full-register set, and new instructions

- To improve efficiency with the improved parameter passing of 64-bit quantities

Not all applications are well suited to a 64-bit data model. If your application does not use or require any of the features listed above, it should probably be left as a 32-bit application. 32-bit applications usually run without problem in a 64-bit environment. 64-bit applications are usually larger in size. Additionally, the use of longer pointers in the 64-bit version could degrade performance because of cache misses. Doubling the size of pointers means that the cache cannot hold as many entries as om the 32-bit version of the application.

# Understanding Differences Between 32-Bit and 64-Bit Data Models

Like Tru64, the Solaris OS supports the LP64 data model. In this convention, longs and pointers are 64 bits in length (hence the acronym LP64) and an integer is 32 bits in length. This is in contrast to the data model used in 32-bit environments, referred to as an ILP32, in which integers, longs, and pointers are all 32 bits in length (hence the acronym ILP32). The following table highlights the differences between these two models:

**TABLE 10-1**   Differences Between 32-Bit and 64-Bit Data Models

| C Data Type | ILP32 | LP64 |
| --- | --- | --- |
| char | 8 | unchanged |
| short | 16 | unchanged |
| int | 32 | unchanged |
| long | 32 | 64 |
| long long | 64 | unchanged |
| pointer | 32 | 64 |
| enum | 32 | unchanged |
| float | 32 | unchanged |
| double | 64 | unchanged |
| long double | 128 | unchanged |

Most of the problems associated with migrating an application to 64 bits arise from the following differences:

- Long values (long) are 64 bits in length, not 32.
- Pointers are 64 bits in length, not 32.
- Integers (int) are not the same size as longs and pointers in a 64-bit environment.

Many of these size issues can be mitigated if the developer uses derived types. These definitions and others can be found in `/usr/include/sys/types.h` and `/usr/include/sys/inttypes.h` in both the Solaris and Tru64 environments. A derived type can specify the size of the attribute (for example, `int32_t`) or its intended use (for example, `blksize_t`), a capability that increases program clarity. The derived types themselves are safe for both ILP32 and LP64 environments, making them 32-bit and 64-bit safe.

All releases of the Solaris OS after and including the Solaris 7 OE support both 32-bit and 64-bit data models. Under most circumstances, binaries that were created under the 32-bit environment can be run in the 64-bit environment.

## Using Large Files to Overcome 32-Bit Limitations

DEC was one of the first computer manufacturers to understand the limitations of a 32-bit environment as it related to file size. In the past, under a 32-bit environment, files could not exceed 2 gigabytes in length. Files are typically accessed relative to a pointer that points to a location within the file. Programmers can move this pointer by specifying an offset, but this offset is a signed quantity because the pointer can be moved forward and backward within the file. Consequently, the maximum offset that could be specified was 31 bits, limiting the file size to less than 2 gigabytes ($2**31 = 2$ gigabytes).

Vendors created a "large file" option that allows the offset variable to be a long quantity. This enables the file to grow well beyond the 2 or 4 gigabyte limit, because the offset variable used to move the pointer is much larger ($2**63$). This technology can be found in many legacy applications but is not necessary in a 64-bit computing environment like Solaris or Tru64.

# Clustering

In today's business environment, time really is money. In the financial markets, applications can be responsible for moving literally trillions of dollars a day. Any significant unavailability of such an application, or even an outage on a smaller system that is responsible for only billions or possibly millions of dollars of daily revenue, can have a significant impact on a company's bottom line. Consequently, highly available (HA) environments are required for certain applications. One strategy for creating an HA environment might include a cluster of computing devices and related storage.

In the following sections, we provide an overview of clustering technology and focus on TruCluster and Sun Cluster 3.0 software. Although our example does not involve the migration from one clustering technology to another, we discuss the technology here to provide background information that will be helpful if you encounter an opportunity to migrate from using TruCluster to using Sun Cluster software.

# Overview

A *cluster* is a group of two or more computers (nodes) that share a common storage device and are connected in a way that allows them to operate as a single, continuously available system. Should an application on one of the computers, or the computer itself, fail, a companion machine in the cluster takes over to provide the same functionality as the failing computer. Whereas fault-tolerant hardware can provide near-continuous uptime by providing specialized proprietary hardware sharing the same memory, clustering technology provides highly available applications through the use of redundancy (redundant servers and redundant interconnects, networking, and storage, even redundant adapters and controllers). All of this redundancy allows work to continue if a hardware or software failure occurs, by transparently switching to a working component.

Clusters provide an enterprise a cost-effective and flexible method for deploying technology. Machines can be added or removed from a cluster as business demands vary. As newer technology becomes available, it can be added incrementally to the cluster, thereby reducing the need to perform a "forklift" upgrade. Clustering provides the following benefits:

- High availability
- Scalability in several directions
- Ease of use and administration
- Cost-effective, incremental growth path

TruCluster software was a pioneering version of cluster technology. Simple to configure and highly reliable, this framework allowed the deployment of campus clusters as well as machines located over great distances.

Sun Cluster 3.0 software is a scalable and flexible solution that is equally suited for a small local cluster or larger extended clusters.

## Cluster Agents—TruCluster and Sun Cluster 3.0 Software

The ability to detect when an application or resource is no longer operating as it was designed to is an integral component of any cluster. When the cluster detects these types of changes, the application can be restarted or moved to a different node.

In the TruCluster environment, this functionality is provided by the Cluster Application Availability (CAA) subsystem. This facility provides a way for the environment applications to determine whether they are operating properly and allows administrators to specify what actions should be taken if problems are detected.

Sun Cluster 3.0 software supports a similar framework that enables IT staff to develop a customized agent that can be used to monitor the health of the clustered application.

Although these subsystems provide similar functionality, they have significantly different implementations. Porting an application from one clustered environment to another requires you to not only transform the application source code to adhere to the new OS APIs but also that you integrate the application into the high availability framework of that clustered so that application failure can be detected. The framework will also have to be programmed to specify the actions that should take place if an application fails.

# Justifying the Migration

The first stage in any migration project involves justifying the migration. In this particular case study, a manufacturing company has a number of systems deployed. Although the company has numerous Sun platforms in place, its inventory application and the associated database run under the Tru64 OS. The custom-written application was written in the C programming language and uses a Sybase database to store inventory data. This database uses third-party tools to manage the database and produce reports.

A simplified overview of the application and the supporting environment is presented in the following figure.

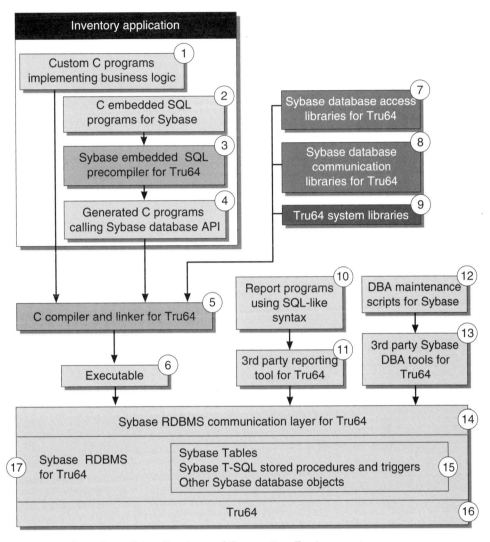

**FIGURE 10-1** Overview of Application and Supporting Environment

# Identifying Migration Motivators

The platform supporting this application is running out of capacity. The enterprise must decide whether it wants to purchase another Alpha server to provide the required capability, or to migrate the application to another vendor's platform that has the capacity to support the enterprise requirements. Two issues suggest that migration to a different platform would be the preferred choice:

- **End of life (EOL) of the Alpha processor.** Industry consolidation has led to the acquisition of DEC by Compaq Computer Corporation. This consolidation resulted in the announcement of the EOL of the Alpha processor after its manufacturing was turned over to Intel.

- **Changes to the Tru64 roadmap.** After Compaq acquired DEC, they were in turn acquired by Hewlett Packard (HP). HP already has its own version of the UNIX OS, HP/UX. The new HP/COMPAQ entity has stated that they will be phasing out Tru64 and consolidating on the HP/UX version of UNIX. To compound the problem, HP has also elected to use the Itanium processor as the basis for its new platform. If the client migrated to HP/UX, they would have to migrate again when the Itanium platform is introduced.

If the enterprise chooses to migrate its inventory application to Sun's Solaris environment, it can leverage its existing Oracle licensing agreement and can reduce expenses by switching their database from Sybase to Oracle.

You will explore these issues during a one-day meeting with all stakeholders from the enterprise. By performing that due diligence, you will gain a better understanding of the drivers and end goals of the migration.

# Identifying Migration Strategies

In this case, the benefits of the migration are well understood. The application provides the business functionality that the enterprise requires. It does not want to move to a COTS application. Because the enterprise's problems relate to IT effectiveness, the system has run out of cycles, and the platform/environment product line they are using has a limited life expectancy, the recommended solution is to rehost the application. The benefits of the migration will be that the IT effectiveness of the platform will be improved and the required capacity will be achieved.

In other situations, the drivers might not be as obvious as they are in this case study. If poor total cost of ownership (TCO) or return on investment (ROI) was the driver, and the goal was to improve TCO or ROI, a more detailed investigation might have to be completed to determine whether rehosting is the correct migration solution.

The result of the meeting is an agreement to proceed with a more detailed assessment of the application environment to determine the associated migration costs. The executive responsible for this initiative then releases a mission statement and the detailed assessment begins.

# Architecting the Migration

The first phase in the SunTone migration methodology involves architecting the solution. At this stage, you assess the existing environment and design a first-cut architecture.

## Assessing the Current Environment

The next step in the migration is the assessment of the existing application and the associated environment. This will allow you to create a risk list that can be used to identify any areas of the project that might require a proof of concept to ensure that the project can be completed. The outcome of the assessment is a risk list (where appropriate) and a work breakdown structure that details the amount of effort required to migrate the application and the associated environment. This work breakdown structure is then used to create a plan and schedule various activities, overlapping independent subtasks, where appropriate.

For custom-written applications, provide the migration team with a snapshot of the application source and associated infrastructure to serve as a baseline for the migration activity. When possible, you should also acquire a build log for the application. This log will provide the following information:

- Tools used
- Options provided to these tools
- Source that is compiled
- Libraries that are linked
- Order in which symbols are resolved

Although development documentation is welcome, a simple build log can serve as a guide to the "facts on the ground." It will show how the application is actually built.

In the following sections, we explore the assessment process.

## Assessing the Application Infrastructure

Scripts provide an easy way for IT staff or administrators to create tools to administer an application, analyze or modify data, and provide functional support for an application. Scripts can leverage utilities that exist elsewhere in the operating environment to perform various administrative tasks. In addition, scripts will identify which utilities are used, as well as the options that are specified.

When the application is migrated, the associated scripts must be migrated to the new environment as well. Although the script tool (for example, Ksh, bash, sh, csh, PERL, or Python) might support the same syntax in the new environment, the location of the programs or files used by the script might be different in the new environment. Additionally, the options of the programs called by the scripts might also require modification.

Ensure that a version of the script tool is available in the new environment.

## Analyze Scripts

The Perl utility is becoming popular as a scripting tool because of its power and flexibility. However, the venerable shell is still the script tool of choice for most developers, primarily because of its availability across a variety of platforms and environments.

When assessing shell scripts, check each command for the following conditions:

- Command is unavailable on the Solaris OS.
- Command is in a different location and the location is not in the user's path.
- Command uses a flag that does not exist on the Solaris OS.
- Command uses a flag that has different functionality on the Solaris OS.
- Output of a command is different and is redirected.

This check can be done manually or through the use of the scriptran tool.

The following sample presents the analysis of the issues associated with the shell scripting used with the Tru64 example.

```
alias     |   27
ar        |   365
cc        |   86
colrm     |   1
df        |   14
du        |   1
e         |   2
ed        |   1
egrcp     |   68
expr      |   11
fold      |   1
get       |   1
iostat    |   1
ipcs      |   45
```

(continued on next page)

(continued from previous page)

```
ld          |   13
lex         |   4
ln          |   177
lpr         |   2
make        |   1
mcopy       |   1
more        |   12
mt          |   3
netstat     |   5
printenv    |   5
sleep       |   94
stty        |   1
style       |   219
tail        |   61
tset        |   1
vmstat      |   26
w           |   5
wait        |   14
whoami      |   2
xconsole    |   3
xhost       |   4
xlsclients  |   1
xset        |   14
xsetroot    |   4
xterm       |   1
yacc        |   4
Total: 40   |   1301
```

## Analyze Build Tools

When working with a custom application, you also have to migrate the tools used to build the application executable. These usually include a compiler, a source code management system, and the build environment used to create the executable. Additionally, any third-party products that were used to build the application must be migrated.

Obtaining a build log created when the application was last built is the best way to ensure that the build process and the tools involved in that process are identified. Be certain that you understand the semantics of the options that were specified when the application was built. Although tools in the new environment will most likely support the required functionality, different options might have to be specified to invoke the desired behavior. For example, static linking, position-independent code, extended symbol table information, and the like might require the use of new and different options.

In this example, the assessment reveals that a number of development tools are currently available on another Sun platform within the enterprise. Although this development environment has not been used to create the Tru64 version of the application you want to port, you can leverage some of the existing tools that are available (for example, compilers and debuggers). Assume that you have determined that this platform can be used for the migration exercise.

## Determine Third-Party Products Usage

While all applications depend on support from the operating environment and associated utilities, many applications are also designed to work with the functionality provided by third-party products that are integrated into the execution architecture. When the application is ported, this supporting software must be ported as well, as part of the application infrastructure. In the example, the most significant piece of third-party software is the Sybase database that is implemented on the Tru64 environment. However, additional third-party software is used to generate reports and administrate the database.

When assessing third-party products, you must ensure that these or similar products are available for both the new OS and the new database.

This migration case study involves the conversion of a Sybase database implemented on the Tru64 platform to an Oracle database running on the Solaris platform. FIGURE 10-1 on page 183 provides an overview of the Sybase implementation.

When attempting to assess the database component of the application, be sure to assess the deployment of database technology, not just the database itself. Databases have evolved to become much more than simple repositories for data. Complex logic can be programmed into the database. Database vendors encourage developers and database administrators (DBAs) to store database-related (or data-intensive) logic inside the database. The program units that are locally stored in databases are often called stored procedures and triggers.

The practice of storing program logic in the database aids in the assessment because the majority of the database-related logic is centralized in a single location, although some interaction with the database will be specified in the programs themselves. For DBAs who are concerned about database performance, storing program logic in the database is encouraged as well, because logic that is locally stored in the database has many positive performance implications. These stored program units are written in a language that is commonly known as the Structured Query Language (SQL).

Regrettably, although there is an SQL standard, the degree of compliance with this standard varies greatly from one database vendor to another. Different database vendors might develop their own extensions to the SQL language to make it more powerful and easier to use and, in some cases, to address specific database performance issues through optimization.

The assessment of the database technology must address the stored procedures as well as database object behavior. Among the different databases, database objects (box 16 in FIGURE 10-1 on page 183) that have the same name behave differently. For example, database objects such as stored procedures, triggers, and temporary tables are supported in both Sybase and Oracle. However, there are no standards for the behavior of these objects. Consequently, procedures, triggers, and temporary tables stored in Sybase behave differently than those stored in Oracle. These differences must be well understood before you can accurately assess the amount of change and effort that will be required in a migration.

Take extra care when migrating application logic from one version of SQL to another. In this example, translating a full-blown Sybase T-SQL application to Oracle's PL/SQL could result in an extensive modification or a total rewrite. You must carefully identify the use of language features that might require the reimplementation of logic on the new deployment because the SQL extensions and their underlying functionality might not be available. For this reason, the conversion of the Sybase implementation will be considered a reengineering or rearchitecture effort.

When assessing the database technology integration with the application, be aware that each database vendor has its own version of SQL and that these versions can vary considerably. Understanding the differences in SQL implementations will help you understand the nature and amount of work that is needed for a project of this nature.

In addition to the Sybase database technology, our example makes use of third-party reporting tools (box 11), and DBA tools (box 13). If the tool vendor supports both source and target databases and platforms, these can most likely be replaced. If a tool cannot be replaced for any reason, then all the components that use it will most likely need to be rewritten. To keep the example simple, assume that you can replace all the third-party tools and libraries.

In the example, all the components that use SQL will be affected in the same manner. These components are:

- **Stored procedures and triggers (box 15).** These are pure native SQL and are discussed above.

- **C programs that use embedded SQL (box 2).** Embedded SQL allows developers to directly use SQL statements inside a programming language they are familiar with. In our example, the SQL statements are embedded inside C programs. These embedded SQL programs are then passed to a precompiler (box 3). The precompiler converts the embedded SQL to statements that directly call the native database API (box 4). The output is a generated C program that is then passed to the C compiler and linker.

- **Report programs that use third-party reporting tools (box 11).** Note that for this scenario, it is not enough to replace the reporting tool. Report programs that use third-party tools usually issue SQL or SQL-like syntax (possibly allowing database vendor SQL language extensions), so they will have to be modified or rewritten.

- **DBA maintenance scripts (box 13).** The database engine (box 17) stores data in objects called tables (box 16). The type of data that is going to be stored is defined at the table level by data types that are native to the database engine being used. When changing database engines, one of the first tasks is to determine whether all the data types used by the source database can be successfully mapped to data types in the target database.

Problems arise when the data types that are used in the source database cannot be mapped to the target database. If a data type cannot be mapped, you must find a way to mimic its functionality in the target database. This simple data type issue could potentially trigger a chain reaction of changes that need to be made to all components that reference the table. The extent of modifications will depend on the nature of the data type in question and how extensively it is used by all the components that are using the database.

In our example, all data types map from the Sybase implementation to the Oracle implementation without difficulty.

## Assess the Application

As detailed previously, you must acquire the code for the application. That code will help you estimate how much effort will be required for the migration. There are two issues to consider when assessing an application:

- **Understanding the composition of the code used by the application.** Many legacy applications have significant size (for example, millions of lines of code). Simply trying to understand the layout of the source tree and the types of files can be a complex task.

- **Understanding which files within the source distribution are actually used to build the application.** As an application evolves, business functionality might no longer be required and new functionality can be added. Although this can be reflected when the application is built, developers seldom remove the old, unused code from the source code directory. Avoid transforming code that isn't being used.

The following appsurvey output represents the composition of the files under the source code repository of the `inventory` application.

```
Module | FileType   | # Lines  | # of Files | # API issues

invtry | .4         | 127      | 1          | 0
invtry | .C         | 429661   | 605        | 44
invtry | .H         | 24570    | 216        | 9
invtry | .Make_files| 20174    | 126        | 0
invtry | .Msg       | 6572     | 24         | 0
invtry | .acf       | 1916     | 86         | 0
invtry | .bak       | 430      | 8          | 0
invtry | .bld       | 1914     | 6          | 0
invtry | .c         | 656575   | 415        | 14
invtry | .cat       | 25       | 1          | 0
invtry | .cfg       | 131      | 11         | 0
invtry | .cl        | 5070     | 34         | 0
invtry | .cpp       | 6017     | 2          | 0
invtry | .ctl       | 27908    | 54         | 0
invtry | .dat       | 20684    | 11         | 0
invtry | .def       | 81       | 1          | 0
invtry | .h         | 116618   | 356        | 1
invtry | .sh        | 2790     | 6          | 0
invtry | .sql       | 301904   | 699        | 0
invtry | .test      | 133      | 1          | 0
invtry | .tidl      | 4780     | 51         | 0
invtry | .tmp       | 453      | 1          | 0
invtry | .tpl       | 8169     | 36         | 0
invtry | .wpm       | 162      | 1          | 0
invtry | .zip       | 146      | 2          | 0
TOTAL  |            | 2672376  | 4066       | 68
```

Remember that it is possible that not all of these files will be used to create the application. An analysis of the build log will reveal which files are used when the application is created.

In this example, you are considering a custom application written in the C programming language. When implementing this sort of migration, focus on the differences between the APIs provided by the Tru64 environment and those provided by the Solaris OS. The following sample breaks down the APIs differences.

```
Total Files: 3717        LinesOfCode: 1185289      Statements: 388262
Issues:
accept          4        Weight: 5
acosd           2        Weight: 5
asind           4        Weight: 5
atand           5        Weight: 5
bind            33       Weight: 5
bind_to_cpu     1        Weight: 25
connect         5        Weight: 5
cosd            15       Weight: 5
endhostent      2        Weight: 5
exp             1        Weight: 5
fork            28       Weight: 3
freopen         6        Weight: 5
fseek           28       Weight: 5
gethostbyaddr   4        Weight: 5
gethostent      1        Weight: 25
getsockname     2        Weight: 5
getsockopt      15       Weight: 25
getsysinfo      6        Weight: 200
gettimeofday    90       Weight: 5
getuid          1        Weight: 3
htonl           44       Weight: 5
htons           63       Weight: 5
inet_addr       18       Weight: 3
inet_lnaof      1        Weight: 5
inet_netof      1        Weight: 5
inet_network    1        Weight: 3
inet_ntoa       14       Weight: 3
ioctl           104      Weight: 25
kill            26       Weight: 5
listen          4        Weight: 5
log             2        Weight: 5
min             9        Weight: 25
mq_setattr      1        Weight: 5
msgctl          2        Weight: 5
msgrcv          31       Weight: 5
munmap          3        Weight: 5
nint            9        Weight: 5
nintf           4        Weight: 5
ntohl           14       Weight: 25

(continued on next page)
```

*(continued from preceding page)*

```
ntohs                       15      Weight: 25
open                        6       Weight: 25
opendir                     13      Weight: 5
pfopen                      1       Weight: 200
pow                         22      Weight: 5
pthread_cleanup_pop         3       Weight: 5
pthread_cleanup_push        3       Weight: 5
pthread_delay_np            21      Weight: 25
pthread_get_expiration_np 13        Weight: 25
pthread_lock_global_np      125     Weight: 25
pthread_unlock_global_np 128        Weight: 25
recv                        14      Weight: 5
recvfrom                    12      Weight: 5
remainder                   1       Weight: 5
sched_getscheduler          1       Weight: 5
semctl                      4       Weight: 5
semget                      1       Weight: 3
semop                       8       Weight: 3
send                        11      Weight: 5
sendto                      8       Weight: 5
sethostent                  1       Weight: 5
setsid                      3       Weight: 3
setsockopt                  20      Weight: 25
setsysinfo                  1       Weight: 200
settimeofday                4       Weight: 5
shmat                       7       Weight: 3
shmctl                      10      Weight: 3
shmdt                       5       Weight: 3
shmget                      7       Weight: 3
sigaction                   5       Weight: 25
sigwait                     5       Weight: 25
sind                        13      Weight: 5
socket                      55      Weight: 5
sqrt                        118     Weight: 5
statvfs                     2       Weight: 3
strftime                    49      Weight: 5
system                      2       Weight: 5
table                       3       Weight: 200
tand                        3       Weight: 5
template                    1       Weight: 3
times                       2       Weight: 3
ulimit                      8       Weight: 25
uswitch                     2       Weight: 200
wait                        40      Weight: 3
waitpid                     2       Weight: 3
write                       2       Weight: 5
```

## Assess the Compute and Storage Platform

In the example, the capacity of the existing hardware platform is determined. Based on this information, a replacement platform is chosen from the Sun product line that will provide the required performance, reliability, scalability, and manageability. The details of hardware sizing are outside the scope of this document.

## Assess the Network Infrastructure

Next, examine the networking facilities inside the enterprise's data center to determine if they can support the required future capacity and load generated by the migrated environment. Where appropriate, additional capacity might have to be acquired (10BASE-T to 100BASE-T). All aspects of the network must be considered, from the transport technology (FDDI, Token Ring, Ethernet, and the like) to the number of ports that are available on the switch or hub that will be used to cable the Network Interface Card (NIC).

Once you determine the networking technology, you can order the correct NIC for the hardware described above.

In the example, the 100-megabyte network has sufficient capacity, and a port is available on the switch serving the data center. A 100BASE-T NIC is required for the platform, as well as a 10-meter cable to make the connection.

## Assess Facilities

During the next part of the assessment, you assess the facilities and any changes that will be required to support the migrated solution. During this assessment, consider power, space, network connections, door frame size, and similar requirements.

In the example, the new platform is roughly the same in size as the older platform. As a result, it can fit through all the doorways. However, it will have to be installed in a previously unused corner of the data center because the old machine will not be retired for some time.

The newer Sun hardware in this example requires more power but produces less heat than the older platform. However, a new electrical receptacle will be required for compatibility with the new hardware. In this case, the client decides to re-route a cable run for cabling efficiencies with existing machines and to bring power to the new location.

## Assess Management Tools

Next, you assess the existing management tools and determine how they can be moved to the target platform. In this case, the client uses BMC Patrol to monitor the old Tru64 environment. This product is also available for the Solaris environment and has already been deployed on other Sun platforms within the data center. Additional ad hoc system monitoring is performed using the `cron` utility, to schedule scripts that use conventional UNIX utilities such as `iostat`, `vmstat`, `df`, and the like.

## Assess People and Process

The skills of the organization must be assessed to determine whether any gaps exist. A curriculum is then developed to address any shortfalls. In our example, the IT staff already supports a number of Sun/Solaris/Oracle environments, which means that no additional training should be required.

# Understanding Threading Models

Applications use threads to implement fine-grained parallelism. Thread libraries have been created for most modern operating environments. The most common threading implementations are POSIX threads and Solaris threads, which have similar semantics. The Solaris OS supports both threading models.

DEC's implementation of threads differs slightly from these implementations. In the example, you would use a compatibility library to replace threading APIs that are found in the Tru64 environment, but not found in the Solaris environment.

# Implementing the Migration to the Solaris Environment

During the previous phase of the project, you produced a work breakdown structure that was used to develop a plan for this phase of the project. Implementation activities can be broken into tasks that relate to hardware and tasks that relate to software. Where appropriate, independent tasks can be overlapped in the schedule, depending on the required completion date, budget, and skill sets available.

In the following sections, we examine the tasks involved with implementing the solution in a Solaris environment.

## Modifying the Facilities

Typically, the facilities must be modified before hardware is installed. Depending on the modifications required, considerable lead time can be required. In the example, you need to reroute a power cable, install the appropriate receptacle, and clear space for the new hardware. These activities are coordinated to reduce their impact on the existing environment.

## Creating the Networking Infrastructure

This task involves preparing the network for the addition of the new platform. Here, you decide things like IP addresses, routing, and network masks. If warranted, new load balancers, switches, hubs, cable drops, and the like will be deployed and tested. Care must be taken to minimize the impact of these activities on the existing environment.

In the example, the networking infrastructure requires minimal change because a cable must be routed from the switch to the machine location. However, if routers or load balancers were required, significantly more time and effort would go into this task.

## Deploying the Compute and Storage Platforms

Because this activity requires specialized skills, it is typically performed by the service organization of hardware vendors (compute and storage). Before installing platforms, the supporting infrastructure (for example, facilities and networking) should be in place. If the compute platform and storage platforms are provided by different vendors, their activities must be coordinated.

In the example, the compute hardware and storage platforms are provided by the same vendor. Once the power and networking are in place, you can arrange for the equipment to be delivered and installed.

## Implementing the Application Infrastructure

When the development environment is in place, you can begin transforming the application source code and any of the third-party scripts that support the application.

With the production hardware platform in place, you can begin creating the application infrastructure. The activities in this task include:

- Installing third-party products used at runtime. These can include the database and any tools or scripts used to administer the database or to produce reports.

- Installing the modified scripts that manage the application.

- Configuring the platform to support the application.

## Implement the Build Environment

The analysis of the build log identified the tools and utilities that were used to create the application executable. Where possible, you should acquire and install the same tools. In certain cases (most likely, the compiler), you might have to acquire a different product with similar functionality.

When installing these build tools, examine the old build log to determine where the tools were located in the old environment. Putting your tools in the same location will minimize the changes that have to be made to the make files.

Modify the make files to use the new tools, utilities, and libraries. Translate the tool options, when required, such that they provide the same functionality. Our usual and preferred methodology is to port and redesign the entire build environment before the application source is modified. If the build environment is well designed, only a few key make files and setup scripts need to be changed. The general approach is as follows:

1. Understand the key files that affect the whole build system, and port those first.

2. Do a global search for hard-coded values in make files, and change them so they benefit from the new design if applicable.

3. Port the disconnected hard-coded instances if any are left.

4. Release the build environment for code porting work.

These steps might have to be performed on a per-module basis because of the project schedule, code availability, and resources.

Distributing this work across a development team can create efficiencies in the project schedule, but if a large number of code-porting specialists make changes to the make files in the module they are porting, then the make files can become inconsistent with hard-coded values that might conflict with each other.

# Translate Scripts

During the assessment process, a number of issues were identified that made the shell scripts that were originally developed for a Tru64 environment incompatible with the Solaris environment. These differences were usually related to the location or options that are used by the shell script. The following example presents the types of changes that will have to be made.

```
#! /bin/ksh
echo "Generated on `date`" >> $longreport
echo "Hostname : ", `hostname` >> $longreport

# __sun: change tr 'a-z' 'A-Z' to tr '[a-z]' '[A-Z]'
# NEW_TARGET=`echo ${TARGET_NAME} | tr 'a-z' 'A-Z'`
NEW_TARGET=`echo ${TARGET_NAME} | tr '[a-z]' '[A-Z]'`

echo "New target: ${NEW_TARGET}" >> $longreport

echo "Current environment" >> $longreport
# __sun: add path
#printenv >> $longreport
/usr/ucb/printenv >> $longreport

echo "Print who's logged in"  >> $longreport

#__sun: 'f' is 'finger' on Solaris
#f \@`hostname`  >> $longreport
finger \@`hostname`  >> $longreport

echo "Check if $filename is a link?" >> $longreport

#__sun: change -h to -L
#if [ -h $filename ]; then
if [ -L $filename ]; then
echo "$filename is a link" >> $longreport
fi

echo "Extract all names from $filename " >> $longreport

#__sun: add path because of option -F
grep -F "^NAME^" $filename >> $longreport
/usr/xpg4/bin/grep -F "^NAME^" $filename >> $longreport
```

*(continued on next page)*

*(continued from preceding page)*

```
echo "Extract all tasks from $filename " >> $longreport
grep "TASK:" $filename >> $longreport

echo "Extract all TOTALs from $filename " >> $longreport
grep "^TOTAL:" $filename >> $longreport

#__sun: change -w to -m. Send mail on completion.
#lp -w -d ${laser_printer} $longreport
lp -m -d ${laser_printer} $longreport

mv $longreport $LOG/${longreport}.old

exit
```

Go through each shell script and make the appropriate changes. As you can see from the preceding example, comments should be inserted to provide history and context.

## Integrate Databases

As with shell scripts, the application might also depend on third-party products for support. In the example, the only third-party products involved with the migration were related to the database technology, so you will be replacing a Sybase implementation with Oracle technology, as shown in the following figure.

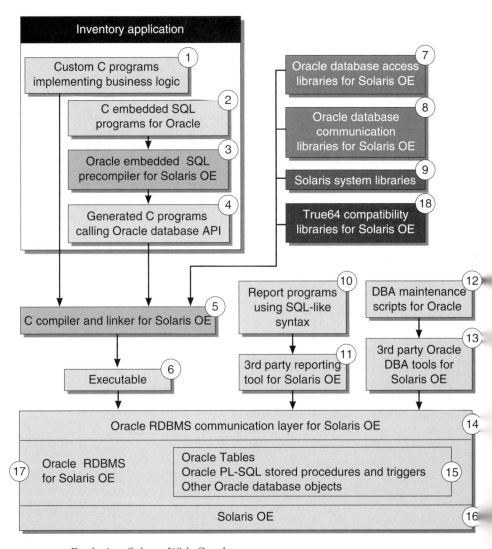

**FIGURE 10-2** Replacing Sybase With Oracle

This assessment indicated that you should address issues associated with the following components:

- Stored procedures and triggers (box 15).
- C programs that use embedded SQL (box 2).
- Report programs that use third-party reporting tools (box 11).
- DBA maintenance scripts (box 12).

As illustrated in the preceding figure, the replacement environment is almost a one-to-one mapping of component technology. When implementing the Oracle environment on the Sun platform, you must acquire and install the appropriate products with their respective licenses as follows:

- The database communication layer (box 14). This is supplied by the database vendor and is usually composed of database client and server libraries.

- The embedded SQL precompiler (box 3). This is supplied by the database vendor, in this case, Oracle.

- The C compiler and linker (box 5). This is usually supplied by the hardware vendor, in this case, Sun.

- The database engine (box 17). This is supplied by the database vendor, Oracle.

Other third-party products you should acquire and install include database reporting tools (box 11) and database management tools (box 13). Versions of these tools exist for the Solaris platform, reducing the amount of change that must be introduced. However, changes will most likely have to be made to the products if they issue SQL statements. These products might have to be rewritten altogether. Additional configuration of these products might also have to be introduced, reflecting different environment variables and path names.

Any API changes introduced in the database technology will have to be reflected in the source code of the applications. At this stage, you are only addressing issues with the database components of the application. The outcome of this stage of the process is new embedded SQL programs that will be compiled with the application source after it has been modified to conform to the new operating environment. These changes are described later in this chapter.

## Data Extraction, Transformation, and Loading (ETL)

After you install the supporting database environment, you can create the database objects to accept the data. You can then extract the data from the old Sybase system by using vendor-provided utilities. Finally, you can load the data into the Oracle database, using utilities that are provided by the vendor.

There are times when database vendor-provided tools can be used. This is usually the case when the database structure is simple and data types can be mapped one-to-one. In such cases, the bulk copy (bcp) utility from Sybase can be used to extract data from Sybase. The output of this command can be an ASCII delimited file. You can then feed this file to an Oracle utility called SQL*Loader.

For more complicated scenarios, the use of third-party extraction, transformation, and loading (ETL) tools such as Hummingbird's ETL or Embarcadero's DT/Studio might be appropriate. Of course, you can also write scripts to perform these tasks.

Although our example requires no data translation, data types that existed in the Sybase implementation that cannot be reproduced in the new Oracle implementation might require that the data be transformed or translated to conform the new data type. Depending on the data type in question and the extent to which it is used throughout the application, this simple change can create significant complexity when attempting to modify the application source code. All references to that data type might require change. In certain cases, depending on the change to the data type, the application logic might also have to change.

## Transforming Source Code

In the assessment process, you identified a number of APIs that were incompatible with the target Solaris environment. Rather than modifying the source code in-line to effect these changes, you should create a compatibility library to implement any changes that have to be implemented to rectify incompatibility issues. You can limit source code modifications to conditional compilation directives that are used to ensure backward compatibility.

The following example shows how to use conditional compilation to ensure backward compatibility.

```
#ifdef _sun
    SunVersion();
#else
    OriginalVersion();
#endif
}
```

The function `SunVersion()` that will emulate Tru64 functionality will exist in a compatibility library.

In the example, you create a compatibility library (box 18) that is linked in when th application executable (box 6) is created. You then modify the source code for the application (box 1) to conform to the application infrastructure and to use the functions provided by the compatibility library, using conditional compilation as discussed above.

# Managing the New Solaris Environment

The management tools and utilities used to monitor the environment should integrate with the existing management policies and procedures. Management processes like trouble ticket reporting should most likely remain independent of the new vendor platform. However, certain processes, such as change management, could be affected by the introduction of operational platforms that support dynamic reconfiguration or hot swapping.

Once the production environment is in place, you can install any tools or agents required to integrate the new environment with the existing management architecture.

In our example, BMC Patrol is installed and configured on the new platform.


# Delivering Training Requirements

System administrators must be able to manage the new environment. You identified areas in which training was required when you assessed the people and process of the IT organization. Enrolment in and delivery of training may be scheduled at any time during the migration effort, but should be structured to minimize the impact on existing IT operations. For example, all the operators cannot take training at the same time, because a certain number of them must provide operational support to the production environment.

In our example, no training was required because the operators were already supporting similar technologies. However, training may be required in areas such as these:

- Storage configuration
- Volume management
- Cluster operation
- Dynamic reconfiguration
- Resource management
- Database configuration and administration

# CHAPTER 11

# Migrating From the HP/UX Platform

The case study presented in this chapter draws on several cases in which Sun Professional Services migrated customers from HP/UX platforms to the Solaris Operating System (Solaris OS). The most significant of these projects involved the migration of one of the United Kingdom's (UK's) leading personal-line insurance companies. This customer was a typical UK-based health care insurance provider in that they primarily sold to corporate benefits managers, but dealt directly with claimants. This organization deployed a commercial-off-the-shelf (COTS) integrated-accounts solution, and enhanced it to support their risk-underwriting and claims-processing business functions. The primary goals of the project were as follows:

- To provide a hardware platform that supported business growth over the proposed lifetime of the platform
- To support the business functionality inherent within the COTS package
- To transition to the target production platform without losing time from the business day

Additionally, the customer was in the middle of a one-year transformation from a legacy application, driving renewals from the legacy system and renewing the customers in the system to be migrated. The customer decided to change the hardware platform to extend the life of the software investment decision. The migration solution we provided needed to be designed in the light of these business goals.

This chapter contains the following sections:

# Justifying the Migration

Before authorizing the project, the customer undertook a due diligence phase to ensure that the company's business goals could be achieved by moving their platforms from HP/UX to the Solaris OS. The engagement and justification tasks required for this migration project were undertaken collaboratively by the customer and Sun. This joint process enabled the discovery of the customer's key requirements and current state, as documented in the following sections.

# Business Background

In this case study, the organization's business strategies involved excellence around process, people, and business tools. The applications the organization used enabled it to run business operations and measure their efficiency and profitability.

The primary reasons for pursuing a migration effort involved meeting the system-capacity forecasts for new business and legacy replacement. The organization was moving customer data files from a legacy mainframe to its client-server environment, which created a demand for an additional disk. The IT department forecasted that they would run out of disk and CPU capacity, and hence the server environment needed to be upgraded. The Sun solution was selected for a number of reasons, including the requirement of the two systems and their associated storage for minimal floor space and the availability of vertical scalability strategies.

The organization expected Sun to migrate the applications and data from the incumbent HP systems to the new Sun servers. The transition needed to be seamless, with minimal impact on business operations, application development schedules, and the legacy migration schedule.

Enabling the legacy migrations became a key design constraint; the customer did not want to pay for a second migration infrastructure, and the benefits case required the retirement of the HP systems. The organization had already developed software and processes to move data from its mainframe to the client-server architecture, and they required the move from HP to the Solaris OS be undertaken as a deployment. The company had deployed the enhanced ledger package to meet the CEO's vision of employing good people, creating and enabling industry-leading processes, and supplying clients with the best technology. The COTS package had created an integrated risks, claims, and ledger solution and was in the process of taking on the current customer base a month at a time from disparate legacy mainframe systems. The target system had to be configured to act as the target for the legacy migration software. In addition, it had to seamlessly support a migration of the underwriting, claims administration, and finance department staff. (The insurance example presented earlier in this book illustrates how an insurance company can buy time for migrations by leveraging natural business-processing cycles.) The migration from the legacy mainframes utilized the annual cycle of insurance underwriting, but the migration from HP to the Solaris OS was unable to take advantage of this cycle; it was necessary to switch off the HP system as soon as possible.

# Technology Background

In this case study, the goal was to replace a number of HP/UX server systems with a lesser number of Solaris Operating Systems. The key services hosted by the HP systems were database services, print management services, and job management services. These services served the risk management, claims administration and reserving systems, and the accounting and ledger systems. In addition, the systems also acted as hosts for the database client programs that undertook journaling services and end-user reports. In accounting systems, much of the referential integrity between ledgers occurs overnight (or on another periodic basis).

The other driver for the migration effort that was contrary to "work load consolidation" in the source estate design was the need to support different management environments, including development, training, quality assurance, production, and management information instances of the organization's software solution.

The COTS package the customer used was GEAC's SmartStream, which was written as a two-task client-server package developed using Powersoft's PowerBuilder and Sybase Software's SQL Server. At the time of the case study, Sybase had completed its takeover of Powersoft and was the product author and vendor of PowerBuilder. GEAC SmartStream's natural architecture consisted of Wintel PC's hosting the client application and UNIX servers hosting the database.

At the customer organization, a PC file-sharing LAN was implemented. File servers were used to locate the client binaries, and user PCs acquired client runtime images with Microsoft's LAN networking protocols. The Sybase SQL servers were deployed on HP/UX servers that also acted as job hosts for the accounting overnight-batch programs. (These were GEAC-provided binaries.) One of the management environments, known as the Quality Assurance (QA) environment, acted as the interface between the legacy systems and the current system. Files with the next renewals were loaded into the QA environment database, transformed with Sybase-stored procedures, and then copied across to the production environment for renewal notice production. The customer also had a development environment for the bespoke risks and claims system, a training environment for training new and existing staff in new functionality, a production environment, and an MIS environment that held an image of the production database as at the close of the previous month. This last environment was used to run reports by the finance department and corporate management. These reports were of data warehousing or online analytical processing (OLAP) profiles, with large reads and small outputs. A separate instance was configured to reduce database contention between these users and business processing case workers. The following figure illustrates the client's application components model.

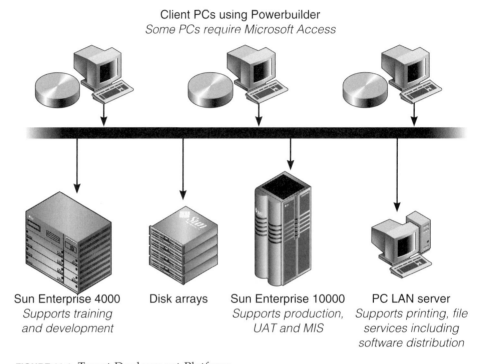

**FIGURE 11-1** Target Deployment Platform

The company ported its database and some of the application infrastructure to the Solaris OS as part of this process, to ensure a degree of confidence that a platform migration was possible within reasonable budgets and that the proposed Sun platform would meet business growth and performance expectations.

# Architecting the Migration Solution

The first task in the AIM methodology is to determine which of the key migration techniques should be applied to each of the source components. This determination requires a component model specific to the purpose of migration planning, that is, a component/technique map. The second output from such a component model is the definition of the scope of the migration. If a software component or function is not a member of the agreed-on component model, it is considered to be out of scope.

The key migration techniques used at the organization in our case study included a rehosting approach, supplemented by replacement and reverse engineering. The key rehosting techniques involved reusing GEAC and Sybase's platform independence and was supplemented with source code porting techniques or some of Sybase objects and HP/UX shell scripts. In this case, the component model included the database servers and their hosted business logic, print management, journaling services, and job management. The key technique driving the migration project was rehosting, using a new installation of a Solaris instance of the COTS package and the runtime software infrastructure. The reason for this is that the independent software vendors (ISVs) support their applications on multiple operating systems and basically support a common applications programming interface (API) for their products. These practices ensure that code or infrastructure changes are minimized.

The boundary of the migration problem is defined by exclusively analyzing components that are currently located on the platform to be retired. Any components located on other systems will communicate with the migrated componentry through the ISV's API. Some testing or research is required to validate that the ISVs have a common API across platforms, but this is a smaller task than attempting to migrate the calling components. The migration process can be focused on the customer's data and proprietary code base.

# Defining the Scope and Approach

The architectural study's two outcomes are a a definition of scope and a technique/component map. The definition of scope means that there are two sets of objects for which no technique will be applied: those determined to be out of scope and those to which a retirement/replacement technique is to be applied. The development of the technique/component map is iterative.

This section describes how to use an architectural approach to define the scope of the project. This approach involves the discovery of business constraints, the application of migration technique to identified components and strategies, and the identification of any external batch or real-time feeds. A version of the component/technique map is presented in TABLE 11-1 on page 216.

The following figure illustrates the scope of the project. Components within the shaded box are in scope for migration and an examination of the arrows crossing the shaded box show the communication protocols used by the migrated components to receive their input and output. Transactional Data Stream (TDS) is Sybase's client-server protocol, which encapsulates their implementation of SQL, Transact-SQL. These protocols are all stable UNIX-guaranteed or ISV-guaranteed protocols, reinforcing the decision to use rehosting as the strategy.

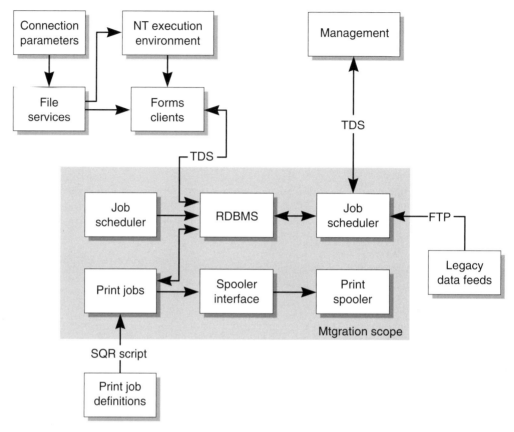

**FIGURE 11-2** Applications Component Model

# Creating a Transition Plan

The creation and design of the transition plan is a separate task within the migration project. It requires the application of project planning skills and might involve prototyping and the application of technical design skills.

## Discover Business Constraints

The migration team consulted with the business and IT departments to discover any business and operational constraints that existed. Fortunately, this was primarily a front-office system for a call center and it was required only during an extended working day. The overnight batch process typically took most of the night during the week, but data load prototyping showed that an overnight run and the copy process could be undertaken on a weekend without impacting business hours.

## Design a Plan

A key feature of the transition plan in this case study was to build in a regression path and a final user acceptance.

The basic plan was to close the source system at the close of business on Friday, copy the outstanding data from source to target, and then run the overnight batch on both systems. This meant that both systems should be at "start of day Monday" state. This would permit the two systems to be compared and either system to operate as the production host on Monday morning. The plan met the goals of testing for success and regression in case final testing exposed catastrophic failure conditions. It also provided a test that the business logic in the overnight batch run was identical on both systems. The inputs to both overnight runs would be designed to be identical, and if the outputs were not the same, the test would fail.

Additional features in the plan included check-pointing the process and inserting test points so that tasks between test points could be repeated should the intermediate tests fail or alternative remedial action be undertaken.

Prototyping both timings and the development of metadata discovery tools led to changes in the strategy/component map. This was reinforced when the downtime window was finally established. The change was to leverage the installation processes of GEAC and Sybase. This meant that metadata and configuration data were prepopulated and other, less-volatile, objects were also precopied. These included the table definitions, views, triggers, and procedures. The precopying of the procedures meant that the project team had to amend the development change control process to ensure that any changes to procedures already copied were applied to both source and target system.

This change of approach leveraged the principle of precopying to minimize the work to be undertaken on the weekend when the transition was to occur. In this case, we reached a point where only data table contents (and hence their indexes) were to be transferred on the transition weekend.

---

**Note** – Indexes are a key to page map and this must reflect the UNIX volume implementation and hence the RDBMSs intermediate structures. This generally mandates the rebuilding of indexes on the target system. Depending on the implementation details of the RDBMS, this can be done before or after the data copy transaction.

---

# Design Test Plans

The key benefit from leveraging both rehosting and reverse engineering is that runtime testing of the new environment is minimized. The underlying assumption that the ISV implementations have a common and stable API requires testing, and the testing process needs to be sufficiently broad to ensure that the assumption is considered safe. This means that testing the input interface for semantic meaning is not required. The basic purposes of testing in this case study were to prove the following:

- The copy process was comprehensive.
- The target system represented the business accurately (or at least as accurately as the source system).
- The required service improvement goals had been met.

A further way of reducing the testing required is to utilize prototyping as a technique. In this particular case, the less critical systems (in revenue-earning terms) were migrated before the production systems, and any bugs in the transition process were discovered and rectified. The copy completion checks were developed and improved during the prototyping process.

---

**Note –** The copy completion checks were based on checking that all rows of a subset of the tables were copied. Additionally, we ran the check sum script against the contents of certain columns.

---

Testing tools consisted of five sets of tests:

- Copy integrity—Precopy
- Copy integrity—Transition phase
- Semantic integrity
- Business acceptance
- Performance acceptance

The copy integrity suites both involved writing programs that read the source and target systems to compare them. These browsed the database catalog tables, and since the query language used was SQL, only one language was used. In addition, critical columns were check-summed. These columns were the critical item level financial columns. One error was discovered at this phase based on a bug in the application. This error was corrected in the production code lines, and a fix was applied to erroneous data. This illustrates a principle of fixing a problem at its root cause, rather than, as in this case, writing a data transformation and fixing the problem during migration.

Semantic integrity tests were limited in this case study. The key area they were applied to was the shell-script-based print management solution. The key question to be answered in this test suite is, does the code behave the same on both systems

We supplemented semantic tests by co-opting members of the business unit's training department and their training scripts to test the unchanged client layer against a Sun-hosted migrated environment. To conduct these tests, we undertook the first full-scale migration test on the training instance of the application.

The performance tests had been specified in the contract prenegotiations and pretests undertaken in Sun's Global Benchmarking center. These tests were repeated on site on an appropriately sized instance of the database before the migrated solution was placed into production.

## Specify the Business Acceptance Tests

The business acceptance tests were specified to meet the following goals:

- To prove the target system accurately represents the business
- To prove the target system meets the performance-based system improvement goals

The axiom of the project was no change in business logic, so the basic acceptance test was running the test chart of accounts, which was a report option within the package. The view taken was that if the target system represented the business accurately, then it was suitable. This view was based on one of the fundamental theories of software development: the primacy of design is in the data model and if the data model implementation is accurate, then the process implementations can change to support changes in process. This view had the advantage that the run times of the test were low and the verification time was also low. Using this test mandated constraints on the transition strategy.

It was decided jointly by the customer and the team that the best way to ensure that the system accurately represented the business was to run a test chart of accounts. To simplify the comparison between the two reports, we ran both of them at the same logical time. These activities leveraged the decision to ensure that both the source and target system were available, because they were at the start-of-day post transition.

Given that the business acceptance test involved running a program that relied on denormalized tables, a risk was identified that the acceptance test be sufficiently comprehensive to test the data migration, so additional instrumentation of the migration process was developed. As stated above, not only was a target container created that held all the non-business/transactional data instances (rows) so that the migration was constrained to business/volatile data only, test programs were also written to ensure that source and target container properties were identical. Test programs were written to ensure that all the contents of business data tables were copied accurately in terms of both number of entries and summing critical columns.

# Implementing the Migration to the Solaris Operating System

The next phase of a migration project involves implementation tasks. In this section, we examine the tasks involved with implementing an HP/UX solution to the Solaris OS.

## Applying Migration Techniques

Migration involves the movement of business logic (for example, code), business data, configuration data, and metadata from the source environment to the target environment.

In this case study, the various objects to be migrated were categorized and a strategy for moving them was developed. Because we were certain that the source system worked satisfactorily, the initial strategy was to copy all the objects from the source environment to the target environment. However, during prototyping, we discovered that the database volume map needed to be recreated and that it would be difficult to port certain configurations and metadata. Because it was going to be more difficult to adopt a "copy everything" strategy than we'd expected, we decided to use the installation scripts provided by GEAC and Sybase to create a container in which the remaining data and executables were installed.

The decision to implement a new disk map was made for the following reasons:

- The target system had a different disk architecture from that of the source system
- The source system disk map had only two virtual disks, which makes implementing database recovery difficult.

---

**Note** – Database recovery requires that database files, the write-ahead log, and the offline images of these objects be held on different disks. Databases with split journals and before-image logs (such as Oracle) might require an additional disk. Database recovery is designed to protect work against a lost disk, so the write-ahead log must be on a different disk from the database or it will be unavailable if the database disks become unavailable. Offline copies should be held on other disks so that they are available if the write-ahead log becomes unavailable.

---

The target system had significantly more disk volumes than were available on the source system. The disk map redesign also enabled a simplification of the database' internal object placement design.

Both Sun and the customer agreed that the rehosting strategy would be applied to GEAC, Sybase, and the Sybase Client reporting tool used. The data migration process would be a logical copy. It was not possible to undertake a physical copy of the source system; Sybase implements certain features of its system differently on the Solaris OS and HP/UX. The methods used to extract the data for the procurement due diligence were based on logical copy technology for this reason.

---

**Note –** Print-report logic and the output formats were defined in another third-party product, originally sold by Sybase, which remained available. The customer obtained a Solaris license for this product. This product and an ISV portability guarantee permitted the interface between the `Print Job Definitions` and `Print Jobs` commands to be defined as a third-party protocol and obviated the need to rewrite the report programs.

---

Solutions for the individual data item types needed to be developed.

The team undertook a volatility analysis of the data objects. The database schema definitions were very stable. The majority of the databases were part of the ISV package (SmartStream); therefore, the schemas were very stable, typically only changing when software updates were applied. At the other end of the spectrum, the online transaction processing (OLTP) data changed minute by minute. Between both ends of this spectrum were the customer proprietary schemas and user identity data.

Sybase data servers organize their catalog tables either in a configuration database called `master` or in the application's databases. `master` holds server wide data, whereas the application databases hold database-specific configuration data as subsets of the data. Each database has its own local catalog tables, including private lists of user objects such as tables, indexes, views, and users. Each database has its own write-ahead log and is therefore a unit of recovery. Identifying Sybase RDBMS metadata is relatively simple. However, GEAC originally architected its distributed-systems solution to hold significant amounts of metadata either in specific application databases that were solely responsible for holding this data or in tables within application databases that had business-functional purposes.

An audit of the available technology to copy data from the source to the target was undertaken. The procurement due diligence resulted in a suite of programs to extract critical business data and metadata from the customer's systems. On the general principal of trying to copy everything, we initially decided to extend the copy and upload scripts from the initial subset to all data objects. We planned to use Sybase's bulk copy program (`bcp`) to transfer the data (and certain other objects) and to use Sybase's `defncopy` utility program to migrate the triggers, views, and procedures. We decided to maximize the advantage of using the Sybase and GEAC capability of running on both the source and target system. A copy strategy also allowed the migration team to minimize their understanding of the GEAC schemas as if they were the same on both systems.

However, Sybase's instance-to-instance copy facilities were limited and needed to be augmented. Sybase had logical copy tools such as bcp or defncopy that could be used for tables or procedural objects. The database was the only larger object that could be made the argument of a copy program: the dump and load commands could be used on it. However, dump and load activities need certain common configuration parameters for the source and target servers. The default collating sequence for a Sybase server is different for HP/UX and Solaris. The team chose to implement the default on the target (Solaris) system for maintainability reasons, so the dump and load commands were not available. An object-by-object copy policy needed to be defined.

The customer had access to two schema extractors. These extractors were part of the two computer-aided software engineering (CASE) tools and could act as reverse engineering tools. Despite relying on the rehosting strategy, we realized that weaknesses in the environment's capability meant that the rehosting strategy had to be supplemented. Reverse engineering techniques and source code porting techniques were used to supplement the strategy.

We chose a schema extractor primarily due to the availability of certain skills and because of current licensing commitments (the customer had two CASE tools licensed and preferred one over the other).

The transfer strategies are summarized in the following table.

**TABLE 11-1**  Application of Migration Techniques to Objects

| Object Type | Transfer Tool | Transfer Technique |
|---|---|---|
| Executables | Reinstall | Rehost |
| Table definition | Schema extractor | Reverse engineer |
| Table data | Sybase BCP utility | Rehost |
| Index definition | Schema extractor | Reverse engineer |
| syslogin table data | Sybase BCP utility | Rehost |
| sysusers table data | Schema extractor | Reverse engineer |
| User datatypes, rules and defaults | Schema extractor, supplemented with bespoke DDL | Reverse engineer, supplemented with source code port |
| Views | Sybase defncopy utility | Rehost |
| Procedures | Sybase defncopy utility, GEAC source files or bespoke DDL files | Rehost, supplemented with source code port |
| Permissions | Schema extractor | Reverse engineer |

Although table definitions and contents are two separate objects in the component map, an index definition contains a description in SQL that is defined in text and held in a catalog table. In the case of Sybase, the index definition possesses either a clustered structure or a B-Tree structure. The definition can be run at any time, but running it involves building the index contents, which, in the case of a clustered index, involves sorting the table. For this reason, a `create index` statement can have significant runtime implications, but it obviates the need to copy index contents.

The disk map redesign made obvious the need to copy the `sysdevices` table that maps the RDBMS's name for a disk volume to the OS name. It also revealed the need to port any named segments. The role of a segment is to provide a location name to which a table or index can be bound. This allows DBAs to manage the location of objects, permitting, for example, a B-Tree index or a log object to be located on specific disks different from their bound table or database. The creation of the `sysdevices` table and the minimum necessary segments was undertaken when the RDBMS and their component databases were installed.

The stored procedures were copied by one of two methods. Procedures that were also implemented as text objects in the catalog tables were copied with `defncopy`. In cases in which there were unresolved external references, the original source code files for the data definition language (DDL) were inspected and rerun unchanged or were massaged. The original author was either the COTS vendor or the customer.

The print management solution was the outstanding piece of code that had yet to be ported. The print queues were reallocated to the file servers, but the print management component had been implemented in UNIX shell script. There was a very limited amount of this code, and rather than install Sun's standard tools and test harnesses, we ported the code manually by inspection and iterative testing. This means that the replacement strategy was applied to the queue management function, and that a source code porting technique was applied to the runtime management functions.

TABLE 11-1 on page 216 shows how the basic strategy of utilizing the COTS vendor's guarantee of platform independence and a consistent API across platforms was supplemented. The initial strategy of copying everything was amended for the following reasons:

- Manifest quality improvement was achieved by a redesign of the disk map.
- The cost of isolating the physical changes that were required and applying separate strategies was too high.
- The time required to transition with this strategy demonstrated a need for a more incremental approach.

Let us consider further the ease of undertaking the creation of a component/ technique map. In the real circumstances of the case study, the axiomatic properties of an RDBMS ease the mapping of object instance to object classes. The descoping of all the client logic also eased the migration task significantly. In many cases, allocating an object to a class of data is not easy. This problem is eased by the facts that a technique can be reused and that object types can have multiple techniques applied to them, as illustrated TABLE 11-1 on page 216. With RDBMS systems, it can be very difficult to define which objects sit in which category. Note that it should be easier for database objects than where significant amount of 3GL code exists, because the types of objects available within 3GLs are far more restricted, and active dictionaries in which metadata are held are less frequently implemented. In the RDBMS case above, the metadata and many runtime objects are held in the data dictionary, alternatively called the database catalog. 3GL systems more frequently build and integrate their metadata within the executables. In this case study, one of the executable database objects was the Sybase stored procedures, which were easy to isolate, although some required significant massage to port because they had unresolved external references. If the stored procedure used a temporary object, which means one that is created and destroyed by the procedure itself, despite the fact that the creation commands exist within the stored procedure, unless the object exists at the time the CREATE PROCEDURE command is issued, the CREATE PROCEDURE command will fail.

An example of a tightly integrated business logic and execution logic is described in the following paragraph. For instance, Cobol 88-level definitions are business logic objects, and are embedded into an executable, or at least into the source code lines.

```
77  BOOL-TEST-1                          PIC(X) VALUE 0.
88      TEST-1-TRUE REDEFINES BOOL-TEST-1   VALUE 1.
88      TEST-1-FALSE REDEFINES BOOL-TEST-1  VALUE 0.

    IF < complex condition true>
        MOVE 1 TO BOOL-TEST-1.
    IF < complex condition false >
        MOVE 0 TO BOOL-TEST-1.

    IF TEST-1-TRUE
        PERFORM TRUE-CONDITIONS
    ELSE
        PERFORM FALSE-CONDITIONS.
```

In this example, data division entries state that a binary test condition exists, for example, it can be true or false, and that the variable acts as a flag. The next two procedural statements evaluate the condition and encapsulate a business rule; the final statement executes the business transaction logic. To simplify the example, we've used the PERFORM statement to invoke a section that undertakes this work. The business rules, business logic, and business data types are all distributed throughout the source code lines. Extracting these three object classes as individual items from a source code file is hard. There are no clear rules for distinguishing among these object classes, and identifying the elements is equally difficult. Fortunately, the richer data types available in an RDBMS solution allow application designers to isolate business rules and transaction logic from implementation detail.

This case study shows how iteration and prototyping were applied to various objects, object types, and classes. For example, an index can contain both business logic (a uniqueness constraint) and implementation factors such as a fill factor. The value of or the necessity for iteration and prototyping might depend on physical design and implementation details of the RDBMS. Other examples of implementation details that are encapsulated in the index include the location where the index was built and the sort order of a clustered index.

In the case study documented here, the RDBMS was implemented with a cost-based query parser and predated the implementation of query hints. For this reason, the index is used as an example, but where rule-based analyzers are implemented, performance-critical transactions need to be tested to ensure that the query plan resolution remains optimal. Query plans are usually calculated at runtime, so prototyping and preimplementation testing might be required because rule-based optimizers can require code changes to permit the analyzer to choose the optimal query plan. This is particularly important when RDBMS version upgrades are undertaken.

TABLE 11-1 on page 216 shows the application of migration strategies and techniques to specific database and execution objects. These strategies and techniques were developed during the architecture stage and were refined during the implementation phase while software to implement the migration was developed.

With an RDBMS, business logic can be held in database objects (such as views, indexes, constraints, triggers, and procedures) or in client-side objects. The definition of scope is critical in defining the techniques used to migrate business logic. As described above, business-object logic can be in scope or out of scope. The scope status of business logic can depend on several factors. The business logic can be redundant, as is the case when the retirement/replacement technique is used. It can be encapsulated in part of the environment that exists in both the source and target environments. In the case of this study, client-side PowerBuilder procedures were executed in both the source and target environments; therefore, they remained out of scope. For this reason, these business-logic entities remained the same in both source and target environments. Given the techniques applied to the migration, the business and presentation logic encapsulated in these procedures and objects was defined as out of scope.

The Print Job component was defined as being within the scope of the project because print queue management had been undertaken by the HP/UX jobs. Actual queue management was moved into the LAN, and the organization's LAN servers were configured to hold the print queues. If the job were undertaken today, it is likely that the printers would manage their own queues, depending on the output management requirements such as restarting and reprinting. Scheduling print jobs against the databases was managed by a series of shell scripts that ran the third-party report generators. The report logic was held in ASCII files holding SQL script definitions that were invoked by the shell scripts. The following example illustrates shell syntax that allows the script to run on either an HP/UX system or Solaris system, and thus supports backward compatibility. Furthermore, it has the advantage of indirectly referencing the UNIX utility in the example (for example, cpio). In this case study, indirection was implemented but backward compatibility was not.

```
#!/bin/ksh
OS=`uname | ${cutpath}/cut -f3 -d' '`
case $OS in
HPUX)     OS_PATH_LIST=${HPUX_PATH_LIST};;
SunOS)    OS_PATH_LIST=${SOLARIS_PATH_LIST};;
*)        exit 1;;
esac
#Original Line
#PATH=${HPUX_PATH_LIST}
PATH=${OS_PATH_LIST}
CPIO=`whence cpio`
.
.
.
$CPIO ${CPIO_FLAGS}
```

*Metadata* is data that describes data. In the case study, this was absolutely critical because the key migration object was an RDBMS that possesses an active data dictionary. Three strategies were applied to the metadata:

- Utilizing the installation processes provided by the COTS and DBMS vendors
- Copying metadata objects from the source environment to the target environment with tools based on the appropriate migration technique
- Applying reverse engineering techniques

Financial considerations were the primary influence over the decision of which strategy to apply. There are several factors in calculating strategy costs. These include the following:

- The cost of identifying objects. In the case study, a number of objects could not be identified and the installation processes were utilized.
- The cost of applying the strategies. SQL-BackTrack was rejected because of cost.
- The runtime cost implications of the strategy.

Not all metadata is held in obvious metadata objects. In the case of the COTS product under consideration, metadata was held in the RDBMS catalog tables, user tables defined by the COTS vendor, and index definitions. One additional piece of metadata included the representation of the system namespace within objects that are available to the application. GEAC SmartStream used multiple databases within a database server and used Sybase remote procedure calls to implement inter-database transactions. This permitted the deployment of a SmartStream implementation across any number of server instances. One of the advantages of this implementation feature is that different application components can be deployed in separate servers on separate hosts. The development of blade technology gives this architecture a new lease on life. This technology requires each server and stored procedure to know about the location of the database within a server. Sybase implements a name service based on flat files, mapping a server name to a TCP/IP address/port location. In addition, when a remote-stored procedure semantic is implemented, this name service must be placed within a security model implemented in the catalog tables. In the case study, most of the COTS metadata was applied to the target the installation scripts were run.

The examination of security data in the context of application name services brought us to security data itself. Within Sybase, both authentication and privilege management functionality is implemented. Privilege management is part of the SQL standard. The permissions row in TABLE 11-1 on page 216 represents the implementation of each object's execution, read, insert, update, delete, create, and destroy privileges. The mapping of a user's identity to a privilege set is a business issue based on roles within the business. At this customer site, the authentication data was treated as data, not as metadata; therefore, it was copied across. This is represented by the `syslogins` row in TABLE 11-1 on page 216. Sybase also implements an alias for each login within each database, and at the time, it presented the team with a referential integrity issue between the database user alias and login. The aliases were migrated with reverse engineering techniques, with manual inspection and adjustment as the remediation techniques used when reverse engineering failed.

## Namespace Migration

In the case study, there are three namespace problems as follows:

- Database object namespace. Objects within the data servers (except `databases`). This includes a need to migrate or transition the server names and address maps
- Applications component namespace.
- System component namespace.

Different techniques were used to manage the namespace implementations to the target environments.

We utilize the application's installation procedures to preserve the database server's internal namespace. This meant that the proprietary extensions to GEAC SmartStream deployed by the customer also needed to be ported and the object namespace preserved. The mechanism used to preserve the object namespace is documented below. It utilized the file system by writing the object definitions to files with the object name in the file system name.

The target data servers were given new names. This was required because the servers had separate TCP/IP addresses and both needed to be on the network at the same time. This policy conformed to the strategies adopted and aided transition because the customer had a good server name management-distribution policy. The server name and address file, `${SYBASE}/interfaces`, was held on a file server and read by each of the user client's systems. This system also allowed the default data server to be configured by the LAN administrator.

The application's component namespace was managed as defined by GEAC, and existing documentation explained how to transition the namespace from HP/UX to the Solaris OS. This transition involved manually updating rows in three tables. The customer had previously moved systems and had scripts we could use to update the system names. Only one of the rows involved specifying the target OS. The system namespace was implemented in `bind`.

## Data Migration

The use of the supplementary techniques is mainly constrained to nondata objects. In the case study, data was defined as only the content of database tables that contained business data. Previous sections discussed the techniques used to identify metadata, configuration data, and security data; what's left is the business data. We had two choices for copying the data:

- Logical copies
- Physical copies

The need to apply data transformation to the source data is one of the primary influences on the decision of what technique to use for copying data. In this case study, copying data from the legacy mainframe required the application of transformation techniques. With one exception, moving the business data from the source environment to the target environment did not require transformational work. This means that a logical copy was simple and that a physical copy was possible. At this site, a physical copy was not possible because of implementation differences in the RDBMS on HP/UX and Solaris systems. Therefore, a logical copy was the only option. In the case of Sybase, this suggests the `bcp` program; in the case of Oracle, it would imply the use of the `export` and `import` commands.

In all cases, object namespace preservation and mapping is required. This means that because we were using different techniques in the case of Sybase to copy the table definitions and table contents, the planners needed to map the target DDL file, table name, and table contents file. (This would not be the case with Oracle's import/ export, but would be if SQL/ODL were used.) This issue was resolved by use of the UNIX file system to preserve the table namespace between systems, as shown here.

```
mkdir ${database_name}; cd ${database_name}
for table_name in ${table_name_list}
do
    mkdir ${table_name};cd ${table_name}
    extract_ddl ${table_name}> ${table_name}.ddl
    bcp ${bcp_flags} out ${table_name} \
    > ${table_name}.data
done
```

In this case, extract_ddl is a script or function that performs the table DDL extraction so that ${table_name}.ddl contains the table DDL code. The queried object might be the database, or it might be a flat file that contains the complete RDBMS-instance DDL, prepared by the selected schema extractor. The following example code can also be used to preserve objects transferred by defncopy.

```
mkdir ${database_name}; cd ${database_name}
mkdir views ;cd views
for view_name in ${view_name_list}
do
    defncopy ${defncopy_flags} ${view_name} \
    > ${view_name}.ddl
done
```

In both cases, input scripts can be driven by parsing the directories for *.ddl files.

In the case study site, migration harnesses were built to parse the database catalogs to extract the ddl and data files, and the input scripts parsed the UNIX file system to drive the database inputs. The input scripts also used symmetrization techniques to leverage the power of the SMP platforms proposed for the target implementation. Each job stream uploaded a quarter of the database bound to a single CPU, and the jobs ran concurrently.

## Specify the Implementation Platform

The procurement due diligence exercise led Sun and the customer to specify the hardware platforms. It was proposed that a system with three domains would support the production, QA, and MIS environments, and a second system would support development and training and act as a business continuity system if the production machine became unavailable. This meant that the customer wanted both a physical consolidation and workload sharing consolidation benefits. These decisions allowed the customer to recover significant floor space through the consolidation of three environments onto a single system. The shared solution also delivered significant floorspace savings.

One of the aims of this project was to reduce the number of system hosts at the customer site. The current estate consisted of five HP/UX systems, and the goal was to reduce this number to two Sun systems. However, because the number of management environments was five, separate instances of the OS were required to allow differing and separate management policies to be implemented and enforced. At the time, an instance of the OS could have only one security model and the business necessity of ring fencing nonoperational users from production systems was, and still is, almost universal. The target platform design established during the customer's due diligence phase consisted of two Sun servers, with only one being capable of hosting multiple OS instances. Both systems were SMP systems, and the smaller was designated to become the development and training system host. This involved the implementation of two application instances within a single instance of the Solaris OS and used an aggregation design pattern. The remaining instances of the application (production, QA, and MIS) were planned to be hosted within a domain in a multidomain system.

## Specify the OE Tune State

We initiated a requirements-capture exercise. This exercise primarily involved collecting the constraints that the superstructure products such as the RDBMS placed on the /etc/system file tunables. The following were the two key tunables for the RDBMS:

- **SHMMAX.** Maximum size of a contiguous shared memory segment. With the versions of Sybase proposed, a limit of 2 gigabytes was the maximum. More recent and current versions support Very Large Memory addressing, so a more appropriate setting is to set SHMMAX to high values.

  If explicit values are set for SHMMAX, the system will require rebooting if the database administrator decides to increase the database buffer cache beyond the SHMMAX limit. Restarting the database server process will cause a service outage to their users. In a shared infrastructure solution, rebooting a system is undesirable because other customers might take a service outage for no benefit.

- **ISM.** The Solaris default is intimate shared memory on which is the advantageou performance configuration. This configuration option had implications for defining the swap partition size.

Prototyping during the test loads of the development and training instances was undertaken to see if the available processor-management tools were necessary or desirable to manage service level provisioning for the multiple communities proposed to use the shared second system. These management tools allowed the system administrator to provide rules to the dispatcher. It was discovered that the Solaris affinity algorithms did not need the help of the process management tools, and the final production configuration for this system did not use them.

## Build a Migration Harness

The copy programs were encapsulated into a harness so that the migration team could undertake relevant jobs of work. These included "extract an instance," "load an index," and "rebuild indexes." These were supplemented by jobs to copy various objects that were planned to be precopied. These latter programs could take an instance, database, or object as argument so that they could be copied incrementally. They were all driven by lists that were created by the developer team or developed by browsing the database catalogs. By creating programs to undertake this work, not only was human productivity enhanced but the programs could be tested and trusted. This minimized the requirement for testing the processes activity; if the jobs reported success, then the prior testing of the programs enhanced the confidence that the job had been performed accurately. It made the process testable.

The transition process was principally tested by migrating the training and QA instances before the production instance of the application. This permitted both real timings for the data extraction and target index builds to occur. It also meant that the user training began on the target Solaris system several weeks before the migrated solution was to be placed into production. This allowed the training team, as well as the trainees, to comprehensively test the migrated application. This was advantageous because it ensured that trainees were introduced to every aspect of the system, and it had the added benefit of thoroughly testing the client-server interfaces.

## Utilize Management Environments to Enhance Testing

The transition plan for this project included testing plans for testing outputs and regression testing. The migration process was pretested, and checkpoint tests were inserted. In addition, checkpoints were designed into the plan to use backup solutions.

The migration team utilized nonproduction environments as part of the enterprise transition plan. The training and QA environments were ported in advance of the production instance, which improved the confidence the team had in the transition harness and the application of basic strategies. The migration of the training department allowed enhanced, comprehensive testing of the client APIs. The migration of the QA instance delivered confidence that the production performance tests would be achieved.

The development and MIS environments were ported after the production transition. The development environment was created by copying the training the environment and then applying the developers' subsequent changes to the new development environment. This is a process that the customer had frequently undertaken and was satisfied with.

The MIS environment was created with the production mechanism, which was to use Sybase's block-level online dump and load. This gave us the advantage of testing that this process/program worked in the new environment. (The technology had been tested before the production transition).

# Managing the New Solaris Environment

The methodology chapter discusses, in detail, the process for the design of a management solution. The case study described in this chapter was a project that was identified to end when the final user acceptance test was successfully completed. Both backup and job management tasks are discussed in this section of the case study, but the key work performed by the migration team was the design and implementation of the solution.

Operations management remained the responsibility of the customer's computer operations department. One of the reasons for this was that while the HP/UX systems were to be retired, the PC LAN and legacy mainframe remained part of the production environment. Therefore, the management problem was a heterogeneous one.

The two key management requirements were to provide off-line recovery capability and to allow business superusers to start and manage application jobs. Both of these functional areas were subjected to a business requirements capture, design, and test life cycle before handover.

## Backup

The move to the Solaris OS gave the customer the opportunity to take advantage of the predecessor product, Sun StorEdge™ Enterprise NetBackup. The source system was also bundled with a backup solution, and the Sun team captured the policies for occurrence, strategy, and tape maintenance and reimplemented them in the new technology. This involved implementing the "No worse than before" strategy. One of the solution-design constraints was the customer's tape pool size policy. The company also dumped the production database directly to tape, using Sybase's online backup utility.

The change in technology mandated a change in the backup technology. Fact-finding was undertaken, user policy constraints discovered, and a suitable backup solution implemented. This involved configuring a small robotic tape device on the production domain of the multidomain system and the second system. Network backups were used for the QA domain. Note that the MIS environment was not backed up because it changed only once a month.

## Job Management

The key problem introduced by the proposed platform architecture was related to job management. The COTS solution had an integrated job manager for which certain jobs (for example, accounts journaling jobs) had to be organized. System tasks could be organized by traditional Solaris/UNIX solutions, but application-related tasks had to be organized by the application's encapsulated job manager. In addition, a solution to the consolidation/workload sharing design had to be found.

Another problem was that the software had not been designed to run in a work-sharing environment. It was network aware—for example, it used TCP/IP for its interprocess communication—but two instances of the job scheduler could not be distinguished in the UNIX process table. System managers could not distinguish between the development and training instances of the job management daemon when using the UNIX utilities. While these daemons were correctly manipulated by an applications component running on remote PC systems, the system's managers felt uneasy about this new feature. A feature in the software was discovered that permitted this problem to be overcome.

# Results

The migration was successfully undertaken. Sun used the Sun Tone Architecture Methodology for Migration to move the customer's business-critical financial and insurance applications from HP/UX to the Solaris OS using a rehosting strategy supplemented by reverse engineering, source code porting, and retirement/replacement techniques. This was undertaken within an acceptable system down-time window with zero business downtime.

The project life cycle articulated in Sun's AIM methodology was a key enabler to the success of the project. The case studies presented in this book show how the application of methodology makes migration projects simpler and less risky.

# Sample JScore Report and Analysis

The sample JScore report and analysis presented in this appendix is referenced in Chapter 7.

**Note** – This sample has been formatted for the printed page. It would appear slightly different when viewed in a web browser.

# Solaris(TM) OE Analyzer for C/C++ and Cobol Source Code Migration Analysis Results

## Table of Contents

## How To Read This Report

This report is created by the "Solaris(TM) OE Analyzer for C/C++ and Cobol Source Code"after analyzing your source file(s).

The report includes an Analysis Summary which displays your input and options to the tool.

The APIs Encountered section lists the APIs which may pose some issues when porting your C/C++/Cobol source file(s) from other operating environments to the Solaris(TM) OE. The weight information was created to give a sense of how much work it takes to port the issue, thus helping in the estimates. It does not translate directly to any time value, and its value and significance is constantly changing from project to project.

The next section is the Detailed Analysis. It documents in which file and on what line the porting issue was found. The "COMMENT" portion gives a more detailed explanation as to why this particular issue may pose a problem. The comment also gives the recommended solutions. If there is no solution, it simply says that the user may have to write his/her own wrapper for that particular issue.

*Back to Top*

## Analysis Summary

| | |
|---|---|
| **Analysis Date:** | 07-07-2003 09:59:58 PDT |
| **Input :** | C:\Documents and Settings\Administrator\My Documents\My Downloads\zzftp |
| - Number of Sub Directories | 5 |
| - Number of C Files | 11 |

| Analysis Date: | 07-07-2003 09:59:58 PDT |
|---|---|
| - Number of C++ Files | 0 |
| - Number of COBOL Files | 0 |
| **Analysis Options :** | |
| - Use Database for Analysis | Yes |
| - Platform Options | Linux |
| - Show all functions NOT in database | No |
| - Show all functions NOT checking for issue | No |

*Back to Top*

## APIs Encountered

| No. | API Name | Level of Difficulty | Occurrences |
|---|---|---|---|
| 1 | recvfrom | Easy | 2 |
| 2 | connect | Easy | 6 |
| 3 | gettimeofday | Easy | 8 |
| 4 | strftime | Easy | 1 |
| 5 | syslog | Easy | 1 |
| 6 | argz_create_sep | Hard | 1 |
| 7 | getopt_long | Easy | 2 |
| 8 | sendto | Easy | 5 |
| 9 | getsockname | Easy | 4 |
| 10 | setsockopt | Easy | 2 |
| 11 | fsync | Easy | 3 |
| 12 | open | Easy | 1 |
| 13 | openlog | Easy | 2 |
| 14 | select | Medium | 4 |
| 15 | argz_next | Hard | 6 |
| 16 | fstat | Easy | 2 |
| 17 | hosts_ctl | Hard | 1 |
| 18 | argz_count | Hard | 1 |
| 19 | bind | Easy | 5 |
| 20 | argz_extract | Hard | 1 |
| | Your Average Level of Porting Difficulty Is : | Easy | |

*Back to Top*

## Detailed Analysis

Back To APIs Encountered Table

**1) recvfrom**

Appears in C:\Documents and Settings\Administrator\My Documents\My Downloads\zzftp\zzftp-0.6.2ftp_io.c on line number(s) :

237
241

COMMENT :

recvfrom ( 2.0 ) - receive a message from a socket

int recvfrom ( int s , void * buf , int len , unsigned int flags struct sockaddr * from , int * fromlen ) ;

These are the error conditions that may be returned under Solaris 8.0 but not Linux LSB

ECONNRESET A connection was forcibly closed by a peer.

ETIMEDOUT The connection timed out during connection establishment , or due to a transmission timeout on active connection.

EOPNOTSUPP The specified flags are not supported for this socket type.

ETIMEDOUT The connection timed out during connection establishment , or due to a transmission timeout on active connection.

EIO An I/O error occurred while reading from or writing to the file system.

ENOBUFS Insufficient resources available in the system to perform the operation.

ENOMEM Insufficient memory was available to fulfill the request.

*Back To APIs Encountered Table*

**2) connect**

Appears in C:\Documents and Settings\Administrator\My Documents\My Downloads\zzftp\zzftp-0.6.2ftpd.c on line number(s) :

429

Appears in C:\Documents and Settings\Administrator\My Documents\My Downloads\zzftp\zzftp-0.6.2ftp_file.c on line number(s) :

101
201
216
494

Appears in C:\Documents and Settings\Administrator\My Documents\My Downloads\zzftp\zzftp-0.6.2ftpd_file.c on line number(s) :

514

COMMENT :

connect ( 2.0 ) - initiate a connection on a socket

int connect ( int socket , const struct sockaddr * address , size_t address_len ) ;

These are error conditions that may be returned under Solaris 8.0 but not Linux LSB

EADDRNOTAVAIL The specified address is not available on the remote machine.

EINVAL The connection attempt was interrupted before any data arrived by the delivery of a signal.

EAFNOSUPPORT Addresses in the specified address family cannot be used with this socket.

EALREADY The socket is non-blocking and a previous connection attempt has not yet been completed.

EINTR The connection attempt was interrupted before any data arrived by the delivery of a signal.

ENOSR There were insufficient STREAMS resources available to complete the operation.

EPROTOTYPE The file referred to by name is a socket of a type other than type s ( for example , s is a SOCK_DGRAM socket , while name refers to a SOCK_STREAM socket ) 0.0

In addition , a different type " is used to define the third parameter on Solaris 8.0

*Back To APIs Encountered Table*

### 3) gettimeofday

Appears in C:\Documents and Settings\Administrator\My Documents\My Downloads\zzftp\zzftp-0.6.2ftp.c on line number(s) :

541
543
620
622

Appears in C:\Documents and Settings\Administrator\My Documents\My Downloads\zzftp\zzftp-0.6.2ats.c on line number(s) :

41
49
112
127

COMMENT :

There is parameter difference
On Linux LSB
int gettimeofday ( struct timeval * TP , struct timezone * TZP )

On Solaris 8.0
int gettimeofday ( struct timeval * tp , void * ) ;

The second argument to gettimeofday ( ) and settimeofday ( ) should be a pointer to NULL.

*Back To APIs Encountered Table*

**4) strftime**

Appears in C:\Documents and Settings\Administrator\My Documents\My Downloads\zzftp\zzftp-0.6.2logger.c on line number(s) :

99

COMMENT :

Some of the flags used are GNU extensions and are not available on Solaris 8.0 For example The following flags are all GNU extensions. The first three affect only the output of numbers

' _ '
' _ '
' 0.0 '
padding with spaces.

' ^ '

possible ( * note Case Conversion ) 0.0

For detail of these flags , see Linux document " 0.0

On Solaris 8.0 , write your own implementation.

*Back To APIs Encountered Table*

**5) syslog**

Appears in C:\Documents and Settings\Administrator\My Documents\My Downloads\zzftp\zzftp-0.6.2logger.c on line number(s) :

113

COMMENT :

syslog - send messages to the system

There are differences in the options and facility which are available on Linux LSB but not on Solaris 8.0
For options
LOG_PERROR is available on Linux LSB
For facility
LOG_AUTHPRIV - security/authorization messages ( private )
LOG_SYSLOG - messages generated internally by syslogd

*Back To APIs Encountered Table*

### 6) argz_create_sep

Appears in C:\Documents and Settings\Administrator\My Documents\My Downloads\zzftp\zzftp-0.6.2ftp.c on line number(s) :

312

COMMENT :

error_t argz_create_sep ( const char * STRING , int SEP , char
* * ARGZ , size_t * ARGZ_LEN )
The ' argz_create_sep '
STRING into an argz vector ( returned in ARGZ and ARGZ_LEN ) by splitting it into elements at every occurrence of the character SEP.

This function is not available on Solaris 8.0 , write your own implementation.

*Back To APIs Encountered Table*

### 7) getopt_long

Appears in C:\Documents and Settings\Administrator\My Documents\My Downloads\zzftp\zzftp-0.6.2ftpd.c on line number(s) :

573

Appears in C:\Documents and Settings\Administrator\My Documents\My Downloads\zzftp\zzftp-0.6.2ftp.c on line number(s) :

815

COMMENT :

int getopt_long ( int ARGC , char * const * ARGV , const char
* SHORTOPTS , struct option * LONGOPTS , int * INDEXPTR )
Decode options from the vector ARGV ( whose length is ARGC ) 0.0 The argument SHORTOPTS describes the short options to accept , just as it does in ' getopt '
options to accept ( see above ) 0.0

This function is not available on Solaris 8.0 , write your own implementation.

*Back To APIs Encountered Table*

## 8) sendto

Appears in C:\Documents and Settings\Administrator\My Documents\My Downloads\zzftp\zzftp-0.6.2ftp_io.c on line number(s) :

79
100
140
170
192

COMMENT :

sendto ( 2.0 ) - send a message from a socket

On Linux LSB
int sendto ( int s , const void * msg , int len , unsigned int flags , const struct sockaddr * to , int tolen ) ;

Solaris 8.0 had different return type
#include <sys/socket.h>
ssize_t sendto ( int socket , const void * message , size_t length , int flags , const struct sockaddr * dest_addr , size_t dest_len ) ;

Solaris 8.0 may not have the following error conditions as they exist in Linux LSB

ENOTSOCK The argument s is not a socket.

EFAULT An invalid user space address was specified for a parameter.

EWOULDBLOCK The socket is marked non-blocking and the requested operation would block.

*Back To APIs Encountered Table*

## 9) getsockname

Appears in C:\Documents and Settings\Administrator\My Documents\My Downloads\zzftp\zzftp-0.6.2ftpd.c on line number(s) :

425
428

Appears in C:\Documents and Settings\Administrator\My Documents\My Downloads\zzftp\zzftp-0.6.2ftp.c on line number(s) :

538
617

COMMENT :

getsockname ( 2.0 ) - get socket name

int getsockname ( int s , struct sockaddr * name , int * namelen )

These are the error conditions that may be returned under Solaris 8.0 but not Linux LSB

ENOMEM There was insufficient memory available for the operation to complete.

ENOSR There were insufficient STREAMS resources available for the operation to complete.

*Back To APIs Encountered Table*

**10) setsockopt**

Appears in C:\Documents and Settings\Administrator\My Documents\My Downloads\zzftp\zzftp-0.6.2ftp_file.c on line number(s) :

361

Appears in C:\Documents and Settings\Administrator\My Documents\My Downloads\zzftp\zzftp-0.6.2ftpd_file.c on line number(s) :

503

COMMENT :
setsockopt ( 2.0 ) - get and set options on sockets

#include <sys/socket.h>

int setsockopt ( int socket , int level , int option_name , const void * option_value , size_t option_len ) ;

On Solaris 8.0 , it does not define SO_DONTROUTE , SO_SNDLOWAT , SO_RCVLOWAT , SO_SNDTIMEO , SO_RCVTIMEO , SO_TYPE , SO_ERROR , EFAULT

*Back To APIs Encountered Table*

**11) fsync**

Appears in C:\Documents and Settings\Administrator\My Documents\My Downloads\zzftp\zzftp-0.6.2ftpd.c on line number(s) :

486

Appears in C:‡ocuments and Settings\Administrator\My Documents\My Downloads\zzftp\zzftp-0.6.2ftp.c on line number(s) :

546
625

COMMENT :

fsync ( 2.0 ) - synchronize a file '

int fsync ( int fd ) ;

These are the error conditions that may be returned under Solaris 8.0 but not Linux LSB EINTR A signal was caught during execution of the fsync ( ) function.

ENOSPC There was no free space remaining on the device containing the file.

ETIMEDOUT Remote connection timed out. This occurs when the file is on an NFS file system mounted with the soft option. See mount_nfs ( 1.0 M ) 0.0

*Back To APIs Encountered Table*

**12) open**

Appears in C:\Documents and Settings\Administrator\My Documents\My Downloads\zzftp\zzftp-0.6.2logger.c on line number(s) :

68

COMMENT :

open ( 2.0 ) - open and possibly create a file or device

Different parameters found in Linux LSB and Solaris 8.0

Linux LSB

int open ( const char * pathname , int flags ) ;
int open ( const char * pathname , int flags , mode_t mode ) ;

Solaris 8.0

int open ( const char * path , int oflag ,
/ * mode_t mode * / 0.0 0.0 0.0 ) ;

These are the error conditions that may be returned under Solaris 8.0 but not Linux LSB

EDQUOT The file does not exist , O_CREAT is specified , and either the directory where the new file entry is being placed cannot be extended

because the user ' that file system has been exhausted , or the user ' where the file is being created has been exhausted.

EINTR A signal was caught during open ( ) 0.0

EIO The path argument names a STREAMS file and a hangup or error occurred during the open ( ) 0.0

EMULTIHOP Components of path require hopping to multiple remote machines and the file system does not allow it.

ENOSR The path argument names a STREAMS-based file and the system is unable to allocate a STREAM.

EOPNOTSUPP An attempt was made to open a path that corresponds to a AF_UNIX socket.

EOVERFLOW The named file is a regular file and either O_LARGEFILE is not set and the size of the file cannot be represented correctly in an object of type off_t or O_LARGEFILE is set and the size of the file cannot be represented correctly in an object of type off64_t.

*Back To APIs Encountered Table*

**13) openlog**

Appears in C:\Documents and Settings\Administrator\My Documents\My Downloads\zzftp\zzftp-0.6.2logger.c on line number(s) :

62
70

COMMENT :

openlog ( ) - opens a connection to the system logger for a program.

There are differences in the options and facility which are available on Linux LSB but not on Solaris 8.0

For options
LOG_PERROR is available on Linux LSB

For facility
LOG_AUTHPRIV - security/authorization messages ( private )
LOG_SYSLOG - messages generated internally by syslogd

*Back To APIs Encountered Table*

**14) select**

Appears in C:\Documents and Settings\Administrator\My Documents\My Downloads\zzftp\zzftp-0.6.2ftpd.c on line number(s) :

241
243

Appears in C:\Documents and Settings\Administrator\My Documents\My Downloads\zzftp\zzftp-0.6.2ftp.c on line number(s) :

245

Appears in C:\Documents and Settings\Administrator\My Documents\My Downloads\zzftp\zzftp-0.6.2ftp_io.c on line number(s) :

225

COMMENT :

select ( 2.0 ) - synchronous I/O multiplexing '

The functions select and pselect wait for a number of file descriptors to change status.

On Linux LSB

```
#include <sys/time.h>
#include <sys/types.h>
#include <unistd.h>
int select ( int n , fd_set * readfds , fd_set * writefds , fd_set * exceptfds , struct timeval * timeout ) ;
```

On Solaris 8.0
```
#include <sys/select.h>
int select ( int , fd_set * , fd_set * , fd_set * , struct timeval * ) ;
```

*Back To APIs Encountered Table*

### 15) argz_next

Appears in C:\Documents and Settings\Administrator\My Documents\My Downloads\zzftp\zzftp-0.6.2\options.c on line number(s) :

41
47
54
57
76
79

COMMENT :

char * argz_next ( char * ARGZ , size_t ARGZ_LEN , const char * ENTRY )

The ' argz_next ' over the elements in the argz vector ARGZ. It returns a pointer to the next element in ARGZ after the element ENTRY , or ' 0.0 ' there are no elements following ENTRY. If ENTRY is ' 0.0 ' element of ARGZ is returned.

This function is not available on Solaris 8.0 , write your own implementation.

*Back To APIs Encountered Table*

**16) fstat**

Appears in C:\Documents and Settings\Administrator\My Documents\My Downloads\zzftp\zzftp-0.6.2ftp_file.c on line number(s) :

527

Appears in C:\Documents and Settings\Administrator\My Documents\My Downloads\zzftp\zzftp-0.6.2ftpd_file.c on line number(s) :

385

COMMENT :

fstat ( 2.0 ) - get file status
int fstat ( int filedes , struct stat * buf ) ;

These are the error conditions that may be returned under Solaris 8.0 but not Linux LSB

EFAULT buf points to an illegal address.

EINTR A signal was caught during the fstat ( ) function.

ENOLINK fildes points to a remote machine and the link to that machine is no longer active.

*Back To APIs Encountered Table*

**17) hosts_ctl**

Appears in C:\Documents and Settings\Administrator\My Documents\My Downloads\zzftp\zzftp-0.6.2ftpd.c on line number(s) :

401

COMMENT :

host_ctl ( - access Control Library ) is available on Linux LSB.
hosts_ctl is a wrapper around the request_init ( ) and hosts_access ( ) routine with a easier interface.

int hosts_ctl ( daemon , client_name , client_addr , ^ client_user )
char * daemon ;
char * client_name ;
char * client_addr ;
char * client_user ;

On Solaris 8.0 , write your own implementation.

*Back To APIs Encountered Table*

**18) argz_count**

Appears in C:\Documents and Settings\Administrator\My Documents\My Downloads\zzftp\zzftp-0.6.2ftp.c on line number(s) :

318

COMMENT :

size_t argz_count ( const char * ARGZ , size_t ARG_LEN )
Returns the number of elements in the argz vector ARGZ and ARGZ_LEN.

This function is not available on Solaris 8.0 , write your own implementation.

*Back To APIs Encountered Table*

**19) bind**

Appears in C:\Documents and Settings\Administrator\My Documents\My Downloads\zzftp\zzftp-0.6.2ftpd.c on line number(s) :

180
427

Appears in C:\Documents and Settings\Administrator\My Documents\My Downloads\zzftp\zzftp-0.6.2ftp.c on line number(s) :

536
615

Appears in C:\Documents and Settings\Administrator\My Documents\My Downloads\zzftp\zzftp-0.6.2ftp_file.c on line number(s) :

351

COMMENT :

bind ( 2.0 ) - bind a name to a socket
int bind ( int sockfd , struct sockaddr * my_addr , int addrlen ) ;

bind on Solaris 8.0 use EADDRNOTAVAIL instead of EFAULT , and it does not have ENOMEM. In addition , a different type " is used to define the third parameter on Solaris 8.0

*Back To APIs Encountered Table*

**20) argz_extract**

Appears in C:\Documents and Settings\Administrator\My Documents\My Downloads\zzftp\zzftp-0.6.2ftp.c on line number(s) :

326

COMMENT :

void argz_extract ( char * ARGZ , size_t ARGZ_LEN , char * * ARGV )
The ' argz_extract '
ARGZ_LEN into a Unix-style argument vector stored in ARGV , by putting pointers
to every element in ARGZ into successive positions in ARGV , followed by a
terminator of ' 0.0 ' pre-allocated with enough space to hold all the elements in
ARGZ plus the terminating ' ( char * ) 0.0 ' 1.0 ) * sizeof ( char * ) ' string pointers
stored into ARGV point into ARGZ--they are not copies--and so ARGZ must be
copied if it will be changed while ARGV is still active. This function is useful for
passing the elements in ARGZ to an exec function ( * note Executing a File ) 0.0

This function is not available on Solaris 8.0 , write your own implementation.

*Back to Top*

## Levels of Porting Difficulty

There are four levels of porting difficulties defined as follows:

**Easy -**
Depending upon your level of expertise APIs that have this level of difficulty will
typically have an estimated porting time of about 2 hours to approximately 4 hours.

**Medium -**
Depending upon your level of expertise, APIs that have this level of difficulty will
typically have an estimated porting time of about 4 hours to approximately 1
working day.

**Hard -**
Depending upon your expertise, APIs that have this level of difficulty will typically
have an estimated porting time of about 1 working day to 2 working days.

**Toughest -**
Depending upon your expertise, APIs that have this level of dificulty will typically
have an estimated porting time of about 3 working days.

**Not Known -**
Estimate is not calculated.

**\* NOTE**

Your average level of porting difficulty is directly related to the number of APIs
discovered which may pose porting issues. Each level of difficulty, Easy, Medium,
Hard, Toughest, is assigned a numeric value. Your total level is porting difficulty is
calculated by dividing the sum of these numeric values by the total number of APIs
discovered.

*Back to Top*

# Index

migration projects (*continued*)
  phases of
    architect, 71
    implement, 107
    manage, 133
  problems with, 6
  reasons for, 3
  Red Hat Linux example, 161
  strategies, types of
    interoperation, 36
    rearchitecting, 35
    refronting, 30
    rehosting, 33
    replacement, 31
    retirement, 36
  Tru64 UNIX example, 177
MUMPS, emulation and, 34
MySQL, example dump, 123

**N**

namespace, migrations, 221
networks
  data, transferring, 118
  design, refining, 98
  infrastructure
    assessing, 194
    creating, 196

**O**

operations requirements, assessing, 80

**P**

partitioning
  functions in a distributed application, 135
  large enterprise-class systems, 125
performance testing, defined, 130
PICK, emulation and, 34
plans, creating
  acceptance testing, 103
  configuration management, 102
  test, 128

plans (*continued*)
  training, 105
  transition, 102
platforms
  compute and storage
    assessing, 194
    deploying, 196
  design, refining, 94
  implementation, specifying, 223
  production, building, 125
  requirements, assessing, 78
port activities
  detailed list, 67
  planning for, 61
Portable operating systems based on UNIX
  (POSIX), standards of, 14
portal management tools, defined, 144
porting
  applications, 107
  defined, 25
  third-party products, 188
probes, defined, 142
production environment
  creating, 124
  tasks involved in creating, 67
project
  objectives, identifying, 50
  plans
    architecture activities, 59
    developing, 58
    implement activities, 62
  resources, identifying, 58
  teams, organizing, 57
prototype activities
  assessing need for, 61
  creating prototypes, 104

**R**

rearchitecture, defined, 35
recompilation, defined, 33
Red Hat Linux migration, example, 161
redevelopment activities, planning, 61
refronting, defined, 30
regression testing, performing, 129